NEW SCIENCE LIBRARY presents traditional topics from a modern perspective, particularly those associated with the hard sciences—physics, biology, and medicine—and those of the human sciences—psychology, sociology, and philosophy.

The aim of this series is the enrichment of both the scientific and spiritual view of the world through their mutual dialogue and exchange.

New Science Library is an imprint of Shambhala Publications.

General editor/Ken Wilber

For my colleagues in medicine,
brothers and sisters in the Great Tradition:
in acknowledgement of what we have done well,
and in anticipation of what we must do better.

BEYOND ILLNESS

Discovering the Experience of Health

LARRY DOSSEY, M.D.

NEW SCIENCE LIBRARY

SHAMBHALA / Boulder & London / 1984

NEW SCIENCE LIBRARY
An imprint of Shambhala Publications, Inc.
Boulder, Colorado 80306–0271

Distributed in the United States by Random House
and in Canada by Random House of Canada Ltd.
Distributed in the United Kingdom by Routledge & Kegan Paul Ltd,
London and Henley-on-Thames

Printed in the United States of America

Library of Congress Cataloging in Publication Data

Dossey, Larry, 1940-
  Beyond illness.

  (New science library)
1. Health.   2. Holistic medicine.   I. Title.
  II. Series.
RA776.5.D67   1984   613   84-5487
ISBN 0-87773-295-7
ISBN 0-394-54123-5 (Random House: pbk.)

Designed by: Judith Yourman
Typeset by: G&S Typesetters, Austin, Texas in Linotron ITC Garamond Light
Printed by: R. R. Donnelley & Sons

With thanks to the following publishers for permission to reprint material copyrighted or controlled
by them: E. P. Dutton, Inc. and Hutchinson & Co., Ltd. for permission to quote from *Essentials of
Zen Buddhism*, by D. T. Suzuki, edited and copyrighted by Bernard Phillips, © 1962; Faber and
Faber Publishers for permission to quote from *A Choice of Whitman's Verse*, by Walt Whitman,
© 1968; Grove Press, Inc. for permission to quote from *The Way and Its Power*, by Arthur Whaley,
© 1958; Holt, Rinehart and Winston, Publishers for permission to quote from *The Poetry of Robert
Frost*, edited by Edward Connery Lathem, © 1969 by Holt, Rinehart and Winston, © 1958 by
Robert Frost and © 1967 by Leslie Frost Ballentine; The Journal of the American Medical Association for permission to quote from JAMA 241(11) and JAMA 242(14) © 1979 by the American
Medical Association; Little, Brown and Company for permission to quote from *Dying: An Introduction*, by L. E. Sissman, © 1967; Macmillan Publishing Company and Macmillan Press Ltd. for
permission to quote from *One Hundred Poems of Kabir*, by Rabindranath Tagore, 1915; Philosophical
Library Publishers for permission to quote from *Classics in Chinese Philosophy*, edited by Wade Baskin, © 1972; Random House, Inc. for permission to quote from *Leaves of Grass*, by Walt Whitman;
and Viking Penguin, Laurence Pollinger Ltd. and the Estate of Mrs. Frieda Lawrence Ravagli for
permission to quote from *The Complete Poems*, by D. H. Lawrence, © 1971.

CONTENTS

PREFACE

There are some thoughts that physicians early on learn to keep to themselves. They have mainly to do with concepts that have not survived the unforgiving scrutiny of science and which have therefore faded from our list of respectable concerns in the profession. They have to do with spirit.

The mention of the word immediately causes the deepest furrowing of the scientific brow. Eyes are averted in the direction of the measurable and the precise when spirit announces itself, and choruses of objection warn of the dangers inherent in any flirtation with "mysticism." Yet for all the problems in addressing such a murky concept, all of us in medicine know privately it is a notion that has never died and that will never die. For, oddly, "spirit" has seemingly thrived on being officially ignored in medicine in the scientific era, peskily asserting its presence in every doctor's encounter with a patient and in every patient's encounter with illness. For something so diaphanous, it has uncanny persistence.

Our habit of ignoring spiritual concerns in medicine has evolved not because physicians are themselves more spiritually bankrupt than any other professional group, but for the quite simple reason that it seemed unnecessary to insert them in our scientific understanding of health and disease. Nowhere did they seem vital in unraveling the anatomic and physiologic complexities of human beings, nor in prescribing proper therapies when the body went awry. The tendency to ignore the spiritual domain reflected a basic economy of thought and doing which is part of the scientific ideal.

Yet for all our official posturing about keeping medicine clean of spiritual concepts, all the while a kind of duplicity has been at work. The towering figures in the profession, for example, have always represented something more than the power of logic and observation. They have stood for qualities that somehow set medicine apart—qualities of soul, spirit, love, caring. These qualities do not appear on diagnostic algorithms or on laboratory flow sheets, but they are there all the while and are as persistently present today as when physicians mixed their own potions, drove buggies on house calls, and actually sat at bedsides. These qualities are timeless. They have hardly been driven from the field by the insights of modern medical science and the advances of "objective" medicine.

This book seeks to explore the timeless quality of spirit in medicine, but with the recognition that there is nothing new here: spirit cannot be *re*-introduced. It cannot be resurrected, for it has never died, even if it has

been half-forgotten in our time. We are blazing no new paths, only tread-
ing ageless trails laid out long ago by innumerable, nameless healers.

Yet, as my colleagues may remind me, it still seems odd to talk of spirit
and health in the same breath today. We are freshly returned from so many
wars won by molecular biology, victorious in so many conquests we can
hardly recall them all. Why muddy the water by introducing a concept we
cannot even define, the notion of spirit, something which cannot be contained in test tubes or seen under microscopes? Why not continue to focus
on the approach of modern bioscience and rely on a strictly physicalistic
orientation? Let those who wish take their concerns of spirit to priests,
ministers, counselors, or shamans, but do *not* leave them on the doorstep
of medical science where they do not belong. They are part of an altogether different category from biomedicine, which can only be contaminated and weakened if suffused with "the spiritual." Medicine did not realize its power until it divested itself from its priestly function, and a retreat
to such a role will be its ruination. So it is said.

These arguments, so familiar by now, have a compelling logic—one that
is internally consistent. But it is wrong—not wrong in the sense of being
flawed, but erroneous because it is incomplete. Just as Euclid's geometry
was eventually shown to be only one of many possible kinds of geome-
tries, each internally consistent, there are "logics of health" other than that
offered by modern bioscience, some of which have room for spirit.

This common contention that medicine should be purified from the
contamination of spirit, that it should pursue its own aesthetic ideal, that it
should aspire to its own brand of scientific truth: Is this not a subtle intrusion of the scientist's own spirit, his own preferential idea, his own ineffable amalgam of logic, thought, and feeling? Perhaps a spirit-free medicine is an impossible ideal, a contradiction in terms.

One of the great agonies of modern medicine is that its practitioners
feel compelled to choose between "the scientific" and "the unscientific,"
between the objective and the subjective, between the precise and the un-
repeatable, between the measurable and the nonquantifiable. These categorizations tear at the inner life of physicians and exact a silent toll. It is
true that many escape the constraints of this either-or world, evolving their
own private landscape of thought and feeling and medical practice. Many
choose unconsciously to ignore the problem altogether. But the call to "be
scientific" is a mighty one, creating enormous conflicts within many modern physicians who aspire to excellence in their profession.

The root problem for physicians is that we find ourselves in a profession that has traditionally emphasized concerns of the spirit, yet whose
modern, recent, scientific tradition denies the importance or even the ex-

istence of such a spiritual element. Impelled by training and a deep respect for the traditions of science, and simultaneously empowered by the whisperings of spirit that are the legacy of the healer, how is the conflict to be resolved?

We cannot give a solution yet, but hints of the form of an eventual resolution are at hand. An emerging conceptual pluralism is at work in certain domains of science, a form of knowing that presages the demise of the either-or structures which now weigh us down in medicine. Pluralistic and complementary concepts have already exerted a conceptual renovation in physics, as is well known. There they have commanded recognition *not* because of totally arbitrary reasoning, but because it is necessary to adopt them to account for actual physical observations. The now-famous wave-particle duality is perhaps the most striking example of complementary thinking at work in the whole of science. The importance for medicine? It is likely that the pluralistic views of the world that stunned physicists earlier in this century will not remain confined to physics where they originated, but will eventually affect the healing professions as well.*

As they do, it should be remembered that the pluralistic approach to envisioning reality flows from the *best* scientific traditions, not the worst, as is clear from the experience in modern physics. Pluralism need not be equated with a wholesale dilution of scientific precision. Thus in medicine we need not feel compelled to protect a monolithic guiding ideal that is utterly spirit-free out of the principle that it is the *only* possible view of man that is scientifically legitimate. If our best observations of ourselves lead to complementary visions of our world, we must have the courage to follow them, just as scientists have already done in domains that are far more exact than medicine.

Perhaps it is unnecessary to expect precise definitions of spirit, mind, or consciousness before we begin to reexamine old assumptions in medicine. If we wait until we fully know something of the world about us, we shall be in for a very long wait. As Einstein reminded us, this problem is really no different in physics where, although much more is increasingly known *about* things, nothing is ever known about the *true nature* of the grand phenomena of the universe such as light, magnetism, electricity, or gravity. Today we know enough *about* spirit, mind, and consciousness to search for grander, more inclusive concepts of ourselves. And the fun— yes, the *pleasure*, in the deepest sense of the word—in this task lies in pursuing the best traditions of exactitude and precision in science *and* in

---

*These implications have been examined in an earlier work, *Space, Time, and Medicine* (Boulder: Shambhala Publications, 1982).

hearkening to the eternal spiritual elements that have always been a part of the tradition of healing. This is the pleasure of all synthetic effort—seeing the formation of wholes from parts, seeing diversity merge into unity.

The following essays flow from my own attempt to resolve some of these questions. They are about patients I have known, and about the larger questions that were raised by their health or illness. In caring for them I sometimes felt myself to be more student than physician. For their lessons I am grateful.

Larry Dossey, M.D.
Dallas, Texas
April, 1984

Many of the clinical cases which follow are taken from the author's practice of internal medicine. The names of all patients have been changed to preserve confidentiality.

Despite the towering intellectual and technological achievements of twentieth-century science, its spell over us has been irreversibly weakened. There are at least two important reasons for this. First, scientist and layman alike have become acutely aware of the limits and shortcomings of scientific knowledge. Second, we realize that our perpetual hunger for spiritual understanding is real and undeniable. It can neither be defined away by subtle logic, nor be satisfied by viewing the universe as sterile, mechanistic, and accidental.

—Roger S. Jones
Physics as Metaphor

I

The Light of Health, the Shadow of Illness: a Living Unity

. . . where there is life, there is death; and where there is death, there is life. . . . But really are there such distinctions . . . or are there no such distinctions? . . . by the Tao this great variety is all brought into a single unity. Whether in construction or in destruction, all things are in the end brought into unity.

—Chuang Tzu
Discourses on Tao

To remain whole, be twisted!
To become straight, let yourself be bent.
To become full, be hollow.
Be tattered, that you may be renewed.
Those that have little, may get more,
Those that have much, are but perplexed.
Therefore the Sage
Clasps the Primal Unity.

—*Tao Te Ching*

Health-as-Experience

"Hi, Doc! Want a cigarette?" the old man whispered, too breathless to speak clearly. He sat upright in the wheelchair, struggling for air. With a cyanotic, leathery, outstretched hand, he offered me his favorite nonfilter brand. Declining, I noticed that he was one of the Brown-Fingered Ones, an appellation we interns gave to our emphysema patients whose decades of dedicated cigarette smoking had left their fingers deeply stained and desiccated.

Buck Scranton came to Ward 5A around midnight. He brought with him a diagnosis of chronic obstructive bronchopulmonary disease, which in his case meant emphysema. With him came eight volumes of hospital records from previous admissions. Buck was truly a regular, having been admitted to this hospital a total of twenty-three times. Most of these occasions were for the same problem, emphysema, but there had been a smattering of other diagnoses through the years: pneumonia, alcoholic pancreatitis, delirium tremens, alcoholic gastritis, gastric ulcers with bleeding, and assorted other maladies. I asked the nurses to admit him to the four-bed ward which we interns called "Marlboro Country," so-called because most of its occupants had developed their illnesses through the injudicious use of tobacco.

This seventy-six-year-old man was different from most patients I had cared for that year as an inexperienced intern. Even though he arrived smoking a cigarette and was having a difficult time breathing, he was amazingly alert and jocular, extraordinary for someone in his state. Buck smoked four packages of cigarettes a day and drank heavily too, and his small tattered travel bag bulged with several cartons of cigarettes he kept in reserve. As I approached him for the first time to begin my medical assessment, I was momentarily disconcerted by his smile. His overwhelming smothering should have banished all his capacity for humor. Sensing my befuddlement, he managed some more words.

He said that he knew I was tired, that it was late, that he didn't want to be any trouble. He said that he would have delayed coming until morning if he could have made it that long. He allowed that he had been through this many times before and had "trained" a lot of interns in how to care for acute respiratory failure. He knew, he said, what it would require to get him through the night. Astonishingly, old Buck began to dictate his therapy, all in precise medical terms. His "orders" were very nearly identical to those I wrote for his care before I got him bedded down in Marlboro Country—not only in terms of the drugs to be used but the actual dosages and frequency as well.

As I knew from his records of previous hospital admissions, he usually responded quickly, and this time was no exception. By morning his condition had improved remarkably, and he was up and about, chatting animatedly with the less vigorous patients. On rounds, after I examined his chest and heart and had reviewed the laboratory data that had begun to filter onto his chart, we talked. My conversation with Buck became the prime event of the day for me, and I realized that whatever I gave this wizened, ribald old man in the course of my care for him, he gave me as much as he took.

Physicians generally dislike caring for patients with emphysema. The illness is almost always due to cigarette smoking, and, as such, it seems self-imposed, which does little to endear such a patient to a doctor—especially when the need for care comes at the end of a long day or in the middle of the night. But with Buck it was different, and he reminded me of the question that one frequently hears from patients in teaching hospitals: "Doctor, are you doing this for me, or am I doing this for you?" With Buck I felt the doctor-patient interchange was being conducted largely for my benefit.

He took a cantankerous pleasure in revealing his irresponsible past—relationships that waxed and waned, marriages that came and went, fortunes gained and lost. One thing was apparent: for this man, life was an ongoing bacchanal, a never-ending Dionysian excursion that had persisted for 76 years. Buck was a walking textbook of pathology, yet he had survived innumerable illnesses that would have destroyed most men.

The singular quality that distinguished this man was that of an *experiential* attachment to life—uniting with it in some umbilical sense of oneness with an enthusiasm that seemed out of context when considering his illness. Why, Buck even smiled when he could not breathe, and put my convenience over his own welfare when it fell my lot to care for him in the early morning hours.

When it came time for me to discharge him I felt the need to do some "pre-discharge planning." I urged him, as an evangelical intern, to "clean up his life" in no uncertain ways. He listened to my exhortations—as usual, with a twinkle and a smile. I felt myself in the full force of his odd wisdom, as if my teaching was little more than feeble preachments. He let me finish, then smilingly offered, "Thanks, Doc." Then he picked up his tattered bag and left—after, of course, lighting a cigarette.

Three days later I was summoned from a clinical conference for a long distance telephone call. Leaving the room, I was told by the secretary that a patient of mine was calling, and that it was an emergency. I walked quickly to the phone, to be greeted with "Hi, Doc! It's me, Buck Scranton!"

Taken aback, I said, "Hello, Buck. Where are you calling from?"

"I'm in Louisville! I just had to call you to let you know I hit it big on a long shot in a horse race. I'm in the money again, Doc. And I still feel great, too. You did a lot for me!"

"Buck?" I asked.

"Yes, Doc."

"You still smoking?"

"Yep!"

"Still drinking?" I asked, knowing the answer.

"Yep!"

"You feeling O.K., I mean *really* O.K.?" I asked.

"I wouldn't lie, Doc, you know I wouldn't lie to you. . . ."

The conversation went on. I could see him, euphoric over his good luck, too short of breath to tolerate the crowds for too long, too winded to walk up the ramps. But Buck Scranton knew something that skilled physicians seldom learn, the simple fact that the ultimate meaning of health cannot be found in objective parameters—in his case not in pulmonary tests nor in chest x-rays.

I only had one more piece of advice for him. "Buck?" I said. He didn't answer, and I knew he was too short of breath to reply. "Buck, keep up your clean living!"

"Thanks, Doc!" I could hear him laughing, or trying to laugh while short of breath on the other end of the line. Yet, in spite of his crippled lungs, this man was effulgent with health, not as demonstrated in his body, but as it resonated in his spirit. Buck Scranton was alive as few people are, even though his body had fallen apart. The quality that set him apart was the ability to cut to the core of *experience*—whether that experience was winning a long shot, or sensing what it was like to depend on a respirator for his next breath. He laughed at, shook his fist in the face of, objective parameters of health.

I never heard from him again, and I do not think he is alive now. But I am certain that Buck left life the way he entered Ward 5A late one night— with eyes atwinkle and a smile on his face—his own personal signature, his own endorsement that health does not merely *reflect* experience, it *is* experience.

THE PROBLEM IN VIEWING HEALTH
AS A MATTER OF PURE EXPERIENCE

This feeling only what you allow yourselves to feel at last kills all capacity for feeling, and in the higher emotional ranges you feel nothing at all. This has come to pass in our present century. The higher emotions are strictly dead. They have to be faked.[1]

Many of us have become inured to health. We have lost what we once knew how to feel, what we once sensed with exuberance, what we early on knew in keen purity, excitement, fulfillment. We are numb to the *experience* of health.

Where did it go? Where *is* the experience of health that we have lost? It is hiding within our true self, the part of us that once felt. The experience of health vanished as we have forgotten our organic relationship with the world. It is this relationship that, like health, is *also* experiential. And to be unable to experience the oneness and unity of ourselves with the world is to be unable to experience health, which at heart is an expression of our organic connection with the world.

We feel, as Lawrence described, only what we allow ourselves to feel. We allow only a piteous counterfeit of the real thing to creep in from time to time. We mistake the map for the territory, in the semanticist Alfred Korzybski's words, mistakenly supposing that lab tests and physical examinations are the same thing as health.

To allow more than objects to enter our experience—*really* enter—would entail a painful reassessment of who we are. It would mandate a redefinition of our relationship with the world, a renunciation of the ordinary subject-object way we habitually define ourselves. It would entail an immersion in the "organic system of life" from which "we shall produce the real blossoms of life and being," as Lawrence put it.[2]

Such immersions can be painful—so wrenching that most persons prefer to chase the *persona* of health rather than the real thing, preferring the symbols of health to the experience itself. Better, perhaps, to accept the doctor's pronouncements of health than to know the immediacy of it ourselves. Better to continue the masquerade of acquiring health-as-object than to undergo the transformation that is required to know health-as-experience. Better to play the game according to the rules of Blue Cross-Blue Shield than according to those required for spiritual growth and spiritual evolution. Better to eat the menu instead of the meal.

Until, of course, we discover that in the "higher emotional ranges" we feel nothing at all—not health, nor non-health—only vacuity, nothingness. That we have deluded ourselves with our ideal body weight, our biochemical nomograms, and our exercise stress test values is the realization that many people eventually come to. At some point the light breaks through. And we discover the naivete of what we have been doing, of mistaking health-as-object for health-as-experience. We see that we have been behaving as if health were something we could *possess*.

But it is not so. We cannot possess health *or* illness. Aldous Huxley knew this. In his *Island*, Lakshmi, the old woman on the verge of death, could see herself over in the corner of the room while her body remained on the bed. She said, "What you discover . . . [is that] nothing really belongs to you. Not even your pain."[3]

Health-as-experience leads us to the understanding that there is, in fact, no such *thing* as health, and, more calamitously, no *one* to be healthy. For

> In the higher realm of True Suchness
> There is neither "other" nor "self":
> When a direct identification is asked for,
> We can only say, "Not two."
>
> One in all,
> All in one—
> If only this is realized,
> No more worry about your not being perfect![4]

No-Health

> We put thirty spokes together and call it a wheel;
> But it is on the space where there is nothing that the
>   usefulness of the wheel depends.
> We turn clay to make a vessel;
> But it is on the space where there is nothing that the
>   usefulness of the vessel depends.
> We pierce doors and windows to make a house;
> And it is on these spaces where there is nothing that the
>   usefulness of the house depends.
> Therefore just as we take advantage of what is, we should
>   recognize the usefulness of what is not.
>
> —*Tao Te Ching*

There is a particular sense of health that cannot be achieved or acquired, promoted or developed. It is not the result of active medical interventions, whether by drugs or surgery. It is not the product of the most vigorous preventive measures. It is so unlike our ordinary concepts of health that we can most properly call it "no-health."

The ancient Taoists had a similar concept of a kind of knowing they called "no-knowledge." This is not knowledge as we know it in the West, not the product of linear reasoning that pursues an object as the goal of knowing, but something altogether different. As Siu puts it,

> It [no-knowledge] concerns an understanding of what the East calls *Wu* or nonbeing. The *Wu* transcends events and qualities; it has no shape, no time. As a result it cannot be the object of ordinary knowledge. At the higher level of cognizance, the sage forgets distinctions between things. He believes in the silence of what remains in the undifferentiated whole.
>
> An important difference exists between "having-no" knowledge and having "no-knowledge." The former is merely a state of ignorance; the latter is one of ultimate enlightenment and universal sensibilities.[1]

Similarly, having "no-health" is not to be confused with "having-no" health. The latter is sickness, despair, dissolution, and eventual death. The former is, as Siu described, the Taoist's no-knowledge, a state of "ultimate enlightenment and universal sensibilities." It is *not super*health. It is *not* to never fall ill, although it does not exclude healthiness and proper body function. It transcends, even, the unity and oneness of body and mind, that highly sought-after goal of holistic health. No-health is not man's mind in tune with man's body, but man in tune with nature in an undifferentiated wholeness that goes beyond distinctions such as health and illness, birth and death, mind and body.

No-health seeks nothing, for there is nothing outside it to seek—not longevity, not freedom from pain and suffering, not freedom from disease and infirmity and death. Thus *it includes everything,* for it is the ground from which all our convenient referents and standards of health take their meaning. It is the origin of opposites, including such contrasting elements as high *and* normal blood pressure, heart attacks *and* proper heart function, even birth *and* death. No-health cannot be reduced to such specifics. It does not appear on lab reports, it does not show itself in the form of blood tests or x-rays. It transcends distinctions between things. It is universal sensibility. It is the silence of the undifferentiated whole.

The Interpenetration of Opposites

This feeling of being embedded in a universal, connected dynamics may not only remove the fear of our own biological death, but also the fear which defends the "survival of the species" as a supreme value. In self-transcendence we reach not only beyond our own limits as individuals, but also beyond the limits of mankind.

In the immovable all, the common origin of evolution, time and space and the not-yet-unfolded—all quality—were one. The highest meaning is in the non-unfolded as well as in the fully unfolded; both reach up to the divinity.

—Erich Jantsch
The Self-Organizing Universe

The notion that there is some dynamic interplay between opposites permeates the Zen Buddhist tradition in Japan, emerging as vital principles in the arts. In his treatise on Japanese landscape and garden design, Mark Holborn describes the Buddhist attitude:

. . . beauty and ugliness were one and part of the same perception. . . . Accordingly, absolute perfection, in which no trace of the imperfect was found, would fail to embody beauty. It was through imperfection that perfection was recognised and beauty appreciated. A form that was perfect would be static and dead.[1]

This understanding was not idle philosophy, but was enacted in everyday life:

This feeling was realised by the tea masters who delighted in the asymmetrical forms of the tea room and the stepping-stones of the tea garden, or in the choice of the irregularly-shaped utensils.

Likewise, the architecture of the Buddhist temple followed no geometrical pattern in Japan . . . but followed natural features. The rhythm of the building became the rhythm of its background.

Solemn, impressive and graceful—symmetry is the manifestation of a logical, calculating intellect. The Japanese had no need for the creation of a new abstract order. They intuitively found their identity in the balance of the landscape and the passing of the season. Throughout the garden the asymmetrical patterns of bridges, paths, stones and trees retain the impression that there is no design at all. The garden becomes the accident of Nature.[2]

The kind of balance that emerges through the tradition of Zen Buddhism stands in stark contrast to our usual way of thinking about opposites—particularly with regard to health and illness. In the Zen tradition, "beauty and ugliness were one and part of the same tradition," Holborn tells us. "A form that was perfect would be static and dead." If we translated this position into the arena of health, we might say that health and illness, like beauty and ugliness, are also one and part of the same perception; to be perfectly healthy is to be static and dead.

On the surface this view seems absurd. An ongoing, constant, static state of health is our *ideal*. Although we know we can never achieve it, at least we can try. Moreover, equating health and illness in the Oriental way is pathological—a *guarantee* of poor health through a passive acceptance of "what is." Such notions may have had appeal to a culture that was Oriental and prescientific, but to transfer such generalizations onto our own traditions just won't work. So the objections go.

And so we continue in our ceaseless struggle for the endless summer of health, striving to banish physiological imperfection forever from the field, reenacting the archetypal search for the fountain of youth with every annual exam, x-ray, and blood test.

And it doesn't work. What is worse, we know it—somewhere in our being we know we're off the mark in our struggle for eternal, unblemished health. And the assurances of modern bioscience that nothing is beyond our reach—what we could call "promissory healthiness"—has, for most of us, come to seem vacuous. I do not even think that those within the community of bioscience really believe such promises and predictions. There is, within us, a gnawing reminder that somewhere, in matters of health and illness, we have it wrong.

The wrongness, I believe, lies in the peculiar way we have come to view the world—as a collection of bit-pieces of things and events which have been wrenched and torn from their organic interconnectedness. In medicine, this way of viewing things, this mode of perception, haunts us and annuls our ability to know health, were it to confront us. We need a new vision of health, one that will reinstate our ability to sense its quintessence—a vision that must include, paradoxically, illness and death as the "moving principles" of the health that eludes us.

TWO WAYS OF KNOWING: PRAJNA AND VIJNANA

The Buddhist scholar D. T. Suzuki has done more, perhaps, than any person in history to bring to Western awareness the way Eastern cultures have dealt conceptually with the notion of opposites such as health and illness. Central to the Buddhist way of perceiving this relationship is the notion of *prajna* and *vijnana*.

> For "intuition" Buddhists generally use *"prajna"* and for reason or discursive understanding, *vijnana*.
> *Prajna* goes beyond *vijnana*. We make use of *vijnana* in our world of the senses and intellect, which is characterized by dualism in the sense that there is one who sees and there is the other that is seen—the two standing in opposition. In *prajna* this differentiation does not take place; what is seen and the one who sees are identical; the seer is the seen and the seen is the seer. *Prajna* is the self-knowledge of the whole, in contrast to *vijnana*, which busies itself with parts.[3]

If we were to take seriously the possibility that there were some essential unity to the experiences of health and illness, Suzuki would remind us that this oneness cannot be known through the intellect. Yet in matters of health, in the Western world, *it is through the intellect* that we approach health. Being healthy and staying healthy have become a matter of *shrewdness*. It has become a matter of "beating the odds":—of cheating decline and death, of staving off the inexorable for as long as possible through the search for a formula that guarantees longevity and well-being—be it periodic physical exams, immunizations, the myriad of vitamin-mineral-trace element combinations, using the latest "body therapy," or visiting the latest spa. An overriding assumption in our approach to health care is that if we are *clever* enough, maybe, just maybe, we can achieve our goal.

This approach to being healthy is that of *vijnana*—the way of the intellect, the way of the discursive mind, which tries to "figure out" how to be healthy. It carves the phenomenon of healthiness up into bits and pieces, assigning them names such as feeling good, vitality, energy, upper respiratory illnesses, polio, and sprained ankles. Health becomes a balancing act, a matter of getting all the parts in the right order and combination—eliminating some, admitting others. If the diastolic pressure is right, if the cholesterol level is normal, and if the aerobic capacity on the treadmill exercise test is acceptable, then I *must* be healthy!

But an approach to health which emphasizes *prajna* is different. Here there are no stark categories such as illness or health. Numerical values for the heart rate and blood pressure carry no ultimate significance. Is my electrocardiogram normal? No matter. For the assemblage of bits of information which go into the formula for healthiness in the world of *vijnana* are subsumed in the whole. A factor analysis approach to health is discarded. And, strikingly, the concept of health as a state "for which" one strives, as if it were an object which could be apprehended as an "out there" phenomenon, is transcended. For *prajna* does not divide the world into seer and seen, subject and object. Health is not a state to be acquired. In this mode of seeing the world, seer is seen, and seen is seer. I *am* health, and it is I. There is no process of becoming, nothing to be gained.

Yet this generalization is no guarantee that the blood pressure *is* normal, or that the concentration of magnesium in my tissues is ideal. Because, in *prajna*, distinctions between "ideal" and "non-ideal" also melt into the whole, and opposites are contained in each other. Thus one can as validly say that I am Illness as I am Health. I am Both, and Both are I. The preeminent reality is the Whole which contains all distinctions.

This perspective may, at first glance, seem to melt the world of things-and-events into some indistinguishable mush. In matters of health everything becomes a blur—health becomes illness and vice-versa; it is not wholeness so much as nonsense that reigns. Yet it is not so, and we do *not* automatically lose all sense and sanity when we recognize that there is an underlying unity that envelops all the disparate events which we perceive in our everyday life. Contrasts do continue to appear. Were it not so, we would not even be able to distinguish these two ways of knowing, *prajna* and *vijnana*. In fact, it is the recognition, the apperception, of apparent contrasts that constitutes the vitality of our existence, as Suzuki makes clear:

> While this way of *vijnana* appraisal is a tragedy because it causes to our hearts and to our spirits unspeakable anguish and makes this life a burden full of miseries, we must remember that it is because of this tragedy that we are awakened to the truth of *prajna* existence.[4]

Even though perceiving the world by carving it up into seer and seen, subject and object, creates human misery, it is also in this "tragedy" that the awareness of *prajna* or the intuitional, wholistic way of seeing the world is born. In this way opposites become the moving principles of each other. So it is with health and illness.

To know through the mode of perception called *prajna* that an underlying oneness pervades the world, and so envelops health and illness in a unifying way, distinctly and definitely does *not* condemn us to a conceptual blur in which we cannot distinguish health from illness, night from day, black from white. What *does* change is the meaning we impart to these events: health ceases to become something to be gained and acquired; and illness and death cease to be malevolent, external forces which may invade and destroy us at any moment. In *prajna*, pain is still pain, and high blood pressure still predisposes us toward strokes and heart attacks. Yet the quality of these events is transformed by our inner experience of them. They cease to appear as experiences to be avoided or exterminated. In fact, they take on a friendlier face—because in *prajna* it becomes apparent that to some degree the experience of them is *necessary*. For without the contrasting experiences of illness and health, we could take no meaning from either. Again, Suzuki makes this clear:

> That *prajna* underlies *vijnana*, in the sense that it enables *vijnana* to function as the principle of differentiation, is not difficult to realize when we see that differentiation is impossible without something that works for integration or unification. The dichotomy of subject and object cannot obtain unless there is something that lies behind them, something that is neither subject nor object; this is a kind of field where they can operate, where subject can be separated from object, object from subject. If the two are not related in any way, we cannot even speak of their separation or antithesis. There must be something of subject in object, and something of object in subject, which makes their separation as well as their relationship possible.[5]

Viewed from this perspective, perfect health becomes a pipe dream, a contradiction in terms. For without its moving principle, illness, we would never know it. To banish illness, then, would be to achieve the hapless result of banishing health. To be healthy, we must acknowledge what we are loathe to admit: *we need illness*.

Such statements inevitably invite criticism, for they sound like an endorsement of suffering and death. And viewed from purely an intellectual point of view, the mode of knowing which the Buddhists call *vijnana*, they are. But not so from the perspective of *prajna*. It is *prajna* that must be utilized to know the necessity of illness and the importance of suffering as components of health. Speaking of this understanding, Suzuki states:

And, as this something cannot be made the theme of intellectualization, there must be another method of reaching this most fundamental principle. The fact that it is so utterly fundamental excludes the application of the bifurcating instrument [the intellect]. We must appeal to *prajna*-intuition.[6]

The "coming together" of opposites, such as health and illness, is a theme not only Eastern in its origins, but one that can be found in all cultures, even our own. The implication that opposites and boundaries are artificial and arbitrary is inherent, for example, in Robert Frost's famous poem, "Mending Wall":

Before I built a wall I'd ask to know
What I was walling in or walling out,
And to whom I was like to give offense.
Something there is that doesn't love a wall,
That wants it down.[7]

Something there is in us, too, that doesn't love divisions, that wants them down—as when, through *prajna* wisdom, we see the interpenetration of illness and health.

"Does This Patient Have R.D.?"

The more we come to understand the human animal in terms of our species-specific biology and developmental sequence, the more "health" tends to become less culturally relative than it is grounded in maturational invariants that can be nourished or starved in the growing human being—and in whose "starvation" we find the pathogenic spectrum of psychopathology, psychosomatic pathology, and what we tend unfortunately to call "real" disease. We need to conduct our therapeutic communication and intervention strategies with our ear attuned to the developmental process underlying sickness and health that is "speaking" to us through the pathology—if we have only the courage to listen.

—Howard F. Stein

"Does this patient have R.D.?"

As an intern in the hospital, this was one of the first questions I learned to ask when encountering a patient. "R.D." stood for "real disease." I acquired the habit of asking the question from the residents—my immediate supervisors who, although they too were physicians-in-training, seemed to know everything. "R.D." was what we yearned for. In fact, the sicker the patients were, the better we liked them. There was real "teaching value" in R.D. Nothing could be more annoying than having to evaluate a "crock"— someone without R.D.—when time was short and the ward was full.

I was not wise enough at that stage in my understanding to know the folly of those habits of thought. I felt my distinctions about two different kinds of disease were accurate. I *knew* they were consistent with the way my peers saw things. There seemed real utility, too, in thinking that way, for if a patient did *not* have R.D.—well, why should I work hard to heal what wasn't sick in the first place?

I look back at this way of thinking with mixed feelings—amazed at my naivete, yet certain that at the time I was practicing medicine in honest fashion. I know, too, that one doesn't leave those habits of thought as easily as one leaves internship and residency training. Regrettably, vestiges of the "R.D. mentality" persist in almost all physicians, affecting not only our ideas of how health and illness originate, but what we decide are appropriate treatments.

THE UNREALITY OF "REAL" DISEASE

The R.D. mentality is an enactment of the dominant theory of human function in medicine today, that of Cartesian dualism.* This way of thinking is *not* specific to immature interns and residents, but appears in the most highly skilled physicians as well. Indeed, it is not even confined to physicians: Our entire Western culture characteristically views humans in this way. There is a fundamental split between body and mind, we say, and non-

---

*Recently, Descartes has had his defenders, who vigorously have protested that he never stated that mind and body were separate. It is certainly true, as Bertrand Russell has pointed out in *A History of Western Philosophy*, that much of what is referred to as Cartesian dualism rests on the influence of his immediate successors and interpreters, such as Gaulinx. It is also a matter of history that Descartes tried to unite mind and body by postulating the pineal gland as the region in the brain where actual transactions occurred between the two. Nonetheless, it can hardly be denied that dualism of mind and body is a dominant force in modern medical theory.

interaction is the rule. The body is material and the mind is not. It is true that we have allowed that the body can affect the mind; but here the interaction stops. For the mind, which is assumed to be nonmaterial, cannot, even in principle, affect the material world. Disease is conceived of as a mechanistic breakdown and is, thus, a material process by definition. It is confined to the body, the only material part of humans. Seen in these terms, mental disease becomes a contradiction in terms—for only matter can break down, and the mind is nonmaterial.

"Real disease," as we interns used the words, similarly became a redundancy in the light of Cartesian thinking. For, since disease was physical by definition, what was physical was obviously real. Disease *had* to be real, or we should not have called it disease at all. To even speak of real disease was as inappropriate as referring to the "real sun" or the "real earth." Disease, like sun and earth, had no counterparts in unreality.

I do not know where in one's growth from child to adult, and in one's education as a physician, the Cartesian way of dividing man into mind and matter most forcefully enters one's life. We *do* know this habit of thought is not universal, nor is it completely pervasive in our own culture. It does not describe, for example, the way the artist, poet, and mystic see the world.

But, for the average physician, Cartesian dualism does enter the picture—and with a vengeance. Oddly, it is seldom recognized as a major force in thought and habit—even by thoughtful physicians. Yet it is a dominant philosophy in medical science today, allied with the reigning theory of how all disease originates—which, it is said, comes about due to breakdowns at the molecular level and is, thus, physical by definition. This way of thinking legitimizes certain forms of therapy over others: Physicalistic approaches—drugs and surgery—that exert actual physical changes are most valued. Other therapies, such as behavioral modalities, are valuable only to the extent that they bring about demonstrable somatic changes; therapies that simply make one "feel better" are said to "really not do anything," and are suspected as fundamentally useless.

It is a mistake to underestimate the force of Cartesian dualism in medicine today. In spite of a growing disaffection of a section of the populace with traditional approaches to health, the dualistic philosophy is alive and well, the guiding light of almost all theoretical and clinical efforts of Western medicine.

MIND OR MATTER: THE WRONG QUESTION

It comes as a shock for adherents of modern dualistic medicine—whether physicians or patients—to realize that the very foundation of our thinking is based on some extraordinarily flimsy assumptions. Uncritically we accept the notion that mind and matter do not interact, that nature is divisible into the living and the dead, and that consciousness and the body are essentially divided. Speaking of these tacit assumptions, the eminent biologist and philosopher Ludwig von Bertalanffy, whom many regard as the founder of general systems theory, said,

> The Cartesian dualism between material things and conscious ego is not a primordial or elementary datum, but results from a long evolution and development. Other sorts of awareness exist and cannot be simply dismissed as illusory. On the other hand, the dualism between material brain and immaterial mind is a conceptualization that has historically developed, and is not the only one possible or necessarily the best one. As a matter of fact, the classic conceptualization of matter and mind, *res extensa* and *res cogitans*, no longer corresponds to available knowledge. We should not discuss the mind-body problem in terms of seventeenth-century physics, but must consider it in the light of contemporary physics, biology, and behavioral and other sciences.[1]

Although we do not think about it in medicine, we reason the question of how mind and matter are related in terms of seventeenth-century physics. This is not surprising because medicine, as well as most other inexact sciences, has always had "physics envy." It has wished to embody the precision demonstrated by physics and has, in some measure, achieved its goal.

Our folly is that in looking for a solution to the most vexing problem in medicine and philosophy—the nature and relationship of mind and matter—we look where the solution will never be found—amid concepts that are now 300 years old. Cartesian dualism depends on an antiquated framework for its very existence, the materialistic and deterministic view of old-fashioned classical physics.

> Only within this view can we speak of the "blind play of atoms" and ultimate building blocks of reality. But not only the blind atoms, but also their directing entelechies are based upon materialistic physics.[2]

Yet the atoms, whose "blind play" sustains the materialistic and deterministic views that are so much a part of modern medicine, have become "dematerialized" in modern physics. Von Bertalanffy states the case:

> According to the world view of classical physics, tiny hard bodies called atoms were moving in empty space, representing ultimate reality. From

them issued mysterious "forces," physical and chemical, determining the play of these minute lumps of reality according to inexorable laws. The world view of modern physics is different. Through wave mechanics it has radically eliminated the classical concept of substance.

"Materialism" in the narrow sense, i.e., the assumption that there exists some "external, indestructible matter" composed of atoms as "rigid building blocks of reality" is definitely finished.[3]

What do these changes in the concepts of modern physics have to do with mind and matter, consciousness and body? The answer can only be: *Everything*. For in redefining matter as something very much unlike the "minute lumps of reality" we generally assume, the rug is pulled out from under the philosophical foundations of modern medicine. It makes no sense in the light of the new understanding of modern physics to say that matter is all, that it is ultimately predominant over the mental. And it makes equally little sense to argue the opposite, that mind is predominant over the physical. The reason? Both arguments suffer from the fatal flaw: *the type of matter they refer to does not exist*. Again, von Bertalanffy describes the situation succinctly:

> Modern physics resolves matter into dynamics. Consequently the mechanistic statement that material units and physiocochemical elements or forces are the ultimate reality is meaningless. Equally meaningless is the vitalistic statement that physiocochemical elements or forces are directed by an entelechy. The world process is neither a blindly working machine nor one which is supervised by an entelechy.
>
> [Modern science] abolishes the dualism between metaphysical mechanism and vitalism.
>
> . . . these arguments now take on a new appearance. Since the concept of "matter" in the old sense disappeared in physics, the physiocochemical problem is no longer how "matter" acts upon "mind" and vice versa.[4]

It has been more than half a century since these new ideas of matter originated. Yet they can hardly be said to have penetrated very deeply into the consciousness of our culture, or into the ways we think about mind, body, health, and illness. I suspect that interns and residents who today are staffing the internal medicine wards and emergency rooms where I trained still refer to "R.D."—"real disease"—or to some equivalent. In medicine, habits change slowly. Conservatism is still the hallmark of the profession, and the words of the physicist Max Planck still apply: "Science progresses funeral by funeral."

Yet the brightest hopes remain that an ultimate revision will occur in which vital new concepts of mind and body will emerge. Indeed there is, I feel, no going back. Today we know too much about the breakdown of the barriers separating the material and the nonmaterial parts of the universe. New conceptualizations of health and illness await us, and we can look forward to the day when tired interns no longer lament having to care for the person who does not have "R.D."

The Indispensable Key of the Universe: The Coincidence of Opposites

One might suggest that when consciousness is turned back upon its own organic basis, it gets some apprehension of that "omniscience" which is the body's total, organizing sensitivity. In the light of this deeper and more inclusive sensitivity, it becomes suddenly clear that things are joined together by the boundaries we ordinarily take to separate them, and are, indeed, definable as themselves only in terms of other things that differ from them.

—Alan Watts
The Two Hands of God

Opposites are abstract concepts that belong to the realm of thought and that are relative. By the very act of focusing our attention on any one concept . . . we create its opposite. . . . a virtuous person is not one who strives only for good and against bad, but one who transcends the limitations of this view by maintaining a dynamic balance between good and bad. The unity of opposites is never experienced as a static identity, but always as a dynamic interplay between two extremes.

—John W. Thompson
The Human Factor

At the dawn of the scientific era lived Giordano Bruno (1548–1600), a rebellious Italian thinker who was eventually burned at the stake for espousing ideas about the universe—ideas for which, ironically, Kepler would later be praised.

It is refreshing to read the words early scientists—men working in areas that only later would come to be called "science"—have left us. These forerunners of today's scientists would have thought some of our ideas about how scientists are expected to think and behave peculiar indeed. They clearly violated the modern notion that science should be dispassionate; that values, emotions, feelings, and attitudes have no place in the scientific process. Their work, in fact, was permeated with these qualities and empowered by them: Philosophy and religious feelings stand side by side with the purely objective, and there is no clear separation between the spiritual and the scientific. Bruno is by no means a single representative of this mode of thought in the dawning days of science. In their writings, Galileo, Kepler, and Newton illustrate a similar kind of reliance on the spiritual and philosophical modes of knowledge, as well as the empirical and analytical.

Bruno spoke of "the indispensable key" for the true understanding of Nature.[1] This key was not a matter of scientific discovery, but an unabashed assertion about how the universe behaved—a statement flowing from Bruno's intuition about how, quite simply, the world worked. The key lay in perceiving the "coincidence of opposites" (*coincidentia oppositorum*).

> Being though logically divided into that which is, and that which can be, is really indivisible, indistinct, and one . . . without difference of part and whole, principle and principled. Everything is in everything, and consequently all is one . . . unity in multiplicity and multiplicity in unity.[2]

Why return to a moment in the history of science when knowledge of the world was primitive by today's standards? What is the relevance of dredging up the personal, unproved assumptions of Bruno, or any other figure from science's early days? Because we want to gain a view of science before it became affected by the view that it should be emotionally desiccated and purged of values. There is much to learn here—for in the visions of certain early scientists such as Bruno, men of immense intellectual capacity, we can apprehend fruitful insights about our goal—the goal of understanding the nature of health and illness, pain and suffering, birth and death. We can acknowledge that the private, heartfelt opinions of pioneers like Bruno would indeed not pass for "good science" in our day. But no matter; for the fact is that "good science" has arbitrarily chosen to be mute on the issues that here concern us. It is unmoved by the domain of the nonquantifiable, the very domain that is our interest.

What, then, can Bruno, standing at the earliest edge of what was to become Western science, tell us about life and death, pain and suffering—those "contraries" which occupied his mind as they do our own? His view is unequivocal:

> . . . we must not fear that any object may disappear, or any particle veritably melt away or dissolve in space or suffer dismemberment by annihilation. [Because] when we consider . . . the being and substance of that universe in which we are immutably set, we shall discover that neither we ourselves nor any substance doth suffer death; for nothing is in fact diminished in its substance, but all things, wandering through infinite space, undergo change of aspect.[3]
>
> This is a vision which denies the possibility of death as annihilation.
>
> You have therefore, this fact: that all things are in the universe, and the universe is in all things—we in that, that in us; and, therefore, all things concur in a perfect unity. You see by this, then, that we ought not to *torment our spirit, for there is no thing by which we ought to become vexed.*[4]

And,

> [There is no] ultimate depth from which as from an artificer's hand things flow to an inevitable nullity.[5]

Not even time is enough to ravage us:

> . . . it is in vain that time raises itself to a cruel stroke, stretches the menacing hand armed with the scythe.[6]

There are, in Bruno's writings, the elements of pathos and anguish, for his concerns about suffering and death truly "tormented his soul and bruised his heart," as Choron tells us.[7] There is the most strenuous effort to work through his concerns carefully, and he brings his entire genius to bear on these problems. For him, as for us, the most grievous problem is the fact of death.

But you would ask me: Why then do things change? Why does particular matter force itself to other forms? I answer you—there is no mutation that seeks *another being*, but rather *another mode of being*. And this is the difference between the universe and the things of the universe— because that comprises all the being and all the modes of being; and of the latter, each one has all the being, but not all the modes of being. . . . Of these (things), each one comprises all the being, but not totally, be- cause beyond each there are infinite others. Therefore it is to be under- stood that all is in all, but not totally in all the modes in each one. There- fore understand that everything is one, but not in the same mode. . . .

Everything we see of difference in bodies, in relation to formations, complexions, figures, colours, and other properties or common quali- ties, is nothing else than a diversity of appearance of the same sub- stance; a *transitory, mobile, corruptible appearance* of an immobile, stable, and eternal being.[8]

It was the quality of *life* that for Bruno was the permeative, fundamental quality of the universe inherent in everything in it. It was this fact which annulled ordinary, common-sense ways of viewing death. For Bruno, death was not only not final, it did not even exist.

The fulcrum on which this view of life and death rested was his vision of the unity and oneness of all things that inhabit the universe. It is this inter- relatedness that subsumes the most radical opposites, even such polar events as life and death. This is the vision which made possible his view of the *coincidentia oppositorum*, the "coincidence of opposites," that har- mony of disparate things and events which typifies the views of the great mystics. For Bruno, it is a *fact* of the universe, an expression of the way things are. No "contraries" fall outside it. There are no disparities which are so immiscible as to be excluded from this principle, not even life and death.

There is a tendency to regard Bruno's vision as somewhat quaint and picturesque, couched as it is in the language of his day. This would be a mistake, though, for at least two reasons. The first is that it is consistent with the mystical vision that has surfaced in cultures throughout history:

Above time all is Brahman, One and Infinite. He is beyond north and south, east and west, above or below. To the unity of the One goes he who knows this.[9]

And,

> Jesus said: I am the Light that is above them all, I am the All, the All came forth from Me and the All attained to Me. Cleave a piece of wood, I am there; lift up the stone and you will find Me there.[10]

And secondly, there is the most surprising coherence between Bruno's vision and the views of many modern scientists of the highest caliber. Consider the statement by Nobelist Sir Peter B. and Jean S. Medawar: "The 'Unity of Nature' is not a slogan but a fact to the truth of which all natural processes bear witness."[11] And the view of the physicist David Bohm that life is a pervasive phenomenon that defies the notion of death-as-finality is remarkably congruent with Bruno's vision: "Everything is alive; what we call dead is an abstraction."[12] In fact, the congruence between Bohm's and Bruno's views are striking. Like Bruno, Bohm has advanced the idea of a fundamental domain which he calls the "implicate order," in which all things and events are contained and rooted.[13] It is utterly incapable of being fully described, as it is not subject to total apprehension. Yet we can comprehend it, at least to some extent, even though we can never adequately describe it. From this domain flows the seemingly disjunct events which make up our lives—including the "contraries and opposites" of which Bruno spoke. Thus, founded as they are on a common bedrock of reality, the opposites are really not contraries at all. They are in fact necessary for the existence of each other, one being the "principle of movement" of the other.[14]

Let us observe, then, for now, that it is not only to the statements of poets, mystics, and philosophers that we are obliged to look in attempting to understand the meaning of the "opposites" of happiness and suffering, life and death, and health and illness. The *tradition* of science has something to tell us, too, in spite of the current insistence that such topics are not properly its concern. For since the dawn of the scientific tradition in the West, and continuing through the present, scientists of the highest abilities have been concerned with these problems. And should it be surprising? For they, like us, face the same dichotomies, contradictions, contraries and opposites in their own lives. *Their* suffering, grief, and fears are as real to them as our torments are to us. There is nothing in the whole of science that spares the scientist his share of human misery. Scientist and layman alike are vexed by Bruno's "bruises of the heart."

THE THREE NOBLE TRUTHS OF MATTER

Underlying Bruno's philosophy of the *coincidentia oppositorum* is the implication that any *apparent* opposition in the universe is only an illusion. "Coincidence" comes about only as a result of our preexisting conceptions that separateness and isolation are the way of nature, while in fact there is nothing coincidental at all about nature's unity.

Many persons tend to regard all concepts of oneness, unity, and relatedness as musings appropriate to sixteenth-century mystic-scientists such as Bruno, and believe that modern physicists have outgrown such reckless tendencies. In "grown-up" science, now at a mature age of more than 300 years old, we leave such notions behind. Nowadays we are back to talking about *things*—be they particles, waves, or the elusive quarks. In our time, it is widely believed, science is preeminently concrete in its pursuits, and nowhere is it necessary to insert the diaphanous concepts which preoccupied Bruno and other early scientists of his persuasion.

But it is not so. The physicist Nick Herbert, in his forthcoming book, *Quantum Reality—Beyond the New Physics*, discusses the strange way in which the ideas of oneness and interconnectedness have become necessary and legitimate concerns of modern-day physicists. Herbert presents what he calls the "Three Noble Truths of Matter" in modern physics:

> Particles (electrons) behave like waves; waves (light) behave like particles. Particles and waves are all there is. Hence, everything in the physical world behaves like both waves and like particles. This is the First Noble Truth of Matter: The entire world is of One Nature.[15]

Herbert further adds that although the ordinary world seems to be made of distinct things, the quantum world ("which is after all only the everyday world examined closely") gives different images, depending on the experimental perspective. For example, there is no single image which corresponds to an electron, a situation which is exemplified in Werner Heisenberg's famous statement, "Electrons are not things." These facts lead to what Herbert calls the Second Noble Truth of Matter: The world is not made of objects.

This does not mean that, at bottom, the world is entirely subjective, shaped only by our thoughts, because different people taking the same viewpoint "see the same thing." But these "things" which people see are not specifiable, hard objects, so that "the quantum world is objective but objectless."

The Third Noble Truth of Matter? Bruno would not have been surprised: "The World is an Inseparable Wholeness." As Herbert states,

> . . . the world is instantly connected to every other part. Mother Nature's scattered children are profoundly and completely united. Bell's Theorem proves that any two systems that have once interacted and then moved apart are still in contact with one another.* Moreover, this contact (1) is not mediated by any force, (2) does not diminish with distance, and (3) acts instantaneously. So we return to Matter's Three Noble Truths with a new respect for Mother Nature's design for the universe. Nature is knit together in subtle ways which we are only just beginning to perceive. . . . all separation is an illusion. It's a remarkable and wondrous revelation.[17]

There are physicists who pull up short of Herbert's Three Noble Truths of Matter, considering them neither noble nor true, choosing instead to look another way, perhaps tacitly holding out for future developments in our knowledge of nature's ways that will vindicate the common-sense, particulate, separatist view of the world. But Giordano Bruno would have had no such reticence. He would likely recognize the Three Noble Truths of Matter as nothing esoteric or arcane, but simply nature's signature underlying his *coincidentia oppositorum*.

"O All Ye Sicknesses . . ."

The poet Gary Snyder once remarked that only those persons who are capable of giving up the planet Earth are fit to work for its ecological survival. With this comment he illuminated a perspective that is frequently forgotten: There is an intrinsic relatedness between opposites, even the extremes of planetary death and survival.

The same unifying power undergirds the extremes of health and illness. There is a deep reciprocity at work, an unseverable linkage between the hideousness of illness and the splendor of health. It seems odd to even

---

*For a discussion of Bell's Theorem, see my previous book, *Space, Time and Medicine*.[16]

suggest that such a relationship exists in view of the common attitude that illness is to be exterminated, that it is the harbinger of death, a precursor of personal extinction. Yet these connections between "opposites" will not die. They remain in our bones and blood. They are part of our collective wisdom, and they still survive intact in many cultures on Earth. Even in our own society we have hardly driven them out in spite of the presidential "wars" on various diseases and a medical technology that promises eventual eradication of the major diseases of the day.

We have forgotten how to think about illness. Indeed, we try mightily to *not* think about it at all—putting it out of our minds until it is time for an annual exam or until we contract an illness of some sort. Part of being healthy, we are told, is to *think* healthy—which, we presume, does *not* include ruminating about illness. We eschew sickness, and we dread attending funerals of deceased friends or trips to the hospital to visit those who are ill, or even visits to the dentist, internist, family physician, pediatrician, or gynecologist.

Yet we cannot *not* think about illness. There are constant reminders of it in the form of common colds we experience, or the illness of friends. Death is a part of the collective social structure. Try as we might, no one can avoid confrontation with disease.

It would seem, then, that the sheer inability to hide from illness, to permanently trade its embrace for that of health, might tell us about the relationship of the two: that they are mysteriously united in some odd way; that to know one is to know the other; that one cannot have one without having the other. Just as one cannot know up from down, or black without white, it appears that we cannot partition our awareness in a way that would exclude illness and death in favor of health.

Indeed, we cannot engage in any kind of health care without asking ourselves the question, "What is it I am trying to prevent?" Even if we engage in something as routine as immunizations, we are confronted at some psychological level with the question, "What is it I am immunizing myself *against*?" If we attend the increasingly popular "health fairs" where, for example, blood pressure is checked for free, the subterranean fear always lurks: "What would happen if I ignore my blood pressure?" All acts of health carry this grayish, dark side to them, because they remind us what we most wish to avoid: Illness and death are inevitable, and, try as we might, we can never separate health from illness, nor death from birth. And our frenzy to be healthy only increases our sensitivity to the phenomena of illness and death, just as light, in a world of objects, always casts shadows. The two go together, they draw each other onward, they cannot be teased apart.

Most premodern cultures seem to have had a deeper understanding of the unseverable nature of health and illness, and their myths and rituals embody this wisdom. In many societies there was the attempt to *live with* illness rather than to *hide from* it. It can be argued, of course, that such cultures did not shrink from illness and death because they could not; and that if they had been as technologically advanced as our own society they would have abhorred disease and death just as we. While there may be merit to this argument, it is more likely that many premodern societies' attitudes toward death and disease were an expression of an organic way of being, a manner of living-in-the-world where acceptance was not a function of helplessness but an expression of a deep understanding of the world.

In *The Golden Bough*, Sir James G. Frazier explicitly describes this attitude:

> . . . in the southern district of the island of Ceram, when a whole village suffers from sickness, a small ship is made and filled with rice, tobacco, eggs, and so forth, which have been contributed by all the people. A little sail is hoisted on the ship. When all is ready, a man calls out in a very loud voice, "O all ye sicknesses, ye smallpoxes, agues, measles, etc., who have visited us so long and wasted us so sorely, but who now cease to plague us, we have made ready this ship for you, and we have furnished you with provender sufficient for the voyage. Ye shall have no lack of food nor of betel-leaves nor of areca nuts nor of tobacco. Depart, and sail away from us directly; never come near us again; but go to a land which is far from here. Let all the tides and winds waft you speedily thither, and so convey you thither that for the time to come we may live sound and well, and that we may never see the sun rise on you again." Then ten or twelve men carry the vessel to the shore, and let it drift away from the land-breeze, feeling convinced that they are free from sickness for ever, or at least til the next time. If sickness attacks them again, they are sure it is not the same sickness, but a different one, which in due time they dismiss in the same manner. When the demon-laden bark is lost to sight, the bearers return to the village, whereupon a man cries out, "The sicknesses are now gone, vanished, expelled, and sailed away." At this all the people come running out of their houses, passing the word from one to the other with great joy, beating on gongs and on tinkling instruments.[1]

Illness is regarded here as if it were almost a living thing in itself, with needs of its own—the need to be addressed and reasoned with, the need to be provided for and attended to. Disease was seen as *reasonable*: bargains could be struck, deals could be made. The inhabitants of Ceram did *not* see themselves in a totally helpless situation when struck with "smallpoxes, agues, measles . . ."—a fact which stands in stark contrast with our own way of seeing ourselves waylaid and struck down by cancer, heart attacks, or strokes. The islanders were part of the *process* of illness and death, and possessed powers of intervention that were substantial.

Today, our sense of connectedness with illness has been all but lost, traded away for technological forms of intervention that have, in the bargaining, cost us much of our sense of connection to health as well. We do not know how to savor health because we have lost the vital connections between health and illness. One cannot replace an organic relatedness with the world with antibiotics, surgical procedures, and promissory immortality without destroying something that is vital, something that is health itself. It is not that modern interventions are "bad," but that they are no substitute for the wisdom of "the way things are," as philosopher of religion Huston Smith puts it.[2] Technology is not wisdom of itself; it is no guarantor of the *experience* of health.

Are we in our own time rediscovering something of the organicity of the world that was known to the primitive peoples of the planet? Perhaps. It is clear that we do not have the answers we wish in understanding health and illness, and our society is aflame with resentment at unfulfilled promises and the perceived inhumaneness of modern medicine. I do not believe, however, that this rage, whose existence can hardly be doubted, is properly directed. It is anger that is overtly directed at the "system," but at a system which is really ourselves. We are disappointed in ourselves at being taken in, at selling out, of forgetting something we once knew, of severing our organic ties with the world we live in. We are learning, painfully and deeply, that longevity is not the equivalent of quality of life. We are seeing though the vacuity of concepts such as "the disease-free interval." We cannot ignore that something vital is missing from our health—something without which health is not health at all.

What is this "something," this missing element? It is, I feel, the shadow that is illness, the shadow that must always accompany the light of health. It is the felt organic connection to the world, the sure knowledge that the world cannot be forced into shapes that are not part of its nature. It is the willingness to take on illness as surely as we take on health, knowing in the process that either experience is meaningless without the other.

It is difficult to entertain such reciprocal necessities as the connectedness of health and illness, for we have come to believe in our culture that we *can* have it "one way or the other"—that we can have up without down, black without white. We *can* have health without illness, or perhaps even birth without death. It is only a matter of more research funding, manpower, and time. To ask that we go beyond this kind of "either-or" way of thinking seems an invitation to a primitive form of thought that does not square with the potential of the modern age.

Yet it is not just the primitive who has understood the unseverable nature of opposites. It is a vision that men of all ages have happened upon. It is an enduring wisdom, part of the lore of the mystics and poets of all ages. It is part of ourselves, too, just as surely as it was part of the islanders of Ceram. We do not have to retreat to primitivity to entertain the possibility that health and illness require each other; we have only to awaken to the wisdom that man has always had, and still has. It is an awakening that was expressed in our own time by Henry Miller:

> To get beyond pain and suffering, beyond suffering, one must learn the equilibrist's art. . . . In walking the slack wire above the opposites one becomes thoroughly and keenly aware—perilously aware. The consciousness expands to embrace the apparently conflicting opposites. To be supremely aware, which means accepting life for what it is, eliminates the terrors of life and kills false hopes. I should say rather, kills hope, for seen from a beyond hope appears as an evil rather than a good.
>
> I say nothing about being happy. When one really understands what happiness is one goes out like a light. . . . All arrangements for a better life here on earth mean increased suffering and misery. Everything that is being planned for tomorrow means the destruction of that which now exists. *The best world is that which is now this very moment.*[3]

On Knowing Health

This is the great image or idol which dominates our civilization, and which we worship with mad blindness. The idolatry of self. Consciousness should be a flow from within outwards. The organic necessity of the human being should flow into spontaneous action and spontaneous awareness, consciousness.

But the moment man became aware of himself he made a picture of himself, and began to live from the picture: that is, from without inwards. This is truly the reversal of life.

—D. H. Lawrence

As recently as two hundred years ago, color blindness was unknown. Then the great English chemist, John Dalton, discovered that he himself was color blind. His awareness led to the discovery that the problem was actually quite common, affecting a significant percentage of the population.

What are we to say about color blindness prior to its discovery? Did it even exist? Most of us would instinctively say yes. Dalton discovered it, but this had nothing to do with its existence or nonexistence.

Thus, so with health. We generally believe that we are either healthy or we are not; our health does not depend on our awareness of it or our thoughts about it. It is an objective fact, and is either present or not.

Yet a moment's reflection gives reason to question these easy assumptions. There was a time for most of us when we gave no thought to health. This was the time of youth, a time when illness had not yet made an appearance in our lives. There were no events of poor health that could cause us to focus on our healthiness, no dark events counterposed with bright ones, no contrasting experience which accentuated our wellness.

At those times, were we healthy? The question is not rhetorical. We hardly had a concept of what health is; we were unaware of health. How could we experience what we were unaware of? Is health an objective "thing" or "event" that exists "out there," or is it tied to our awareness of its existence? Does it have some fundamental status all its own, or is our own consciousness of it necessary to bring it into being?

We can recognize here an ancient philosophical problem that is still significant: if a tree falls in the forest, and no one is there to hear it, does it make a sound? Unless an event impinges on the consciousness of an observer, can it be called an event? Are *we* necessary to lend validity to the existence of all classes of events? Can a "happening" be called in any sense real if it occurs outside human awareness? I am neither inclined by disposition nor capable by training to reason my way through these epistemological conundrums that have thwarted (and continue to thwart) Western philosophers for hundreds of years, but shall offer some observations that bear on what we mean by health.

"DOES CONSCIOUSNESS EXIST?"

Bertrand Russell, in his classic treatise, *A History of Western Philosophy*, states:

> It had, until then [the year 1904], been taken for granted by philoso-
> phers that there is a kind of occurrence called "knowing," in which one
> entity, the knower or subject, is aware of another, the thing known or
> the object.[1]

The event in 1904 to which Russell is referring was the publication of an
essay by the American philosopher William James with the startling title,
"Does Consciousness Exist?" The main purpose of this essay, Russell states,
was to deny that the time-honored subject-object relationship is fundamental. Russell continues:

> The knower was regarded as a mind or soul; the object known might
> be a material object, an eternal essence, another mind, or, in self-
> consciousness, identical with the knower. Almost everything in accepted
> philosophy was bound up with the dualism of subject and object. The
> distinction of mind and matter, the contemplative ideal, and the tradi-
> tional notion of "truth," all need to be radically reconsidered if the dis-
> tinction of subject and object is not accepted as fundamental.[2]

And Russell, the thoroughgoing skeptic, allows that,

> For my part, I am convinced that James was right on this matter.[3]

What did James have to say about "knowing"? Russell adds:

> Consciousness, [James] says, is "the name of a nonentity, and has no
> right to a place among first principles. Those who still cling to it are
> clinging to a mere echo, the faint rumour left behind by the disappear-
> ing 'soul' upon the air of philosophy." There is, he continues, "no ab-
> original stuff or quality of being, contrasted with that of which material
> objects are made, out of which our thoughts of them are made." . . .
> [James] . . . is not denying that our thoughts perform a function which is
> that of knowing, and that this function may be called "being conscious."
> What he is denying might be put crudely as the view that consciousness
> is a "thing." He holds that there is "only one primal stuff or material,"

out of which everything in the world is composed. This stuff he calls "pure experience." Knowing, he says, is a particular sort of relation between two portions of pure experience. The subject-object relationship is derivative: "experience, I believe, has no such inner duplicity."[4]

James was challenging the common sense notion indigenous to all of us, that there is something "out there" that we, the knower, actually know. This natural way of viewing the world typifies modern medicine, as when we make statements in which we assign to health and illness an "out there" status: "I contracted an illness," or, "I lost my health." James would ask us, what are these things that we "contracted" and "lost"? He challenges us to give up the "inner duplicity" of subject-and-object thinking in which we adopt an "us against it" stance, on the grounds that this particular way of viewing the world is an illusion.

James does *not*, however, ask us to give up consciousness, or being conscious. This point is greatly misunderstood. Many persons fear that if the subject-object way of dividing the world is abandoned, some inchoate, illogical, nonverbal mush will invade the mind, and we shall not be able to differentiate a snail from Mount Everest, nor ourselves from either. This is a distorted view, and one contradicted in the actual experience of the mystics who *do* abandon the subject-object mode of seeing the world. Indeed, a *greater* clarity most frequently follows, a clarity that reveals the prior subject-object way of dividing the world to be erroneous, deceptive, and impoverishing.

Thus, the answer that James would give to the question, "Does consciousness exist?" is that it does *not* exist as a fragment isolated from the rest of the world that it perceives.

THE WORLD AS ONENESS

This idea suggests that there is a unity in nature that is fundamental. Not only does this oneness unite what we call "things" in the world, it unites the seer and perceiver with these "things"—through what James referred to as "pure experience." It is *experience*, according to this view, that is the "only . . . primal stuff or material" out of which everything comes.

It is the recognition of this fact that is the core of the mystical experience. This understanding is embodied in a remark by the great scholar of mysticism, W. T. Stace:

The whole multiplicity of things which comprise the universe are identical with one another and therefore constitute only one thing, a pure unity. The Unity, the One . . . is the central experience and the central concept of all mysticism, of whichever type.[5]

A frequent impulse on encountering this nondual way of viewing the world is to dismiss it as the fuzzy thinking of mystics or primitives who had no intimations of the sheer complexity of nature. It is wrong, however, to ascribe to this view a backwardness that we in our current age of enlightenment have cleverly escaped. Indeed, we encounter it at every turn in our own time, running headlong into it in the views of both modern philosophers and modern scientists. Consider Whitehead's comment:

> Nature gets credit which should in truth be reserved to ourselves; the rose for its scent, the nightingale for his song and the sun for its radiance. The poets are entirely mistaken. They should address their lyrics to themselves and should turn them into odes of self-congratulations on the excellency of the human mind. Nature is a dull affair, soundless, scentless, colorless, merely the hurrying of material, endlessly, meaninglessly.[6]

Whitehead, whose vision of the unitary qualities of the world is comparable to those of the most thoroughgoing mystics, suggests the sheer impossibility of regarding nature as something standing apart from ourselves. There is some nexus in which we and nature unite, some matrix in which the distinction between "us" and "it" melt away.

In speaking of "scent," "song," and "radiance," Whitehead is speaking of *experience*—the cognizing capacity of the human mind combined indissolubly with the world to produce consciously recognizable phenomena. We do not think *about* the scent of the rose, the song of the nightingale, or the radiance of the sun. There are no external "its" waiting about to be registered by our consciousness in this nondual view; and there is no stuff called consciousness that is lurking, ready to do the registering. To believe that such a dynamic actually exists is to fall prey to the "inner duplicity" that James warned against.

And it is a warning that has arrived—unexpectedly—from modern science. For if there is a quality that distinguishes the science of this century from the science that has come before it, it is the transcendence of the view of reality that emphasizes the subject-object, knower-known distinction. The duality of mind and matter has yielded to a new view that emphasizes, surprisingly, the view of consciousness that is very close to that of James as well as the views inherent in most mystical traditions. Consider Einstein's comment:

Pure logical thinking cannot yield us any knowledge of the empirical world; all knowledge of reality starts from experience and ends in it. Propositions arrived at by purely logical means are completely empty of reality.[7]

And the physicist Max Planck, who defined for us the concept of the quantum, felt that ". . . not even the existence of the real world could be logically proved."[8]

Planck's view of the relationship of consciousness and the physical world is akin to Einstein's, who further noted that

. . . the concept of the "real external world" of our everyday thinking rests exclusively on sense-impressions.[9]

Thus, the frequently heard notion that consciousness and the world are intimately connected only in the thinking of naive, primitive, and uneducated mystics is far from the case. Striking similarities are to be found in the views of mystics and modern scientists. While it is true that it would be an exaggeration to imply that there is uniform agreement among modern physicists as to the precise degree to which consciousness and the physical world interrelate, or what, for example, is the origin of the "ordering principles" by which we make sense from our impressions of the world, there is general agreement that the notion of a fixed, external world that stands totally apart from humans—the cornerstone of an older science—has been transcended. The new view gives due regard for an integral role of consciousness, and is expressed in a famous remark by the physicist John Archibald Wheeler:

Nothing is more important about quantum physics than this: it has destroyed the concept of the world as "sitting out there." . . . In order to observe . . . the observer has to reach in. . . . The universe will never afterwards be the same.[10]

And,

"Participator" replaces the "observer" of classical physics. It is impossible in principle to separate what happens to any system, even the Universe, from what this participator does. This principle of Bohr's of the "wholeness" of nature . . . may be expected to come to the fore in a new and far deeper form.[11]

This idea strikes down the term "observer," a notion that belonged to the classical way of looking at the world. The observer could stand safely apart from the world. He could approach it, measure it, and extract data without taking part. But this cannot be done in the new view.

There are, thus, threads of similarity running through the presentiments about consciousness and experience of a great variety of thinkers—mystics, philosophers, and modern scientists—which span millenia. There is a core insistence in the views we have cursorily surveyed on the inter-relatedness of consciousness and the physical world.

CAN HEALTH BE ACQUIRED?

From this perspective it is impossible to postulate health as set apart from a distinct "I." For if there is no definite "I," there is no health to acquire—for the simple reason that there is no "I" to acquire it. Quite simply, the acquisition of health demands an acquirer, and depends on the dual way of splitting the world up into subject-object, knower-known categories. Without this distinction there *is* no health-as-object, nothing to take on, nothing to become, and nothing to care *for*.

Yet there *is* an experience of health, just as the mystics experience a world around them without exhibiting a strong sense of "I." And, moreover, the experience of health *without* a burdensome sense of "I" is *heightened*, not diminished. This is the accentuation of perception and feeling that is part of the mystical legacy, the clarity and enhancement of feeling that bursts forth in literary and artistic expressions through the ages. It stands in stark contrast to the perception of health that most persons feel in the ordinary dualistic world we live in, in which health becomes the mere absence of disease—an experience which, surely, is itself sick.

There is nothing in the whole of my experience as a physician that leads me to believe that health is an external entity that can be acquired. Neither can I believe, even, that it is "something" that lies latent within us, waiting to emerge in full flower. I reject the idea, moreover, of health "care," for I have never observed this "thing" that is in need of being cared for. I can only conceive of health as *experience*—a result of a nondual interrelationship between human consciousness and the physical world.

Health is a realization, not an acquisition. Evidence for this assertion is implied in the aphorism, "Money can't buy health!" We all know something of the wisdom of health-as-experience, perhaps in faint memories of nondual relationships with the world in which health was felt not as an object, but something in the core of our being. And I am certain that physicians see evidence pointing to the same view of health every day, as the following experience illustrates.

OLD HUNTER'S STORY

It was my first day as an intern on the medical ward, having "rotated off" the emergency room service. It was early morning, wintry outside, and not yet daylight. The hospital corridors felt chilled, and in the soft light I saw a patient seated in a wheelchair huddled in several blankets. He was assigned to a fellow intern, and I knew nothing about his particular case. I spoke to him, though, and was surprised that he did not respond. In fact, he seemed to register nothing. He stared straight ahead, motionless, and I noticed his hands were white from his forceful grasp of the arms of the wheelchair. Although I perceived him to be in middle age, his face was aged and bore an expression I shall never forget—that of stark terror. He sat still, transfixed in fear, his wheelchair in his tetanic grasp.

"What's wrong with him?" I asked the resident.

"Oh, nothing. That's old Hunter, nothing at all the matter with him," he replied.

I asked the obvious. "Then why is he here? Are you just trying to keep the beds full?" This was a feeble attempt at humor, for any empty bed was a rarity.

The resident went on to describe how Hunter, when in his thirties, began to experience chest pain. The cause of the pain was an enigma to his physician, but Hunter was sure it was originating from his heart. Every conceivable test to decipher the origin of the pain proved normal. His physicians (he accumulated several) searched for well-known etiologies of chest pain—cardiac, esophageal, pulmonary, pleural, neurogenic, cancerous, infectious, etc.—to no avail. Hunter's belief that he had heart disease grew firmer as the list of negative diagnostic studies lengthened. He quit his job as a butcher, certain that the physical exertion would provoke a heart attack. He gradually receded into inactivity, focusing on the pain which no one could demonstrate as "real." He became crippled by it, utterly devastated and consumed by his attention to it. His personal relationships deteriorated. His wife, emotionally unable to support the cripple he had become, abandoned him, as did all his friends. Bereft of funds, he came under the care of the charity hospital system. He withdrew more and more to the point of seldom communicating at all, and eventually was committed to the psychiatric ward with a diagnosis of cardiac neurosis, the appellation given to persons who develop morbid concerns about heart disease yet who have healthy hearts.

One night he awakened on the psychiatric ward with one of his many episodes of chest pain and he was once again shipped over to the medical floor "just in case," and to "rule out" a heart attack. After this event was repeated many times it seemed simpler to let him remain on the medical floor in order to avoid shuttling him between the psychiatry and medical services. It seemed to make little difference to old Hunter where he was, since by this time he seemed oblivious to his surroundings. What meant most to him was being in the hospital, since this affirmed his worst fear, that of heart disease.

The resident allowed flippantly, "His hospital record's volumes thick. All normal numbers. A real monument to ol' Hunter's health!"

As he spoke, there sat Hunter—immobilized with his fear, stolid, hearing nothing, terror-stricken—with a chart full of normal numbers.

But a monument to health? The thought was as absurd then as it is now. The objective and subjective meanings of health here seemed discrepant.

I looked at this poor human being, not knowing if he saw or heard anything at all. I heard the resident say in the background, "Yep! Healthy as he can be!" A quotation related by a former patient floated into my head as we left Hunter alone in his inner world: "Such men must have doctors to threaten and flatter them, to give them the only pleasure they can enjoy— the pleasure of not being dead."

Old Hunter's case seemed to affirm that any definition of health that doesn't hinge on the experiential is bound to be hollow. Health will never be adequately described by numbers alone, or by fat charts detailing normal studies. Hunter was right and we were wrong. He *was not* healthy, and he knew it.

Sometimes we insist that health is present when it is not, as in the case of old Hunter. And occasionally we believe that health is *absent* when it is *present*, as the following case illustrates.

JOHN'S STORY

The old man lay dying in the intensive care unit, affixed to a myriad array of cables and wires that led from his body to monitoring devices of various sorts. Blood pressure, heart rate, pulmonary "wedge" pressure, urine flow, and body temperature were measured and displayed in silent, red digital forms. The greenish hues of the oscilloscopic sweep revealed the pulsing spikes of his heart's artificial pacemaker that now kept him alive.

John was ninety-eight years old, the oldest patient in my practice. Yet his lively spirit concealed his age, and I never thought of him as ancient. All the nurses and physicians in my medical group knew and loved him dearly. Every time he visited my office for an appointment the entire clinic buzzed with excitement, for it was a remarkable experience to see him and talk to him. He would hobble in, using his cane both for walking and gesticulation, defying the pain I knew he felt in his swollen, arthritic joints. It was as if he had come to take care of *us*, for he was alive with concerned inquiry: "How has your week been?" to the receptionist; "Are you married yet?" to the single nurse; "You're working too hard, try to get more rest," to me. He never complained. He smiled much, even laughed, and seemed immune to his many ailments. I felt at times that my care of him was a charade, a curious inversion, that he was simply indulging me by patiently enduring my treatments and medications. If I wanted to prescribe another drug, well, that was all right with him, if it would make *me* feel better to do so. He seemed wise in ways that constantly took me off guard.

John's heart failed as its electrical activity dwindled and spent itself, and he said yes, he thought he did want an artificial pacemaker. But, following the implantation, the surgical incision became infected, and the infection spread to the blood. He developed pneumonia as well. As his blood pressure fell to dangerous levels, his kidneys ceased to work. And there he lay, still alive on morning rounds in the critical care unit, most of his major organ systems artifically supported and poorly functioning except one: his brain. As usual, and for reasons I could not explain, he was intensely alert, even chipper.

As I fussed over the numbers—blood pressure, urine output, body weight, etc.—and as I listened to heart and lungs and felt and observed his body, our eyes met and locked. He broke into a smile—an alert, clear-eyed smile that came from the deep reservoir that I knew by then to be a part of him, just as surely as his pulse and blood pressure were parts of him. He didn't say anything, though; he didn't need to say anything. But I did, and clumsily searched for something that might offer him some hope. Recalling that his failing kidneys had produced a meager amount of urine the past hour, I offered, "John, your kidneys started working again; you're better!"

His smile relaxed as he thought about the revelation, and I knew at once that he saw through it, that he sensed the meaninglessness of it. He accepted my comment, though, as I meant it—as a gesture of care and love. Then he smiled again and said, "Thank you, Doctor. Now tell me: Better than what?"

Better than what? He cut through my officious pronouncement, my paltry criteria for "better," grateful but not needing it. His reply transfixed me, and I could not respond for a while. The nurse in attendance was uncomfortable too and nervously found something to do. I held his hand silently for a time, eventually telling him when I would return.

As I stood there I was taken with a thought that made no sense at the time: *This man is healthy.* Lying helplessly, affixed to various gadgets, this gentle, wise, alert man seemed *beyond* the distinctions of health and illness. John seemed to transcend the easy classifications of "sick or well," "better or worse." And he *knew* it, too—he *experienced* this transcendence, radiating a kind of healthiness even while moribund.

An hour later John died—I am convinced, in good health.

Our ability to know health-as-experience hinges on our capacity to transcend the common-sense feeling that the world, and thus health and illness, exist "out there." We *can* develop this capacity, this way of knowing the world, in which we cease to set ourselves apart from the illusory "things" we experience. It is the way of sensing the world that emphasizes unity of knower and known, subject and object. It is the mode of being described by Emerson:

> For the sense of being which in calm hours rises is not different from things, from space, from light, from time. It is one with them and proceeds from the same source.[12]

Being Blank: The Health Strategy of Doing Nothing

> . . . the adherence of all under heaven can only be won by letting-alone.
>
> —*Tao Te Ching*

"If you look for the Buddha, you will not see the Buddha." "If you deliberately try to become a Buddha, your Buddha is samsara." "If a person seeks the Tao, that person loses the Tao." "By intending to bring yourself into accord with Suchness, you instantly deviate." There is a Law of Reversed Effort. The harder we try with the conscious will to do something, the less we shall succeed. Proficiency and the results of proficiency come only to those who have learned the paradoxical art of simultaneously doing and not doing, of combining relaxation with activity, of letting go as a person in order that the immanent and transcendent Unknown Quantity may take hold.

—Aldoux Huxley
Tomorrow and Tomorrow and Tomorrow

Every move we make to solve or work out a distress simply reinforces the illusion that we are that particular distress. Thus, ultimately . . . to try to escape or solve a distress merely perpetuates that distress, or that distress in a disguised form. What is so upsetting to us is not the distress itself, but our *attachment* to that distress. We identify with it, and that alone is the real difficulty.

—Ken Wilber

In a poem called "Blank," the writer D. H. Lawrence says,

At present I am a blank, and I admit it . . .
So I am just going to go on being a blank,
   til something nudges me from within,
and makes me know I am not blank any longer.[1]

In this poem, Lawrence is announcing that he is giving up—because he knows this is only a temporary state. Something is bound to happen, something will stir him again, filling the emptiness he now feels. It is a strategy of doing nothing—not out of resignation and hopelessness, but out of an awareness that through inactivity and nonaction substance will arise.

This principle—let us call it "divine waiting"—is foreign to most of us in our health strategy. It is equated with doing nothing but standing idly by until we are stricken with cancer, heart disease, or high blood pressure. Only through vigorous efforts can disease and infirmity truly be thwarted. Isn't that the literal meaning of preventive medicine? Keep the parts fit, don't give them a chance to break down. Diet, exercise, periodic health exams, maybe even megavitamins and meditation thrown in—who knows? You can't be too careful . . .

And so we spend staggering sums on health care, with no end in sight. We live out the notion that if it isn't costly it probably isn't worth much, and that if it doesn't hurt it isn't valuable. After all, "No pain, no gain!" These attitudes reflect an underlying assumption that the road to health is paved with dollars and sweat. Health is something we have to *work* at.

There are times in our health strategy when action is called for. The mysterious pain that won't go away may need to be evaluated, just as the chronic sore that won't heal should be checked. But at other times action is *not* called for, but is something that just gets in the way. Sometimes, instead of promoting health, it obstructs it. There are times when we, with Lawrence, need to be blank.

Numerous health problems illustrate the wisdom of this approach. Most headaches, for instance, are either related to tension (so-called "muscle contracture headaches" from the tightness of the muscles, ligaments, and tendons that overlie the skull), or are vascular headaches, of which migraine is a variety. Our approach to a headache is to reach for medication—aspirin, Tylenol, Excedrin, Anacin, or some more potent prescription drug. In our action-oriented perspective, headache equals medication, a course of action that survives because it works: it *is* possible to suppress the pain of most headaches with drugs. But there is another way. Fully three-fourths of all headaches can be abolished through doing nothing—by learning to be blank.

It comes as a shock to most persons who have had lifelong headaches to be told this. Yet methodologies have arisen that are more effective than any pain medication for those who are open to their use—such as biofeedback, meditation, and various forms of relaxation. They have one thing in common: they emphasize doing nothing, achieving profound physiological and psychological relaxation, quieting the body and mind. As this is done, the headache falls away and the person begins to experience a diminution in the frequency and intensity of pain. Often the headaches cease to occur altogether.

Doing nothing, becoming Lawrence's blank, is therapeutic not only in "nuisance" disorders like headaches, but can be important in life-or-death situations as well. Friedman has shown that if persons who have survived a heart attack learn to modify their behavior through a program which involves the "doing nothing" of certain relaxation techniques, the ensuing death rate and rate of recurrent heart attack is lessened when compared to groups of persons who do not incorporate these skills following a myocardial infarction.[2] Doing nothing saves lives.

It can also alter our physiology profoundly. Elevation of the cholesterol level is a major risk factor for the development of coronary artery disease, the commonest cause of death in our society. If men who have high cho-lesterol levels learn the "do nothing" art of meditation, the cholesterol level falls on the order of one-third, a result that cannot be regularly achieved through the use of any drug.[3]

For Lawrence, being blank was a calculated strategy toward future ac-tion. It was a path toward creativity and artistic expression for him. We know, too, that it can be a path toward heightened health, as in the above examples. It isn't a substitute, for sometimes action is needed. Comple-mentary approaches are required, the way of action and the way of divine waiting, the way of active emptiness and the way of being blank. Each ap-proach has its place, and we need to know the wise applications of each, and not vacillate in uncertainty between the two. The Buddhist injunction would serve us well here: "When walking, walk. When sitting, sit. Don't wobble!"

There is paradox here, for one of the most difficult tasks is to "go on being blank," as Lawrence put it. At every turn we feel impelled to do, to act, to think. In an odd way, then, doing nothing demands the most potent discipline. Yet this discipline is not the hurly-burly sort of doing that we are accustomed to, but a kind of cooperation with what is, a state of mind and body that leads to a quiet awareness in which the sought-after blank-ness and nothingness are transformed into the most fecund understand-ing. One of the clearest expressions of this state is given by Aldous Huxley, whose understanding was later to be put to the test during his experience with cancer:

Total awareness, then, reveals the following facts: that I am profoundly ignorant, that I am impotent to the point of helplessness. . . . This dis-covery may seem at first rather humiliating and even depressing. But if I wholeheartedly accept them, the facts become a source of peace, a rea-son for serenity and cheerfulness. I am ignorant and impotent and yet, somehow or other, here I am, unhappy, no doubt, profoundly dissatis-fied, but alive and kicking. In spite of everything, I survive, I get by, sometimes I even get on. From these two sets of facts—my survival on the one hand and my ignorance and impotence on the other—I can only infer that the not-I, which looks after my body and gives me my best ideas, must be amazingly intelligent, knowledgeable and strong. We know very little and can achieve very little; but we are at liberty, if we so choose, to co-operate with a greater power and a completer knowledge, an unknown quantity at once immanent and transcendent, at once physical and mental, at once subjective and objective. If we co-operate, we shall be all right, even if the worst should happen. If we refuse to co-operate, we shall be all wrong even in the most propitious of circumstances.[4]

We ought to remember that we can never beat the body into line, even with our most vigorous and aggressive health strategies. Without exception, even while "doing" in the most spectacular ways—performing coronary artery bypass surgery, administering potent "fourth generation" antibiotics, transplanting kidneys or livers or hearts—throughout it all we rely on the "unknown quantity at once immanent and transcendent" which Huxley described. The fact is that the healing process begins before, and lasts after, the drug is administered or the surgery has been performed. These medical acts, heroic though they may be, are for nothing but for the body's inner wisdom—what we glibly call homeostasis, self-direction, hierarchical interaction of subsystems, and the like. Every physician knows that there is a limit to therapies of every sort, beyond which they become downright meddlesome, interfering, even dangerous, the progenitors of one of the commonest "diseases" of our day, that of iatrogenic illness (illness that is caused by the doctor). It is this amazing intelligence and strength that is part of the body, and that is part of the world encompassing the body, that makes heroes of surgeons and seers of diagnosticians.

Being blank, then, is not what it seems. It is a call to action, though of a sort we have forgot. "Letting alone" is not a commitment to ruination. There is Wisdom in the universe that does not make a noise. There is Strength that does not announce itself. Sometimes, if we allow, it invades hospital rooms, surgery suites, emergency settings, and, if we are quiet enough, our own body.

Health and Illness as Perfection

These roses under my window make no reference to former roses or to better ones; they are for what they are; they exist with God today. There is no time to them. There is simply the rose; it is perfect in every moment of its existence.

—Ralph Waldo Emerson
"Self-Reliance"

Lying deep in the depths of the human psyche is the sure knowledge that adversity is an essential component of any existence, if that existence is to be complete. The steel must be hardened, and the trial must be by fire if it is to be a trial at all. The mythic archetypes of all cultures represent this idea, enduring enormous physical onslaughts, pains, tortures, woundings—finally coming through, emerging greater and more complete than before—as the examples of Achilles, Prometheus, and Oedipus demonstrate in Western mythology.

Suffering has always been part of the maturation process of the saint and the mystic. This process has been called "mortification" by the mystics of the West, and is an essential part of the mystic way. As the great English writer on the subject, Evelyn Underhill, states:

> Mortification takes its name from the reiterated statement of all ascetic writers that the senses, or "body of desire," with the cravings which are excited by different aspects of the phenomenal world, must be mortified or killed.[1]

One gains the decided impression that the mystics actually seek out suffering—or in any case do not turn from it—for some elemental reason. And the reason is that suffering and illness constitute a necessary adjunct to the process of spiritual purification which is the mystic's goal, the "change of life and turning of energy from the old and easy channels to the new," as Underhill puts it.[2]

> [This change] is a period of actual battle between the inharmonious elements of the self, its lower and higher springs of action: of toil, fatigue, bitter suffering, and many disappointments. Nevertheless, . . . the object of mortification is not death but life: the production of health and strength of the human consciousness.[3]

And there is a definite correspondence between the degree of suffering and the grandeur of the mystical flight. John Tauler, the mystical genius who lived circa 1300–1361 and who was a pupil of the great Dominican scholar Meister Eckhart, stated:

> The stronger the death the more powerful and thorough is the corresponding life; the more intimate the death, the more inward is the life. Each life brings strength, and strengthens to a harder death.[4]

There is, thus, a collective statement from mystics of diverse sources that affirms the place in life for difficult, painful experience. Perfection of the spirit is, in fact, impossible to attain without it, we are told. Suffering, ill-health, and pain are not so much grotesque facts of life as they are prerequisites for the opening of the doors of perception. Without the conjoined fact of the good and the bad, of health and illness, there is no advance of the spirit, only stasis and stagnation.

It is this recognition that has led to some of the great lyrical, poetic descriptions of the perfection implicit in things just as they are. Life, to be perfect, need not be purged of all things disagreeable. The hurtful, the painful, are *part of* the perfection. This vision was stated by Whitman in his "Song of Myself":

> I have heard what the talkers were talking, the talk of the beginning
> and the end,
> But I do not talk of the beginning or the end.
>
> There was never any more inception than there is now,
> Nor any more youth or age than there is now;
> And will never be any more perfection than there is now,
> Nor any more heaven or hell than there is now. . . .
>
> This minute that comes to be over the past decillions,
> There is no better than it and now.[5]

Whitman shares the vision of Emerson's perfect roses, complete in their existence *now*—beyond time, beyond comparisons, beyond imperfection and containing thus their own harmony.

This is the recurring vision that confronts us in the statements of the mystics and the poets. And the relevance for us, in our quest to understand the place in our lives of health and illness, is this: "The whole multiplicity of things" which "constitute only one thing"[6] includes both the morbid and the sublime, the painful and the pleasurable, and the facts of illness as well as health. This is the vision of health as wholeness, a vision which in our technologically oriented age we have done our best to forget. But we cannot—for the vision of the oneness of health and illness is an archetypal one which the most fanciful achievements of biotechnology and modern medicine in all their grandeur can never banish from our deepest, inmost wisdom.

The response of many persons to such observations is to regard them as so many pretty phrases. It is the reality of pain and suffering that is primary, not the musings of saints, mystics, or poets. No matter how sublime the expressions may sound, when it comes to the individual experience of pain, this horrible event, and the illness of impending death which it represents, annuls all flowery philosophy. Pain, suffering, and death are malevolent and grotesque and evil. Philosophical discourse about "unity"* and "oneness" of health and illness are nice-sounding phrases when we are healthy and fit, but when we are in the grasp of the darker experiences of life they come as no consolation and are hardly persuasive.

As William James reminded us, a living metaphysic, like a living religion, is a matter of vision and not of argument.[7] This is another way of saying that all visions, to be ultimately convincing, must eventually be translatable into the plain terms of human experience. Can health and illness as perfection be translated in ways that would be persuasive to those who do not know it as such?

Although the vision of the interconnectedness of health and illness is a uniform component of "the most highly developed branches of the human family,"[8] the mystics, this wisdom is not at all restricted to this class of human beings. It is part of the experience—as well as the vision—of the "plain man." The mystic vision merely confirms what we repetitively experience in our own lives and emerges as commonplace experiences that, as Whitehead said, are "momentous in [their] coordination of values." It is in the here-and-now of our daily life that we discover ". . . the understanding of tragedy in nature and in human life as it expresses itself in the inevitability of transformation, decay, and loss," and that "beneath the immediacy of the flux lies the Harmony of Nature as a fluid, flexible support."[9]

The knowledge that health and illness come together in harmonious perfection, this paradox that is difficult to grasp in our logical moments, lies within us all. With only a slight change in perspective, we can grasp the fact of the unity of these opposites. We can begin to know that absolute distinctions between health and illness are illusions which, in our clearest moments, begin to fall away. The relationship between these facts of life appears as a complementary oneness, a facet of reality beautifully described by the fifteenth-century Indian mystic, Kabir:

The river and its waves are one surf: where is the difference between the river and its waves?

When the wave rises, it is the water; and when it falls, it is the same water again. Tell me, Sir, where is the distinction?[10]

Illness: The Necessary Dimension

What? The ultimate goal of science is to create for man the greatest possible amount of pleasure and the least possible amount of pain? But suppose pleasure and pain were so linked together that he who *wants* to have the greatest possible amount of the one *must* have the greatest possible amount of the other also?

—Friedrich Nietzsche
The Gay Science

. . . "illness" and "sickness" . . . to most medical practitioners . . . are *the* enemy, something to be rid of in the patient, a noxious intrusion into normal life. Yet, cannot one also learn from, and in, illness? The famed German orchestra and opera conductor, Bruno Walter, (1876–1962), tells how, for years, he championed the symphonies of the Austrian composer Anton Bruckner, yet somehow never truly understood the logic or organization of such massive, expansive scores. Then, when ill and hospitalized, he experienced that proximity to death and "eternity" which lie at the root of Bruckner's deeply devout music. Through his illness, Walter learned a deeper sense of life; the inner logic of Bruckner's scores revealed itself to him. Illness, far from being only an adversary, was for him a teacher, an experience, not only of frightening decay but of growth as well.

—Howard F. Stein

In his essay, "The Suffering Body of the City," Robert J. Sardello describes how our culture has come to shrink from illness and disease.[1] We withdraw from unlovely and grotesque things—including the sick and dying. We have developed repositories for them on the margins of society, as Sardello puts it, calling them hospitals, nursing homes, retirement villages, and state "schools." In many cases they may actually serve a benevolent and humane purpose, a fact we hide behind in justifying our reluctance to touch the infirm, the sick, the dying.

Our efforts to sequester the dark, diseased elements of our society express a deep inner urge to escape illness in favor of health, to have one without the other. Illness denied is a prettier world. If we can shut it out, if we can know health only, if we can conquer cancer and exterminate the endless chain of illnesses we are told are our enemies, that is our goal, and, indeed, the alleged purpose implicit in all of bioscience.

We ought to begin to question this goal, for it is a pitfall—not because we could not eventually exterminate disease, but for subtler reasons. *If* we were able to achieve total success in eliminating all residual shreds of illness and disease in our world, we would correspondingly eliminate health. A great paradox is at work here. In some sense medical progress is a boomerang, banishing the very health it would enthrone. Why?

First let us observe that our folk wisdom contains hints that such a hidden dimension exists, that to have no illness is to have no health. For example, we frequently hear statements such as, "We don't appreciate our health until it's gone," implying an epistemological connection between health and illness. It has even been advocated that physicians should periodically become ill to sharpen their awareness of what they do, a position affirmed by the flood of recent accounts by physicians of their own illness—the "my encounter with death" genre of medical writing. These kinds of statements point to a fundamental relationship between health and illness that, in our mad rush to cure everything and to usher in the millenium of perfect health, we have forgotten. It is a relationship that goes beyond health and illness to the question of how we know anything at all.

DIFFERENCE AND AWARENESS

Whitehead said,

> The first principle of epistemology should be that the changeable, shifting aspects of our relations to nature are the primary topics for conscious observation.[2]

In other words, if we never experienced a shift or change in our relationship with nature, we would likely know nothing. It is the *flux* of experience in the world that makes possible our knowledge of anything at all. Lest we dismiss this point of view as merely an unimportant philosophical point, we should note that it comes to us also from modern biology through our knowledge of how the senses work. For example, the developmental biologist Davenport states,

If we examine the experiences from which our knowledge of the world arises, we can see that they consist of various types of differences. Without difference, there can be no experience. The experience of difference is basic to our notion of existence, the latter being derived from the Latin *ex sistere*, which means "to stand apart," i.e., to be different. . . . The foundation of any valid epistemology must be the recognition that, since all properties must be experienced as difference, the physical world exists for us only in terms of relationships. . . . Recognition of the nature of the experience that underlies our knowledge is important for the realization that physical reality does not exist before us as an object of study but *emerges from our consciousness during our changing experience within nature.*[3]

Again, this view is identical to that of Whitehead: ". . . our whole experience is composed out of our relationships to the rest of things."[4]

By and large the vast complex of physiologic processes in the human body is silent. We do not attend to them consciously, and have no need to. They lie deep below our level of awareness. Indeed, when we try to pay attention to some of them we may disrupt their smooth functioning. A classic example of this is the medical syndrome of hyperventilation, in which one begins to actually notice his breathing. The subliminal worry begins to surface: "I am not getting enough breath!" and one begins to "help" the respiratory cycle by intentionally taking in great draughts of air, far too frequently. If this process of overbreathing continues, the carbon dioxide level in the blood falls, the pH level changes in body fluids, the ratio of ionized to deionized calcium in the blood shifts, and severe muscle spasms and pain, changes in the sensorium, and panic may occur. Most processes in the body, like breathing, work best when left alone.

What is the lesson here? It is this: Without shifts in our relationships to nature we are unaware. As long as our breathing, for example, is on an unchanging steady course we are largely unconscious of it. And we can expand on and generalize this principle: as with breathing in particular, so with health in general. Without some shifting aspect of our relationship with the world, we would be utterly blind to health.

There are some who consider it perverse to view health in this way. They say it is a sellout to disease to say, in effect, that sickness and death are the guarantors of health and life. Is it not inhumane to wish for sickness and death? But we are not *wishing* for sickness and death, we are only recognizing that without *each* of them their counterposed opposite would be unknowable, for the reasons that Whitehead and Davenport have pointed out.

The position I am advancing, then, is that the goal of medicine, that of banishing illness; and the goal of individuals, that of achieving perfect and enduring health, is nonsensical. These goals cannot be justified in view of our understanding of our relationship with the world and how we acquire knowledge.

THE "AGITATIONS OF EXPERIENCE" AND THE SENSE OF "I"

The leap in our understanding of the *necessity* of disease comes when we restructure our basic views of what we mean by "I," the I who knows, the I who experiences health and illness, the I who knows anything at all. Again Whitehead is helpful in showing the way:

> So long as nature was conceived in terms of the passive, instantaneous existence of bits of matter, according to Newton or Democritus, a difficulty arises. For there is an essential distinction between matter at an instant and the agitations of experience. But this conception of matter has now been swept away. Thus bodily activities and forms of experience can be construed in terms of each other. Also the body is part of nature. Thus we finally construe the world in terms of the type of activities disclosed in our intimate experience.[5]

Whitehead, in reminding us of the "conception of matter [that] has now been swept away," is illuminating one of the great revelations of twentieth-century science: the world does not exist as a given. It does not possess a material "out there" status that renders it totally separate from a nonmaterial "I." There is interplay between ourselves and nature, and it is *only* because of this interplay that we can know anything at all. It makes no sense in this view to ask which is primary, mind or matter, for the "essential distinction between matter at an instant and the agitations of experience" has dissolved.

And so, too, must the old conceptions of health and illness. We still hold to an idea of health and illness that is solidly based on the "passive, instantaneous existence of bits of matter, according to Newton or Democritus," as Whitehead states. As long as the bits of matter are in working order, health results, we say. But this view of health and sickness is outmoded, and in sharp contradiction to *modern* science. It is in the *bits of matter* that health and illness reside, according to our traditional views, and consciousness is only along for the ride. This view is archaic, even if still dominant in medicine. It violates the "first principle of epistemology" of which Whitehead speaks, that "the changeable, shifting aspects of our relations to nature" constitute the primary stuff of conscious awareness.

In the old view of nature as an external, primary, objective entity, there was no reason to attribute any importance to correlations between "matter at an instant and the agitations of experience," to borrow Whitehead's term again. Now, however, they are seen as inseparable, the very basis of knowing; for it is the *flux* of this relationship between matter and the senses, the fact of *difference* that allows us *any* concept of the world. This is akin to the position of the physicist Niels Bohr, who said, ". . . we must never forget that in the drama of existence we are ourselves both actors and spectators."[6]

The very idea that my "I" could consciously attend to all the stimuli that impinge on it, and thereby be in a position to "decide" reality for itself is a baseless and arrogant stance, once we think about it. Nothing we know about human physiology and psychology justifies the idea that we can stand apart from the world, recognize all the stimuli that have an impact on us, and glibly decide what is real. Whitehead, again in his incisive way, describes the situation all of us are in:

> Unless the physical and physiological sciences are fables, the qualitative experiences which are the sensations, such as sight, hearing, etc., are involved in an intricate flux of reactions within and without the animal body. These are all hidden below consciousness in the vague sense of personal experience of an external world. This feeling is massive and vague—so vague that the pretentious phrase, namely, personal experience of an external world, sounds nonsense.[7]

Since Whitehead wrote these words, we have learned just how dynamic the boundary between the body and the world actually is. Each year 98 percent of the multitudes (the actual number is 1 followed by 28 zeros) of atoms in the body are renewed; and by five years, *100* percent of them are replaced, down to the very last atom. The bone in the body is only a temporary stopping place for a phosphorous atom that originated millions of years ago in a distant star, and that has since been recycled through the lives of yet other stars. Seen in such a perspective, it is arrogant to suppose that the body owns *any* of the atoms that briefly stop over in their cosmic journey.[8] But we forget this dynamism of our bodies, our connections with nature. We trade these awarenesses instead for the concept that we stand apart from a world we perceive with an isolated "I."

So, returning to our notions of health and illness, the common view seems doubly flawed. One, sickness and death are *essential* to perceiving, even, health—for it is only through the perception of differences, of shifting relationships, that we can know anything at all. And, two, if the idea of a personal experience of an external world is nonsense, as Whitehead maintained, then so, too, are our ordinary ideas of personal experience of health and illness. We know that no body separated from the world can, in fact, *be* healthy or sick, for we must say with Whitehead that "we cannot define where a body begins and where external nature ends." And, what is most important, the idea of "personal experience," wherein we suppose the sensations of health and illness reside, is a "massive and vague" illusion, one that can be kept intact only by ignoring the countless ways we meld with the world, and by pushing aside the avalanche of shifting stimuli and sense impressions that tie us inextricably to the universe.

Power and Control as Illness

In order to find one's place in the infinity of being, one must be able to both separate and to unite.

—*I Ching*

Just as zero is both plus 10 and minus 10 at the same time, we are composed of complementary properties. If we seek ultimate order or ultimate chaos, we create a monster.

—Fred Alan Wolf
Taking the Quantum Leap

The metamorphosis which results in physical disease is no autonomous act on the part of our deficiencies: illness is no isolated occurrence. Rather, it is brought about by a particular emphasis upon health, an emphasis which serves self-seductively in its compulsive and limiting nature. Somatization is inconceivable unless it is preceded by a "going astray" of our particular talents. Nature seems to tolerate only a limited measure of one-sidedness—when the limits are exceeded or if too much energy is devoted to one-sidedness, Nature counterbalances the tendency through our bodies as if seeking a more effective or impressive means of demanding recognition for her chimerical plans. *The insensitivity of our healths determines our illnesses.*[1]

One of the most decidedly odd impressions (admittedly unproved) which I have acquired as a physician is that persons who strive and struggle the most tenaciously to be healthy develop more than their share of illness. It is by no means obvious why this should be so. Our culture affirms the value of purposiveness, of resolve, of goal-directed behavior. Why, when it comes to health, should many of those who strive for health the most vigorously be the very ones who seem to be denied it?

On the other hand there are persons, surely obvious to all physicians, who seem utterly healthy yet who laugh at any serious effort to be so. It is not that they consciously set out to abuse their health, just that they seem to do very little to ensure it. Health for them seems to come naturally, effortlessly, almost as if it were a grace. These persons are dismissed by many observers in medicine as "genetically gifted"—that is, it is not *they* who are responsible for their good health, it is the work of their genes.

This interpretation has it that the healthiness of such persons lies in ordinary physiology and biochemistry. There is some *mechanism* (that the rest of us don't have) at work deep inside them that guarantees their healthiness in spite of the fact that they may flaunt the ordinary precautions of prudent health care. And, in due course, we shall unravel them, bringing the physical explanations to light.

There is an important issue at stake here, one not acknowledged by our culture or our medicine. If an overbearing emphasis on health were actually to serve as a guarantor for illness, the consequences for our society would be enormous—infatuated as we are with healthiness in so many forms: youthfulness, athletic prowess, slimness, jogging, nutrition, health retreats, wellness symposia, and on and on. What if healthiness were a life-event that, in order to be attained, ironically must be *not* sought after with the purposiveness we take for granted? What if it is something that comes paradoxically with ease more than with difficulty? What if it were an event in life attainable more by "letting go" than by "holding on" and by "doing"? If that were true, we would find ourselves with misguided concepts, in error by monstrous proportions, pursuing a proper goal by grossly improper means. We would be like the proverbial monkey trapped outside the simple bar-cage, unable to free his hand from inside the bars because he will not release his clenched fist that holds the desired morsel of food.

Only by relaxing his grasp and letting the food fall away can he free himself from the cage, easily slipping his hand from the trap.

There are clues that our passionate struggle for health backfires in the same way—clues based not just on conjecture and speculation, but on the findings of current bioscience. Let us consider that many persons whose fears about contracting illness do seem to materialize—an impression, albeit unproved, that confronts most physicians quite frequently. The individual who most fears "the big one" does indeed die from heart disease. The woman who most fears breast cancer does contract it. In dealing with persons who harbor these sorts of worries, one gets the impression that they actually live out their perceived fate. They actualize their fears; they become what they fear the most.

Ordinary bioscientific thinking finds it laughable that the "mere" thought of a specific disease can actually be translated into such a disease. Something as ethereal as "fear" and "imagination" can, in no way, become flesh. Disease is caused by mechanism, we are told, and mechanism is, by definition, something physical, not mental. It is thus reckless to suppose that one's fears about developing a specific illness could materialize in a cause-and-effect manner. The excessive drive toward being healthy, born of a fear of becoming ill, cannot doom one to illness. If illness does occur in such persons, whatever the specific disease involved, it is material factors that are at work and not the mind.

There is good evidence that this conservative, standard interpretation of the actual origins of illness is limited and off-base in certain individuals. There are ample studies that phenomena as diaphanous as "fear" and "feeling" *can* cause illness—even, I suspect, *specific* illnesses in certain (though not all) individuals who experience them. We are thus not contending that *all* is mind, just that all is not body.

THE WEAKNESS OF POWER

In 1983 researchers studied the relationship between the personality styles of sixty-four dental students and their ability to resist disease. The students were determined, on the basis of psychological evaluation, to be either more motivated to form and maintain close relationships, or to be more "power-motivated." During periods of high psychological stress, such as the period surrounding difficult examinations, the researchers measured the amount of immunoglobulin A, or IgA, in the saliva of the students. (IgA is a protein that protects against viruses such as those that cause upper respiratory illnesses.) In all the students the amount of IgA fell; but the drop was most drastic in those students who showed a greater need for power and control than in those students who showed a greater need for close relationships. In addition, the immunoglobulin levels of the power-motivated students continued to drop far after the difficult examinations were over, persisting even into the period of summer vacation, while those of the other group began to rise again following the stressful period. The researchers conjectured that being idle for the power-motivated group during vacation, or possibly worrying about the upcoming school year, might be as stressful as the actual experience of being in school itself.

According to the researchers, this study verifies a long-suspected belief that stress lowers resistance to infection by inhibiting specific facets of the immune response in the body. Moreover, the decrease in immune activity was linked to something as "flimsy" as feelings—the need to have power and control, or the need to have friendships and close relationships.[2]

Other studies have shown that adrenalin, which is secreted in increased amounts during psychological and physiological stress, can inhibit immune function;[3] and that in persons who cope poorly with stressful situations, defects in so-called cell-mediated immunity (which protects one against cancer and certain types of infectious disease) occur.[4]

We can ask: What is the relationship between the "power-motivated" persons in the above study and those who tenaciously strive to acquire health? Certainly it seems reasonable to suppose that persons who are frantically chasing after healthiness desire power of a sort—the power to defy illness, to cheat disease and infirmity, to shake their fist at death.

The need for power over illness may, then, be the motivating drive behind many persons' goal of wellness. This need can disguise other feelings, such as the fear of disease itself. And the need for power, as the above study implies, can actually predispose one to disease. Thus, the desire for wellness, *if* it is a disguised need for power over disease, is much more than a desire for healthiness: it is a veritable risk factor for becoming sick—for becoming what one is seeking to avoid, what one eschews, what one flees: the fact of sickness and infirmity.

HELPLESSNESS AND ILLNESS

Events are bound to eventually occur which, no matter how hard we try, we cannot possibly change. Disease and death are two such events which await us all. And although we like to think we have control over them, in the end it is not so. For in spite of the array of health-oriented behaviors we design to push back the inevitable, it is only a matter of time before our controls simply no longer work. At that point there is no escape from the fate which all humans share.

Why is this important? If we morbidly dwell on this prospect, we actually may bring it about, as the following study suggests.

In 1983, Laudenslager and his colleagues conducted an experiment with animals which sheds light on the effects of inescapability and inevitability. His study suggests that the actual perception of doom and the loss of control may actually translate into physical disease. Three groups of rats were studied and were given either a series of electrical shocks which they could escape, or which they could *not* escape, or no shocks at all. Then, twenty-four hours later, they were re-exposed to the shocks, after which their immune function was tested—specifically, the aspect of the body's immune function which protects us from "cellular" disorders such as cancer and certain forms of infections. The results? Immune function was significantly inhibited in the group of rats who could *not* escape from the shocks; but was not suppressed in the group of rats who *could* escape from the shocks. In other words, it seemed to matter less whether the rats were shocked than how much control they perceived in the situation. It was not the stress itself, but what they could do about it that seemed to count. Could they escape or not?—that seemed the crucial determinant of whether the immune system was suppressed or not. "Thus the ability to exert control over the stressor completely prevented immunosuppression," the researchers noted. And, "Regardless of the mechanism involved, these findings suggest a link between psychological factors and disease. . . . These results also suggest that the immune system might be altered by . . . variables . . . such as learned helplessness."[5]

The potential consequences of such studies are striking. With the admitted caveat that it is not always reliable to extrapolate the results of animal experiments to the human situation, it is at least a concern that we, like the animals in one of the experimental groups, are also faced with a hopeless, inescapable situation—that of inevitable disease and death. The most that many of us hope for is to "go quickly," "without decline." But there is for us no escape, and we know it—at some level of awareness. And our most vigorous protestations and health-oriented activities make absolutely no difference in our ultimate fate.

In the face, then, of research such as that above, we can wonder to what degree our own sense of inescapability generates our individual illness. A leading authority in mind-body interactions, Professor George Engel at the University of Rochester Medical School, has proposed a "giving up—given up" syndrome, where, in the face of overwhelming perceptions of doom, one sickens and dies.[6]

In the recesses of our psyche hides the most ineluctable fact of life: that of death. To the extent that we perceive this ineluctability as inescapability, we must be prepared to entertain the possibility that it is not only death that destroys us, but our thoughts about it as well.

A SOLUTION?

What do you think has become of the young and old men?
And what do you think has become of the women and children?

They are alive and well somewhere,
The smallest sprout shows there is really no death,
And if ever there was it led forward life, and does not wait at the end
   to arrest it,
And ceas'd the moment life appear'd.

All goes onward and outward, nothing collapses,
And to die is different from what any one supposed, and luckier.[7]

—Walt Whitman

[A] marriage with death . . . evokes the general mythologem of something particularly desirable joining with something dreadful and, thereby, "dying"—a monster containing something of hidden value. The unusual conjunction with "death" results in a sense of expanding horizons—as if the sufferer experienced "eternity." It is as if the individual's life for the first time acquired unmistakable and incorruptible uniqueness, particular limitation and freedom simultaneously. It is as if this recognition conferred an unassailable security amid the hustle and bustle of human existence.[8]

—Alfred Zeigler

There is no death, only a change of worlds.[9]

—Chief Seattle

Observations such as these strongly suggest that our disguised dread and fear of death and ultimate extinction, disguised as a maniacal drive toward wellness, healthiness, and power may exert a boomerang effect. Instead of propelling us toward higher health, these feelings guarantee the opposite, working for our sickening, not for our well-being. The ever-present, although repressed, fact of our ultimate demise creates an inner knowledge of inescapability from which we cannot hide. In our gyrations which we call health strategies, we are running not "to" something but "away" from something—an eventual decline, the inevitability of death.

This perspective implies that any comprehensive health strategy must be at the same time a death strategy. Living well must include at once a plan for dying well—for the plain fact that living and dying are tied together, hand-in-glove, both as facts in our lives and as realizations in our psyche. Yet in our passionate struggles for health we have become decidedly one-sided. We focus only on how to be healthy, ignoring the fact of the dual nature of healthiness, that its other side, the side of death, is as much a fact of our life as is wellness.

A cursory reading of the records of many non-Western cultures tells us that it has not always been so. Preparation for dying was judged to be an essential part of life, and one who did not know how to die would never have been considered healthy in the fullest sense. The duality of health and illness was transcended in these cultures in a way that joined the two in a unified whole, poles not in opposition but tied together in mutual, interdependent oneness. For these societies, living *was* dying—not in any morbid sense but as a plain and simple fact of existence.

We are wont to say in our technologized society that this attitude came about in primitive societies mainly because they had no options. Lacking any capability of "real" health care, one simply makes the best of things, such as by devising philosophies which assert that sickness and death are an essential ingredient of life. This attitude need not preoccupy us, though, because "times" are different: our biotechnology can make a difference. We can declare official "wars" on individual illnesses—and, moreover, win them, as we did with the international war against smallpox. "Life extension" is a popular preoccupation of researchers today, and is much more than a fanciful dream. It is a realistic possibility. Had primitive societies our capabilities, they would not have had the need to resort to simplistic, consoling philosophies which affirmed that illness and death were valuable parts of life. It was essentially their backwardness and primitivity that condemned them to such silly notions.

For my part, I cannot agree with this criticism. I feel that we have lost a wisdom that many pre-modern cultures knew and felt—the sure understanding that birth and death, health and illness stand in a kind of unseverable relationship; that to despise one is to despise the other; and that an overemphasis on one is to contaminate one's experience of the other. There is nothing in the achievements of modern biomedicine that persuade me against this view, for I can see that we have accomplished nothing through our technological approaches to health care that sunder in any way the mutual interdependence of the chimeric principles of health and illness and birth and death. And to the extent that we have allowed ourselves to be carried away by our infatuations, and have forgotten that "death care" is as essential a part of life as "health care," we have cheated ourselves of any possibility of knowing what true health is all about.

What is needed that will allow us to think in these counterintuitive ways? Perhaps the flexibility implied by Lewis Carroll in *Alice in Wonderland*:

> Alice laughed. "There's no use trying," she said: "one can't believe impossible things."
> "I dare say you haven't had much practice," said the Queen. "When I was your age, I always did it for half-an-hour a day. Why, sometimes I've believed as many as six impossible things before breakfast."

Beyond Illness

> Thirty years ago, before this aged monk (i.e., I) got into Zen training, I used to see a mountain as a mountain and a river as a river.
> Thereafter I had the chance to meet enlightened masters and, under their guidance I could attain enlightenment to some extent. At this stage, when I saw a mountain: lo! it was not a mountain. When I saw a river: lo! it was not a river.
> But in these days I have settled down to a position of final tranquility. As I used to do in my first years, now I see a mountain just as a mountain and a river just as a river.
>
> —11th century Zen Master Ch'ing Yuan

The real reason why human life can be so utterly exasperating and frustrating is not because there are facts called death, pain, fear, or hunger. The madness of the thing is that when such facts are present, we circle, buzz, writhe, and whirl, trying to get the "I" out of the experience. . . . While the notion that I am separate from my experience remains, there is confusion and turmoil. Because of this, there is neither awareness nor understanding of experience, and thus no real possibility of assimilating it. To understand this moment I must not try to be divided from it; I must be aware of it with my whole being. This, like refraining from holding my breath for ten minutes, is not something I *should* do. In reality, it is the only thing I *can* do. Everything else is the insanity of attempting the impossible.

—Alan Watts
The Wisdom of Insecurity

What are persons like who actually manage to "go beyond" their illness, who transcend the resentment, fear, and anger of being sick, and who eventually seem transfigured by the event itself? I have known a few of them, as, I suspect, have most physicians. One fact stands out more than any other: they are decidedly ordinary. There are no celestial halos or shimmering auras that set them apart, yet something about them *is* different. What is it?

These persons suffer with their sickness, too. They request pain medication, they lose weight during illness, they decline and die just as other people do. What is this "going beyond," then, that they experience?

The transitions that these special persons make during the course of illness correspond sharply to the stages of understanding experienced by many people on diverse spiritual paths. The clearest delineations of these stages of growth can be found in the literature of Zen Buddhism, which has concerned itself with these transformations for centuries. In one of the clearest and most poetic descriptions of Zen to appear in years, Toshihiko Izutsu has described this process.[1]

The initial stage corresponds to the experience that is typical for ordinary persons. There is a sense of being in a world of objects, surrounded by things and events "out there." There is a strong sense of "I," the one who does the perceiving, the one to whom things happen—such as getting sick and suffering.

The middle stage witnesses the dissolution of this bifurcated world. The distinctions between the knower and the known undergo a unification, and the very notion of an external world fades. In this state there is nothing to know and no one who does the knowing, for they have become one. This is a spiritual state of absolute unification and absolutely undivided awareness. Experiences are not events happening in a world "out there," for there is no "out there" as opposed to an "in here," no "it" versus "I." Experience is ineffable. Ordinary language cannot describe it, and thought, couched as it is in language, is also inadequate. This is the domain of pure, undivided experience that goes beyond all characterization.

For the sick person, this is a stage of *immersion* in illness. It is a stage in which illness ceases to be something "contracted" by an "I." This is the stage of illness as pure experience, and is totally uncharacterizable in words, and is even beyond thought. It is the experiential region of undivided knowing. At this level there is literally nothing to be cured, because there is nothing that has been contracted, and no "I" to which a cure could be applied.

The final stage is a resolution of this Oneness once again, into subject and object—but this time, unlike the initial stage of awareness, the sense of oneness is not destroyed. The "undivided Something" remains intact, in spite of the drawing apart of subject and object. As Izutsu describes this process,

> . . . the result is that the subject and the object . . . are separated from one another, and merged into one another, the separation and merging being one and the same act of the originally undivided Something.[2]

Thus, as the "I" and the "illness" come out of the One, they merge into one another and become one; and this one thing establishes itself as the principle of Unity that envelops and unifies all the overtly external things and experiences called "illness"—or, for that matter, "health."

It would be a mistake to suppose that this process is something that applies only to persons with a peculiar inclination toward Zen or other non-Western modes of thought. Indeed, none of the patients I have witnessed who undergo these transitions have had any inclination whatsoever toward Oriental philosophies, but have been ordinary persons who would likely have denied they held any type of formal philosophy at all. These stages of experience are a generic path for persons who come to the deepest wisdom about health and illness, and are not unique to any particular religious or spiritual tradition.

Persons who traverse these stages during the course of illness seem ordinary. They speak of illness *as if* it were an object, and perform the health rituals that other sick persons perform: having surgery, taking medication, etc. Superficially, it would appear that they are stranded in a world of objects and events just like everyone else. But there is a difference: in their inner experience the subjects and objects are given their proper place. This is *not* the old world of empirical experience that preceded their awareness. As Izutsu puts it,

For our old familiar world, this time, reveals itself in its pristine purity and innocence. The empirical world which has once lost itself into the abyss of Nothingness, now returns to life again in an unusual freshness.[3]

He quotes the thirteenth-century master Dogen who observed,

Here we realize that the mountains, the rivers, and the great earth in their original purity and serenity should never be confused with the mountains, rivers, and the great earth (as seen through the eyes of ordinary people).[4]

Sick persons who achieve this awareness in the course of illness seem to radiate an unmistakable freedom *from* illness, even though they are afflicted by it and are immersed in it. This is paradoxical, for it is obvious that they are *not* free from disease: they hurt like other people, they may orient their lives around taking medications on schedule, following certain treatment programs, etc. Where does the freedom they emanate come from?

It arises because they are not fixated on the fact of illness as if it were an external event that is controlling their lives. Their world, originally a conglomeration of subjects and objects, has undergone the fusion and subsequent disjunction described above as the final stage of understanding in which the freeing quality of Oneness is retained. It is this unity of opposites that allows freedom from particulars, such as illness and disease. As Izutsu puts it,

. . . Man [at this final stage] is a *total* actualization of the Field of Reality, is on the one hand a Cosmic Man comprehending in himself the whole universe . . . and on the other he is this very concrete individual "man" who exists and lives here and now, as a concentration point of the entire energy of the Field. He is individual and supra-individual.[5]

The person who has gone beyond illness is indeed a Cosmic Man, a person who takes the distant view, the grandest perspective, the view of the Whole. In this context he experiences the freedom to act in concrete ways that do not sever the unity and oneness implicit at this stage of understanding.

There is, then, in the behavior of such persons the capacity for freedom from the constraints of illness while being in the throes of it, even while experiencing pain and suffering, even when undergoing deterioration and decline. There seems in such persons the ability to accept things just as they are—not a nihilistic giving up to the inevitable, but an awareness of the intrinsic harmony of the One which overcomes even the most inharmonious moments of life. They embody the description rendered by the Third Zen Patriarch:

> The Great Way is not difficult
> for those who have no preferences.
> When love and hate are both absent
> everything becomes clear and undisguised.
> Make the smallest distinction, however,
> and heaven and earth are set infinitely apart.
> If you wish to see the truth
> then hold no opinions for or against anything.
> To set up what you like against what you dislike
> is the disease of the mind.
> When the deep meaning of things is not understood
> the mind's essential peace is disturbed to no avail.[6]

The mistaken notion frequently surfaces that persons who have managed to reach this stage of "no preferences" are totally imperturbable and do not experience pain, grief, or suffering. It is not so. These qualities, like illness itself, remain; and, although there is a radical transformation in the way the world is sensed following the development of the inner wisdom we have examined, these dark features of life are not extinguished. There is a famous Zen story which describes a Zen master who is accosted by robbers on a lonely road at night. He is killed; but before dying he releases a shout that is loud enough to be heard for miles across the countryside. This act was counted as in total coherence with deep wisdom: to be free enough and spontaneous enough to vent emotion at any moment in a way that was appropriate for the occasion, not to be so distant from the reality of the moment that one feels *no* fear or pain.

There is the most elegant ordinariness to persons who go beyond illness. This is the "nothing special" quality of the world that is sensed by those who know it deepest. It is the stage where once again mountains become mountains and rivers become rivers. It is the awareness wherein suffering becomes suffering, and illness becomes, once again, illness.

If anything, a realized soul is more in touch with the grief and sorrow that is part and parcel of the human condition, knowing that it too needs to be accepted and lived as all life needs to be lived. To reject the shadow side of life, to pass it by with averted eyes—refusing our share of common sorrow while expecting our share of common joy—would cause the unlived, rejected shadows to deepen in us as fear, including the fear of death. . . . The peace that comes when a man is hungry and finds food, is sick and recovers, or is lonely and finds a friend—peace of this sort is readily intelligible; but the peace that *passeth* understanding comes when the pain of life is not relieved. It shimmers on the crest of a wave of pain; it is the spear of frustration transformed into a shaft of light.[7]

NOTES
Health-As-Experience

1. D. H. Lawrence, *Sex, Literature, and Censorship*, ed. Harry T. Moore (New York: Viking, 1959), pp. 88–90.
2. D. H. Lawrence, *Phoenix: The Posthumous Papers of D. H. Lawrence*, ed. E. D. McDonald (London: Viking, 1961), pp. 610–611.
3. Aldous Huxley, *Island* (New York: Harper & Row, 1962), Chapter 14.
4. Dōshin, *Shinjinmei*, in D. T. Suzuki, *The Essentials of Zen Buddhism* (New York: E. P. Dutton, 1962), p. 127.

No-Health

1. R. G. H. Siu, *The Tao of Science* (Cambridge, Mass.: MIT Press, 1957) p. 75.

The Interpenetration of Opposites

1. Mark Holborn, *The Ocean in the Sand* (Boulder: Shambhala, 1978), p. 22.
2. *Ibid.*
3. D. T. Suzuki, *Studies in Zen Buddhism* (New York: Delta, 1955), p. 84.
4. *Ibid.*, p. 93.
5. *Ibid.*, pp. 93–94.
6. *Ibid.*, p. 94.
7. Robert Frost, *North of Boston* (New York: Dodd, Mead & Co., 1977), p. 6.

"Does This Patient Have R.D.?"

1. Ludwig von Bertalanffy, "The Mind-Body Problem: A New View," *Psychosomatic Medicine* 26 (1964): p. 32.
2. Ludwig von Bertalanffy, *Perspectives on General Systems Theory* (New York: George Braziller, 1975), p. 71.
3. *Ibid.*, pp. 69–70.
4. *Ibid.*, pp. 71–72.

The Indispensible Key of the Universe

1. Jacques Choron, *Death and Western Thought* (New York: Collier, 1963), p. 106.
2. Sidney Greenberg, *The Infinite in G. Bruno* (New York: King's Crown Press, Columbia University, 1950) p. 161.
3. Dorothea Singer, *G. Bruno, His Life and Thought* (New York: Henry Schuman, 1950), pp. 243–244.
4. Greenberg, *The Infinite*, p. 161.
5. *Ibid.*, p. 245.
6. *Ibid.*
7. Choron, *Death*, p. 108.
8. Greenberg, *The Infinite*, pp. 162–165.
9. Ken Wilber, *The Spectrum of Consciousness* (Wheaton, Ill.: The Theosophical Publishing House, 1977), p. 62.
10. *Ibid.*
11. Sir Peter B. and Jean S. Medawar, *The Life Science* (New York: Harper and Row, 1977).
12. David Bohm, "A Conversation with David Bohm," interview by Renee Weber in *ReVision* 4 (1981): p. 26.
13. David Bohm, *Wholeness and the Implicate Order* (London: Routledge and Kegan Paul, 1980), p. 147.
14. Bohm, "A Conversation," p. 26.
15. Nick Herbert, *Quantum Reality—Beyond the New Physics* (New York: Doubleday, forthcoming).
16. Larry Dossey, *Space, Time and Medicine* (Boulder, Colo.: Shambhala, 1982), pp. 98–101.
17. Herbert, *Quantum Reality*.

"O All Ye Sicknesses. . ."

1. James G. Frazer, *The Golden Bough* (New York: Macmillan, 1922), pp. 652–653.
2. Huston Smith, *Forgotten Truth* (New York: Harper Colophon Books, 1976), pp. 1–18.
3. Henry Miller, "The Enormous Womb," in *The Wisdom of the Heart* (New York: New Directions, 1942), p. 99.

On Knowing Health

1. Bertrand Russell, *A History of Western Philosophy* (New York: Simon & Schuster, 1945), p. 812.
2. *Ibid.*, p. 812.
3. *Ibid.*
4. *Ibid.*, p. 813.
5. W. T. Stace, *Mysticism and Philosophy* (New York: J. B. Lippincott Co., 1960), p. 66.

6. J. de Marquette, *Introduction to Comparative Mysticism* (New York: Philosophical Library, 1949), p. 15.
7. P. A. Schilpp, ed., *Albert Einstein: Philosopher-Scientist* (New York: Harper, 1959), p. 391.
8. *Ibid.*, p. 140.
9. *Ibid.*, p. 132.
10. J. A. Wheeler and C. M. Patton, "Is Physics Legislated by Cosmogony," in Ronald Duncan and Miranda Weston-Smith, eds., *The Encyclopedia of Ignorance* (New York: Pergamon Press, 1977), p. 21.
11. *Ibid.*
12. Ralph Waldo Emerson, "Self-Reliance."

Being Blank

1. D. H. Lawrence, *The Complete Poems*, (New York: Penguin Books, 1977), p. 501.
2. Friedman, M. et al., "Feasibility of Altering Type A Behavior Pattern After Myocardial Infarction," *Circulation* 66:1 (1982): pp. 83–92.
3. M. Cooper and M. Aygen, "A Relaxation Technique in the Management of Hypercholesterolemia," *Journal of Human Stress*, December 1979: pp. 24–27.
4. Aldous Huxley, *Tomorrow and Tomorrow and Tomorrow* (New York: Signet, 1964), p. 54.

Health and Illness as Perfection

1. Evelyn Underhill, *Mysticism* (New York: E. P. Dutton, 1961), p. 220.
2. *Ibid.*, p. 217.
3. *Ibid.*
4. *Ibid.*, p. 218.
5. Walt Whitman, *Leaves of Grass* (New York: Modern Library, n.d.), pp. 25, 42.
6. W. T. Stace, *Mysticism and Philosophy* (New York: Lippincott, 1960), p. 66.
7. William James, "A Pluralistic Universe," Hibbert Lectures, London, 1909.
8. Underhill, *Mysticism*, p. 3.
9. Albert William Levi, *Philosophy and the Modern World* (Bloomington: University of Indiana Press, 1959), p. 527.
10. Rabindranath Tagore, trans., *One Hundred Poems of Kabir* (New York: Macmillan, 1961), p. 14.

Illness

1. Robert J. Sardello, "The Suffering Body of the City," *Spring: An Annual of Archetypal Psychology and Jungian Thought*, 1983, pp. 145–164.
2. Alfred North Whitehead, *Modes of Thought* (New York: Macmillan, 1938), p. 29.
3. Richard Davenport, *An Outline of Animal Development* (Reading, Mass.: Addison-Wesley, 1979), p. 353.
4. Whitehead, *Modes of Thought*, p. 31.

5. *Ibid.*, p. 115.
6. P. Schilpp, ed., *Albert Einstein: Philosopher-Scientist* (LaSalle, Ill.: The Open Court Publishing Co., 1949), p. 236.
7. Whitehead, *Modes of Thought*, p. 121.
8. Larry Dossey, "The Biodance," in *Space, Time and Medicine* (Boulder, Colo.: Shambhala, 1982), pp. 72–81.

Power and Control as Illness

1. Alfred J. Ziegler, *Archetypal Medicine* (Dallas: Spring Publications, Inc., 1983), p. 13.
2. J. B. Jemmott, J. Z. Borysenko, and D. C. McClelland, "Academic Stress, Power Motivation, and Decrease in Secretion Rate of Saliva Secretory Immunoglobin A," *Lancet* (June 25, 1983), pp. 1400–1402.
3. B. Crary et al., "Decrease in Mitogen Responsiveness of Mononuclear Cells from Peripheral Blood after Epinephrine Administration in Humans," *Journal of Immunology* 130 (1983): pp. 694–697.
4. B. Bahnson, "Stress and Cancer, the State of the Art," Part 1, *Psychosomatics* 21 (1980): pp. 975–981, and, Part 2, *Psychosomatics* 22 (1981): pp. 207–12. For an extensive review of this broad area, see S. E. Locke and M. Hornig-Rohan, *Mind and Immunity: Behavioral Immunology* (New York: Institute for the Advancement of Health, 1983).
5. M. L. Laudenslager et al., "Coping and Immunosupression: Inescapable but Not Escapable Shock Suppresses Lymphocyte Proliferation," *Science* 221 (5 August, 1983): pp. 568–570.
6. George Engel, "A Life Setting Conducive to Illness, the Giving-up—Given-up Complex," *Annals of Internal Medicine* 69 (1968): 293–300.
7. Walt Whitman, "Song of Myself," in *Leaves of Grass* (New York: Modern Library, n.d.), p. 29.
8. Zeigler, *Archetypal Medicine*, p. 40.
9. Chief Seattle, 1786–1866, Chief of the Squamish and Duwamish tribes, in *Indian Oratory*, compiled by W. C. Vanderwerth (New York: Ballantine, 1971), p. 102.

Beyond Illness

1. Toshihiko Izutsu, *Toward a Philosophy of Zen Buddhism* (Boulder: Prajna Press, 1982), pp. 108–109.
2. *Ibid.*, p. 209.
3. *Ibid.*, p. 51.
4. *Ibid.*, p. 61.
5. *Ibid.*, p. 55.
6. Stephen Levine, *Who Dies?* (New York: Anchor, 1982), p. 69.
7. Huston Smith, "The Sacred Unconscious," in Roger Walsh and D. H. Shapiro, eds., *Beyond Health and Normality* (New York: Van Nostrand Reinhold, 1983), pp. 269–270.

II

The Jonah Complex and the Fear of Being Healthy

> Now the word of the Lord came unto Jonah . . . saying, Arise, go to Nineveh, that great city, and cry against it; . . . But Jonah rose up to flee . . . and he found a ship . . . and went down into it . . . from the presence of the Lord.
>
> —*The Book of Jonah*

The American psychologist Abraham Maslow observed that we all have inner impulses to improve ourselves, the urge to achieve higher aims, the need to realize our inner potential. But frequently we do not. It is as if there is something that is holding us up, blocking us, obstructing what we know is possible—if only we could achieve it. Almost all of us know we could be better and do more. The question is, "Why don't we?" As Maslow said,

> We fear our highest possibilities . . . We are generally afraid to become that which we can glimpse in our most perfect moments, under the most perfect conditions, under conditions of great courage. We enjoy and even thrill to the godlike possibilities we see in ourselves in such peak moments. And yet we simultaneously shiver with weakness, awe, and fear before these very same possibilities.
>
> So often we run away from the responsibilities dictated (or rather suggested) by nature, by fate, even sometimes by accident, just as Jonah tried—in vain—to run away from *his* fate.[1]

This defense against growth Maslow called the Jonah complex. The Jonah complex is an attempt, sometimes unconscious, to *under*achieve, to do less than the do-able. We adopt the position that we could be greater than we are *if only we wanted to*—telling ourselves that our underachievement is *our* choice. It is *we* who are still at the controls, still in charge of our fate. And if we are less than we know to be, well, maybe next year we will decide differently.

Maslow describes also how we not only are ambivalent about the higher potential we see in ourselves, but are ambivalent about these possibilities as they exist in other persons as well. Sometimes this reaction turns into downright hostility.

> . . . could anybody who has looked into the depths of human nature fail to be aware of our mixed and often hostile feelings toward saintly men? Or toward very beautiful women or men? Or toward great creators? Or toward our intellectual geniuses?
>
> We surely love and admire all the persons who have incarnated the true, the good, the beautiful, the just, the perfect, the ultimately successful. And yet they also make us uneasy, anxious, confused, perhaps a little jealous or envious, a little inferior, clumsy. They usually make us lose our aplomb, our self-possession, and self-regard.[2]

We resent the fact that others have done what we *know* to do, but have not done—namely, live out our potential. Great achievers remind us of our frailty, our failings. Perhaps we know inside that they are mortals just like ourselves, and once were not great but were fleshly humans as ourselves with the same doubts and misgivings and fears. But *unlike* ourselves, they set them aside and overcame them. Knowing this seems to accentuate our sense of inferiority and worthlessness. In the presence of the great, there is no place to hide from our inner messages of weakness and failure. It becomes easier to hate the great than to hate ourselves.

Maslow's observations provide a background against which we can ask a question that is seldom asked: Why aren't we healthier? Why aren't we as healthy as we know how to be? It is a striking fact that almost all of us understand how to realize a higher state of health, yet we do not. What keeps us from doing so?

It is one of the oddest experiences in my life as a physician to continually perform histories and physical examinations on persons, to do laboratory tests of various sorts, and then to counsel them about how to be healthier only to be told, "But I *know* that already." It is usually fruitless to respond, "Then why did you come for my advice? Why didn't you save your money and do what you already knew to do?" It becomes painfully obvious to the patient and to me at such times that something bizarre and illogical is transpiring in our conversation, and that the patient did not come to be harassed about his or her failings. As such, I can keep my comments and preachments to myself. *Whatever* the reason this patient chose to come, it was decidedly *not* to be reminded that he or she is a weak-willed, illogical, self-destructive human being. And so I remind myself silently: Maslow was right. We underachieve in areas of health as well as in other areas of human endeavor. We actualize less than we know to do. And although my thoughts never make it into the patient's chart, I make a diagnosis: the Jonah complex.

In matters of health it is astonishing how pervasive this problem is. Who could doubt, for example, the statistics showing the effectiveness of seat belts? Yet only a small percentage of the populace uses them. We hide behind excuses: "I had a friend who was killed because he couldn't escape from his car's seat belt." Who can ignore any longer the destructive effects on health from prolonged, unalleviated emotional stress? Yet I continually hear the comment, "I *love* that keen feeling of excitement, Doc! It gives me my 'competitive edge' in my job. Take that away from me and I might as well quit!"—the Jonah complex in action. Or consider the middle-aged, sedentary, overweight executive who makes an effort to "turn it all around" and embarks on a diligent program to lose weight and exercise—but refuses to give up cigarette smoking.

These are obvious examples that occur again and again in physicians' offices everywhere. There seems to be no limit to the extent we will go to in attempting to underachieve in health. Sometimes we violate common sense so flagrantly that our efforts appear to be attempts to deliberately sabotage our healthiness.

During my training as a resident in internal medicine I was assigned for a few weeks to the pulmonary service in the teaching hospital. Most of the patients were there for reasons related to long-term cigarette smoking—chronic bronchitis and emphysema. Every morning the volunteers made their rounds to the patients with a large cart that was stocked with a variety of items for sale—newspapers, magazines, shaving cream—and, unbelievably, cigarettes. Not even an incapacitating cigarette-related disease was enough to deter the habit. And efforts to delete cigarettes from the cart were unsuccessful because of violent patient protest. One patient was particularly famous in this respect. He had end-stage lung disease from the effects of smoking, and was so breathless even at rest that it had become necessary to perform a permanent tracheostomy, a surgical procedure wherein an opening is made in the windpipe. From this opening the tenacious secretions could be suctioned, since he was too weak to cough them up on his own; and oxygen and medications could be delivered through the tracheostomy via breathing machines. I shall never forget this intrepid old man, for he had discovered that the diameter of the indwelling tracheostomy device was exactly the same diameter of a cigarette—and he would lie on his back, light a cigarette, place it in the hole in his neck, and smoke through his artificial airway with the cigarette protruding vertically from his airway! Not even the certainty of an impending pulmonary death was enough to dissuade him from his habit.

Most often our immersion in the Jonah complex is far more subtle, of course, subtle enough that we can fool ourselves into ignoring the consequences of what we are doing. Our violations of common sense may be as simple as failing to brush our teeth, or ascribing rectal bleeding to hemorrhoids when we know it can be a sign of colon cancer. We may ignore a breast lump, telling ourselves it is only a "cyst," or we may fail to have periodic Pap smears because "there has never been any cancer in my family." Just as we frequently resent, as well as admire, those persons who appear godlike and perfect, we frequently experience hostility to those who embody a high degree of health. I frequently hear patients refer to a friend, once as slovenly as they but who has "turned things around" by losing weight, stopping smoking, exercising, and changing self-destructive behaviors, with the comment that "Joe has turned into a real, honest to god, health *nut!*" Joe somehow has become imbalanced in his quest for healthiness; his perspective is off base, too radical for sensible people like me! It's the "let's not get carried away" objection. No matter that Joe feels marvelous for the first time in his adult life, or that he appears more creative and happy.

Sometimes, after making sweeping changes in health strategies, people will resort to their old unhealthy, self-defeating ways. An example is the "rebound" weight gain following massive weight loss through dieting; or the person who has stopped drinking, who resumes his or her previous level of unrestrained alcohol intake. A frequent comment from such persons is, "Doc, my friends told me that if I was going to be this cantankerous, they'd rather I start drinking again. They just couldn't stand to be around me after I gave up the booze!"

These types of experiences are examples of the fact that *we are not strong enough to endure perfect health*—an application of Maslow's observation that, when it comes to peak emotional experiences, our capacity to tolerate them is limited. We cannot survive the intensity of transcendent psychological and spiritual experience every waking moment. It is as if we contained a thermostat for such events which is set at a certain level and shuts off above a certain threshold. So it is with health. We all know how to be healthier, and most of us *have been* healthier. We ignore the obvious:

we *could* be healthier if we wanted to. But we choose the other path—lesser health, a diminished sense of well-being, a truncated vitality. Why?

The answer, I think, lies in the fact that health involves more than proper body function. If healthiness were a straightforward process involving the care of a machine—if our body functioned, for example, like our car—we would all be enormously healthy. But bodies *don't* behave like cars; they cannot be described in sheer mechanical terms. The fact is that all efforts to improve our health go beyond our physical body to affect our emotions, feelings, and spirit. Pure body health is an illusion. It does not exist. All attempts to improve the body extend to the mind and consciousness.

To put it another way, health is not a matter of *doing*. It is a way of *being*. It comes down to asking the question of *not* "What shall I *do* to be healthy," but "How shall I *be* to realize healthiness?" Because healthiness involves the way we feel, the way we experience life, it has enormous repercussions on our ability to tolerate it. Sometimes healthiness becomes too much. We cannot endure it, we shrink from it. And we concoct the flimsiest reasons for doing so, always justifying to ourselves why we have no choice but to destroy our health.

As an example of the "being" aspect of health, consider the problem of elevation of the blood's cholesterol level—a major risk factor for the commonest cause of death in our society, coronary artery disease, which sets the stage for heart attack. We have always conceived that the cholesterol level in the blood was determined by straightforward factors: genetic, as well as behavioral, such as diet, exercise, and body weight. Thus we have said that attempts to lower it involve *doing*—which (since we cannot re-program ourselves genetically) mainly center on diet, weight control, exercise, and taking medications. Yet we are learning that the problem is not as objective as we have always assumed, because there are "being" factors that are important in determining the cholesterol level. For example, certified public accountants have displayed an increase in the cholesterol level on the average of 100 milligrams per 100 cubic centimeters of blood (100 mg%), a striking elevation, between January 1 and April 15—when tax returns are due.[3] Before academic exams, the blood cholesterol of medical students rises significantly.[4] On the other hand, if men who have high cholesterol levels are taught to meditate twice daily as a form of mental relaxation, the cholesterol level *falls* on the order of 30 percent. (There are no drugs available which consistently are as effective, and as safe as meditation.)

The point is that, even when it comes to something as specifiable and objective as the serum cholesterol level, there are factors of being which enter. It is how we live, not only what we do, that counts. Here we have a clue to why we shrink from healthiness, why we find it hard to endure good health, why we do not embrace it more enthusiastically. Good health places demands on us. It extends to the level of feeling, emotion, behavior—to the roots of our *being*. Thus, it can become uncomfortable to be healthy, as healthy as we know how to be. It is easier to deride those who choose the other path as cranks, oddballs, and health nuts. But deep inside most of us know it isn't so.

There is a great emotional safety in maintaining that health is purely a physical phenomenon. As long as we divorce healthiness from feeling, we insulate ourselves from the necessity for self-scrutiny, self-knowing, for change. Far better to scrutinize the chest x-ray and the complete blood count than to peer into our own psyche. Yet the evidence is mounting, in one disease after another, that "being factors" are crucial. Sometimes they have life-or-death consequences.

In a study done at Harvard Medical School's teaching hospital, Reich and his colleagues examined a group of patients who were admitted to the coronary care unit for life-threatening disorders of the heartbeat, so-called cardiac arrhythmias. These were not the trivial "palpitations" which many persons with normal hearts experience, but problems which, if untreated, have a significant mortality rate. Reich found that in the twenty-four-hour period preceding the onset of the arrhythmias, 20 percent of the patients experienced profound emotional upheavals involving anger, acute depression, and fear. And, interestingly, these patients had, by and large, *less* actual disease in their coronary arteries than the remainder of the group.[5]

Any approach that would emphasize the mode of *doing*—having examinations, stress tests, taking medications, monitoring the blood pressure, etc.—and neglect the mode of *being* for this group of patients is bound to be incomplete. This is a dimension of health that cannot be neglected in spite of the fact that it places new demands on the physician and creates, sometimes, uncomfortable awareness for the patient.

It must also be said that the Jonah complex extends frequently to the physician—for the doctor may find himself shrinking from giving the best advice he knows. He may know that his patient is engaging in self-destructive forms of behavior, that he is on a collision course with a catastrophic illness if he continues to behave in a particular way. Yet, how can he be explicit about the negative effects of emotional stress and destructive, hectic schedules when his own life mirrors these problems? How can he confront a patient with the negative effects of a sedentary lifestyle and obesity and cigarette smoking when he himself engages in these behaviors? He cannot endure the advice he knows he should give—and thus he evades the issues. If he has lived out the Jonah complex and has hidden from higher health—"I'm too busy, it won't happen to me," etc.—it is unlikely that he can bring up these issues with his patients for fear of creating discomfort for himself. The age-old injunction, "Physician, heal thyself," can be painful. Better not to complicate things, better to regard health as just a body function. After all, the physician has enough to do and then some, addressing just the physical aspects of the disease. We don't expect ministers to do appendectomies, so why should we expect physicians to minister to all the needs of their patients? So the rationale goes.

Because the Jonah complex affects both patients and physicians alike, there is a kind of "settling out" process that goes on—that is, patients choose physicians who are rather like themselves. When a patient meets a physician, and both are afflicted by the Jonah complex, enormously complex games are played. In the process, the unstated rules operate something like this:

Patient to physician: "Now let's get some things straight. I'm here for you to take care of what *I* want taken care of. I pay the bill, and I define the rules. You are to focus only on my physical problems—and only on the ones I select. None of this 'total patient care' approach for me."
Physician to patient: "That's OK with me. After all, it's all physical anyway, right? I won't make you uncomfortable by any of this 'emotional-spiritual' stuff. We'll keep it down-to-earth, and talk about only what you elect. That way you won't threaten me, either. I'm no saint, you know. God knows that 'emotional-spiritual' talk always made me uncomfortable too. Yep, it's all in the body, that's what I say. You know, I think we're going to have a good relationship."

I have always marveled at how compatible physicians and patients seem to find each other. Through the years many patients and physicians seem to evolve together—even to the point, frequently, of resembling each other in manners of speech, dress, and affect. There are exceptions to this generalization, of course—but the practice of many physicians is heavily affected by this process, wherein patients seek doctors who are rather like themselves, and who are willing to play by tacit rules that obviate the need for deep inner scrutiny.

What is the way out? If the Jonah complex limits our healthiness, and if it affects, even, the physicians to whom we look for wisdom and guidance, what can we do? Maslow said,

You *must* be aware not only of the godlike possibilities within but also of the existential human limitations. You must be able simultaneously to laugh at yourself and at all human pretensions. If you can be amused by the worm trying to be a god, then in fact you may be able to go on trying and being arrogant without fearing paranoia or bringing down upon yourself the evil eye. . . .

Conscious awareness, insight, and "working through,". . . is the answer here. . . . This is the best path I know to the acceptance of our highest powers, and whatever elements of greatness or goodness or wisdom or talent we may have concealed or evaded.[6]

Sometimes the "working through" of which Maslow spoke comes through actual physical illness, which results when we carry the Jonah complex to extreme limits. But hopefully we can see through our own Jonah complex before physical illness strikes.

Perhaps the question we should ask ourselves is not, "Am I healthy?" but "*Am I as healthy as I know how to be?*" I believe that for almost all persons the answer will be an unequivocal no. Almost everyone knows how to implement a higher order of healthiness. And if a "no" answer doesn't make us unmistakably uncomfortable, it is likely that we haven't squarely asked it. Answering "no" means that we have hidden from ourselves. We have shunned an inner wisdom.

Jonah's story did not end tragically. Although he tried to run away from his fate, he was unsuccessful, even though a transient occupancy of a whale's belly proved necessary for his enlightenment. His story tells us that it is possible to find our course once again, that there is nothing inexorable about the Jonah complex. We *can* emerge, as did Jonah, wiser, healthier, and whole.

NOTES

1. A. H. Maslow, *The Farthest Reaches of Human Nature* (New York: Viking, 1971), pp. 35–36.
2. *Ibid.*, pp. 36–37.
3. R. S. Eliot and J. C. Buell, "The Role of the CNS [Central Nervous System] in Cardiovascular Disorders," *Hospital Practice*, May 1983: pp. 189–199.
4. *Ibid.*
5. Reich, P., *et al.*, "Acute Psychological Disturbances Preceding Life-Threatening Ventricular Arrhythmias," *Journal of the American Medical Association*, 246:3 (1981): pp. 233–235.
6. Maslow, *The Farthest Reaches*, pp. 39, 37–38.

III

Beyond Pain and Death: An Impossible Dream?

> The alternative to this uncertain world is a certain world. In such a world . . . all life would stop. For life as we know it can only exist through the blessing of uncertainty, and security is a myth.
>
> Yet security is there. We feel its presence. But . . . we must accept the uncertainty of our positions. Without that uncertainty, there is no world.
>
> —Fred Alan Wolf
> *Taking the Quantum Leap*

In the foregoing sections we have examined the comments of a diverse number of persons about the nature of pain and suffering, grief, horror and death. From several philosophical points of view we saw that there was cause for hope, cause for going beyond our morbid sentiments about pain and death. Some of these philosophical viewpoints, we saw, are coherent with certain emerging perspectives from key areas of modern science. But here lies the difficulty with many such propositions: they are *logical*. Their appeal is to the rational, verbal, thinking mind. Their avenue for persuasion is through the intellect—an avenue that has not been convincing in influencing the thoughts and feelings and lives of human beings in these matters. No matter that they might be "airtight" in their logical coherence; when it comes to issues of pain and suffering, life and death, our minds are not much influenced by logic. For, at heart, these are simply not logical concerns. They are first and foremost emotional issues, not affairs of the intellect. And the human heart does not catch fire with dry ideas, but from the heat of feeling. It is not enough, then, if the philosophers and the scientists might speak to us with a single voice (although they, of course, do not), providing us with a surfeit of reasons to defuse our festering fears of death and anguish. The plain fact is, that is not enough.

This is not to say that the lives of many persons have not been affected by the force of ideas. One cannot read the lives of great thinkers and deny the potency of intellectual insight. But is it the ideas themselves that exert the transformative power over those who come in contact with them, or some more fundamental force? I believe it is the latter—a power that goes beyond the rational mind and the thinking, reasoning intellect, something that touches the heart as well as the head. A reading of the lives of two of the preeminent scientists of the scientific era, Newton and Einstein, affirm this belief. Both men embodied in their being deeply felt ideals about how the Universe worked—ideals which helped to shape their efforts, and not vice versa. They seemed to defy the notion of the cold, dispassionate scientist purged of values and emotion. Their scientific insights, in fact, seemed impelled and empowered by something deeper than the mere formation of hypotheses, data gathering, and information analysis. Whether the visions of these two men were accurate and valid in every detail is here beside the point. What is important is that even when great ideas seem to figure as powerful events in persons' lives, we must look deeper for the source of the power of the transformation, finding it less in the force of logic and reason than in emotion, feeling, vision, and soul.

We do not ordinarily see that our own attitudes are frequently shaped in this way. For instance, if asked what will happen to us when we die, our answer is likely to begin with, "Well, I *believe* that . . ."—when a more accurate response for most of us would be, "I *feel* that . . ." For the fact is that most of our "beliefs" about suffering and death are not rational, logical constructs at all, but notions that hinge fundamentally on feelings and emotions. We speak from our hearts on these matters, and later dress our ideas in the garb of reason.

In the course of interviewing sick persons who come to my office with medical problems, I have become fascinated by their use of words to describe their situation. In taking a history of the problem, I usually ask at some point, "Why did you decide to come at this particular time?" And the answer that I eventually hear is not, "Well, I believe something is wrong," but "I *feel* something is wrong," or "I *know* something isn't right"—the "knowing" being something of a nonverbal awareness having nothing to do with cold reason and logic. The responses of patients show that sometimes, especially when taken off guard, our reliance on our irrational, inner wisdom erupts before we can disguise it in linear thinking.

We want to know, then, not whether there might be compelling philosophical or even scientific reasons why we ought to revise our horrific ideas of suffering and death, but whether we can find ways to transcend our fears which will speak to us in our hearts. Is there any other way—a way of the heart, a way of the soul—that would deliver us of the dread, the pain, the fear of suffering and death? Is there a kind of understanding that might marry the deepest, inmost kind of knowing with the "mere" understanding of the intellect?

It is important to emphasize the use of the word "marry." If possible, there should be a fit in the two modes of knowing that we employ, the intellectual and the inner-directed. For if there is not, the misfit will continue to emerge as it has historically in the dissonance of "science versus religion," "reason versus intuition," "mind versus spirit," or some variation of the "head versus heart" dichotomy. Our goal is to unite the head and heart if possible—not in the sense of maintaining that the two ways of knowing are identical or that they spring from the same source, but that the picture of the world that is apprehended by each be harmonious.

And it is important not to fall at the outset into the trap which will doom our efforts in this task, the trap of implicitly supposing that there is an eternal, unbridgeable chasm that has forever and that shall forever separate man's reason from his intuition. I reject at the outset this notion, and I think it lies at the heart of much of the "versus" type of controversy mentioned above. As long as we insist there is but one picture of the world, and that it can be lit *only* through the light of reason, or that it can be apprehended *only* through the power of inner wisdom and intuition, we shall deny ourselves a vision of the world and of ourselves that can only be known through the full use of all our ways of knowing—the rational *and* the intuitive, the logical *and* the spiritual. These ways of knowing are decidedly *not* the same—but the picture of the universe they give us need not necessarily be unbridgeable.

Our goal in this book has been to re-examine our assumptions about health and its correlates: what we mean by birth and death, health and illness, pain and ecstasy, lassitude and vitality, malaise and energy, fear and hopefulness, depression and joy, horror and elation, feeling good and feeling bad. A postulate has been that there is an intrinsic oneness that unites these opposites. They *are* inextricably intertwined—and most emphatically not just conceptually and philosophically, but as a matter of pure experience as well. If it were possible to *know* this fact at the deepest level, an astonishing revolution in our personal experience of life itself would occur. For the dark negatives that drag at us, the fear and loathing that diminish us, would themselves be transformed.

THE TWO MODES OF KNOWING

We have, then, available to us *two basic modes of knowing* . . . : one that has been variously termed symbolic, or map, or inferential, or dualistic knowledge; while the other has been called intimate, or direct, or non-dual knowledge.

. . . these two modes of knowing are universal, that is to say, they have been recognized in one form or another at various times and places throughout mankind's history, from Taoism to William James, from Vedanta to Alfred North Whitehead, from Zen to Christian theology.[1]

With this observation, Ken Wilber, in his remarkable work, *The Spectrum of Consciousness*, denotes the complementary ways of knowing the world which we alluded to above. Our way of *thinking* about health in all its facets—birth, death, pain, pleasure of various expressions—is in the symbolic, map, inferential, or the dualistic mode, as Wilber puts it. It is this way of knowing that distorts the world in a way that can be deceptive, a way which can hypnotically entrance us into mistaking the symbolic for the real.

PAIN AS COUNTERFEIT

Consider but one of many possible examples—the experience of pain. When we attach the word "pain" to our experience, the pain is transformed by our mind into a kind of counterfeit. Thereafter we utilize an intrepid way of mistaking the symbolic—the *word* "pain," or the thought or the remembrance of pain—into a kind of "thing." And we react to this "thing" as if *it* were real.

There is a confusion at an actual physiological level, too, with the symbolic and the real. For thoughts of pain can generate actual physiological changes in the body—an elevation of the heart rate and the blood pressure, cold and clammy palms, rapid breathing and, in some cases, the actual sensation of the original pain itself. In this way the symbolic becomes so real that we trick ourselves into believing, as it were, in ghosts—because we have transformed ghostly things such as concepts and words and memories into something which *seems* real. So, in our emotional reactions we respond to these "things" as if they were objects—as if they possessed some substantial, concrete quality all their own, as if they actually occupied points in space and time, as if they were "real" in every sense.

It is not only the experience of pain that evokes this kind of response in us. All the concepts we include in the larger category of health do the same.

We reify our concepts of birth, death, illness, and well-being in the same way, responding to them as if they were objects-in-the-world. It is not the experience that we are dreading or fearing (such as the experience of pain), so much as the *memory* or the *expectancy* of experience, that we are responding to—regardless of whether the experience is one of pain or of the other several qualities drawn from the grand category of health.

There is a decided difference in this counterfeit type of pain and the real thing. In the counterfeit type, where the symbolic is taken to be real, we sense there is something set apart from us, something we take to be "out there," something external to and removed from us. We fear "it." "It" is painful and hurtful; "it" is what is causing the suffering. Yet in the actual experience of severe pain there is nothing, or very little, of the "it" experience. When we "really" hurt, we *are* the pain. In severe pain we lose ourselves in the discomfort; we become the pain. We do not pause to form concepts, we do not stop to formulate fears of pain and what it might do or mean to us. Distinctions between self and others melt as we become the experience.

How different than other types of pain, the less-than-overwhelming kinds of hurt which constitute the usual types of discomfort we experience. In moderate or mild pain, we invoke the most ingenious ways of tampering with the experience. Pain is seen as an "it"—something malevolent which is about to cause actual suffering and we invest it with the most colorful qualities drawn from previous experiences of painful events. The boundaries between actually experiencing the pain and between fantasy meld; and what emerges is something quite different from the actual pain itself. The result is part pain, part fear, part dread and horror and grief. As if the actual pain were not enough, we have increased its potency.

This is the mode of knowing Wilber calls "map knowledge." For we are using a representation, a map—drawn from memories and expectation—in place of the thing itself.

Yet we have continual warnings during our lifetime that there is another more valid way of experiencing health and illness. Just as intense pain may eradicate our tendency to confuse the map with the territory as we experientially become the pain, when we are *seriously* sick the same process occurs. We become our illness. We do not posture as if we were separate from it; we unite with it and cease to sense it as an "it." During the depths of illness and malaise that accompany many diseases, patients frequently state the experiential truth: "I *am* sick." This is the identification of self with illness, the cessation of converting illness into something standing apart from oneself. There is an "isness" at work in the throes of significant illness, a process wherein sufferer and suffering become one.

It is a mistake to think that it is only during catastrophic illnesses that this realization can occur. It does not require having cancer or a heart attack to experience an existential oneness with illness and pain. In fact, it can occur in the throes of a lesser illness, such as the common cold or the flu. Any illness that saps one's vitality, both physical and mental, is likely to evoke from us the identity of self with suffering. It may be more difficult to identify with the spectacular diseases of our day—cancer, heart attack, stroke—because they have become hopelessly symbolized into various "its" which we either "get" or are "gotten by," attacked unaware from the outside by "the big one," struck down by some "thing" when we least expect it. The fact is that the common cold is the chief cause of days lost from work in our society—because of the utterly draining malaise that is part of it, the sapping of physical and psychological energy. Thus the "minor" illnesses such as common colds can be great teachers when it comes to uniting with experience, in sensing the immediacy of the health-event.

ILLNESS AS TEACHER

In various historic periods and in many cultures illness has been considered a great teacher. We can begin to see one of the reasons why. When we become one-with-illness we are invoking the second mode of knowing we have referred to, the knowledge that comes through "intimate, or direct, or non-dual" ways.[2] Every illness-event that calls us into unity and oneness with it is a living experience of this way of knowing. The direct experience of illness, pain, and suffering, unmediated and uncontaminated by symbolism, fantasy, memory, or expectation, is an exercise in the nondual way of knowing.

It is this way of knowing the world that has been utilized by the great mystics who appear in every cultural tradition. For the goal of the mystic is to apprehend an unmediated reality, to experience the world directly—a task in which illness seems to play a crucial role for many. Illness-as-teacher prompted the great authority on Western mysticism, Evelyn Underhill, to speak of the "heroic acceptance of labour and suffering" of the mystic: "Often even the sick come forth from ecstasy healthy and with new strength; for something great is then given to the soul."[3]

And the source of this "new strength" that is "given to the soul" comes at least in part from the ability to know the world as it is, even the part of the world which we ordinarily consider reprehensible—the part of the world that is made up of illness, pain, and suffering.

This attitude toward the discomforts of life is not simply an example of "Christian long suffering," for the same realizations appear in many other great religious traditions, including Buddhism. In his classic work on Zen Buddhism, *The Three Pillars of Zen*, Philip Kapleau (quoting the Zen Master Yasutani) describes "the fundamental principle or doctrine or philosophy of Buddhism": that the "matrix of all phenomena," what is referred to in Buddhism as Buddha- or Dharma-nature, is "living, dynamic, devoid of mass, unfixed, [and] beyond individuality or personality . . ."[4] This world is beyond the realm of imagination and intellect, so that any picture one makes of this real world that underlies everything is in fact nothing more than that—a picture and not reality itself. But although we cannot imagine this underlying substratum or even think about it accurately, we can nonetheless directly realize it and "grasp the world" experientially. What result does this direct experience have on one's concepts of pain, suffering, and death? The most profound alterations occur:

> Having once perceived the world of Buddha-nature, we are indifferent to death. . . . [We realize that] what we call life is nothing more than a process of transformations. If we do not change, we are lifeless. We grow and age because we are alive. The evidence of our having lived is the fact that we die. We die because we are alive. Living means birth and death. Creation and destruction signify life.
>
> When you truly understand this fundamental principle you will not be anxious about your life or your death. Even though heaven and earth were turned upside down, you would have no fear.[5]

We glimpse here the central theme of many great religious teachings: The world is not to be understood by severing it into an unending series of incompatible, mutually exclusive sets of opposites such as birth and death or pain and pleasure. Only through comprehending the interpenetrating oneness underlying the apparently isolated events in the world can "the way things are" be correctly seen. This unity spares nothing, or it would be something other than unity. It extends, thus, to health and illness, birth and death.

It is important to note that the unseemly facts of life with which we concern ourselves—those events we seek to banish through our assorted strategies of health—do not vanish in some mystical puff of smoke with the capacity to directly perceive the Dharma-nature. Pain and death remain. They are still here for us to experience. But the employment of the mode of knowing that is nondual, direct, intimate, and unmediated transforms the experience of these life-events into something altogether different than we ordinarily conceive. There is the sense that they *belong*, not that they are "unnatural" or that they are foreign intruders like some pathogenic bacteria or viruses that are constantly upsetting the apple cart of ecstasy and pleasure we generally view as our richly deserved lot in life. The stones and bruises are evidence *of* the apple cart, the complementary meaning of the ecstasy and pleasure, the evidence that we are alive enough to know the very pleasure we seek. The pain remains, and it must remain— but so too must its opposite. Both are essential parts of the Buddha-nature. It is the becoming-one-with-experience that transforms it without abolishing it:

> . . . if you are caught in a holocaust, inevitably you would be burnt. Therefore become one with fire when there is no escaping it! If you fall into poverty, live that way without grumbling—then your poverty will not be a burden to you. Likewise, if you are rich, live with your riches. All this is the functioning of Buddha-nature.[6]

What does it mean, then, to go beyond pain and death? Is it possible? If we approach the question in our ordinary way of thinking—the way that opposes pain and pleasure, birth and death, the answer is no, for we can never trick ourselves through logical means that there is anything about these opposing qualities of life that could be reconciled. But if we are willing to employ the nondual way of knowing, the inner-directed, intimate, and direct way of experiencing life, the answer is unequivocally yes.

NOTES

1. Ken Wilber, *The Spectrum of Consciousness* (Wheaton, Ill.: The Theosophical Publishing House, 1977), p. 43.
2. *Ibid.*
3. Evelyn Underhill, *Mysticism* (New York: Dutton, 1961), p. 61.
4. Philip Kapleau, *The Three Pillars of Zen* (Boston: Beacon Press, 1967), p. 74.
5. *Ibid.*, p. 75.
6. *Ibid.*, pp. 75–76.

IV

Of Time, Evil, and Health

There are said to be creative pauses,
pauses that are as good as death, empty and dead as death itself.
And in these awful pauses the evolutionary change takes place.

—D. H. Lawrence
Nullus

The ultimate evil in the temporal world, as Whitehead has . . . shown, is deeper than any specific evil such as hatred, suffering, or death. It lies in the fact that time is a perpetual perishing and that being actual involves elimination. The nature of evil may be epitomized therefore in two simple but ultimate metaphysical propositions: "*Things fade*" and "*Alternatives exclude*." In the temporal world . . . the passage of time entails loss, and . . . the characteristics of many things are mutually obstructive. (italics added)[1]

It is the nature of our thought to accept uncritically what passes for common sense. Human history is littered with ideas that seemed self-evident, but which later were tossed onto the garbage-heap of fallacy: the notion that the earth is flat; that the sun revolves around the earth; that there is an invisible ether which serves as the carrier of all energetic wave phenomena in the world; that the earth is the center of the universe.

When it comes to health, a future reading of the history of our own time will likely show that we accepted, in the name of common sense, ideas that were as fallacious as these.

There are two notions which lie at the heart of our thinking about health and illness that, if we are courageous enough to do so, we may eventually transcend. They account for the most grotesque qualities of pain and suffering and death, and lie at the source of untold human misery—misery that for the most part is self-inflicted because it is caused by wrong thinking. What are these two ideas? Simply put, they are: one, we live in a world of separate objects, which, two, exists in a linear time that flows inexorably from past to present to future.

HEALTH IN A WORLD OF OBJECTS

In *Space, Time and Medicine* [2] we examined reasons why both these ideas are suspect in the light of the discoveries of modern science. They belong to a science of an older day, a science that rested more on commonsensical ideas of how the world behaved than on what could be proved to be so.

The world for the earliest scientific thinkers was a world of noninteract-ing objects. After all, there were two fundamental entities in the universe, massive objects and empty space. From the Greeks—for example, from Democritus—came the notion of atoms, conceived as the primordial, quintessential building blocks of nature. These units could be combined in ways in which forms of increasing complexity could evolve. Because they were fundamental, they maintained their individual identity in the process as nature's irreducible objects.

It is by now well-known that this concept of nature as comprised of solid subunits has run into trouble in our century. One of the central mes-sages of twentieth-century physics is that the attempt to visualize nature in terms of such objects leads to models which cannot be verified by experi-ment. The concept of "object" was one idealized from the world of mac-roscopic experience, and which finds no support when put to the tests of modern physics. Entirely new concepts have come into being to replace that of object, such as the concept of "field." Massive objects and empty space are *not* inseparable, we are told, each determining the "geometry" of the other. When we attempt to observe the energetic events which we previously called objects, we cannot entirely separate from them, for the very attempt to study their behavior affects the characteristics we ob-serve. We have come, thus, to a view of nature in which there are no essen-tial objects; and no-thing, not even ourselves, can assume a posture of noninteraction.

Most importantly, this principle of relatedness and interaction extends not only to the depths of nature's microscopic domain but to the macro-scopic world of living things as well. This situation is clearly stated by Whitehead, whose vision of a world of oneness solidly incorporates these modern principles:

. . . neither physical nature nor life can be understood unless we fuse them together as essential factors in the composition of "really real" things whose interconnections and individual characters constitute the universe.[3]

We have almost completely abandoned this concept when it comes to fashioning our ideas of health and illness, birth and death; for then we resort to almost a pure "object thinking." It is noninteracting objects who are born, live, decline, and die—objects called persons, individuals, human beings. We pride ourselves on individuality; we promote it on every hand, and even think poorly of those who do not demonstrate it in our culture. We build our health ethic around the individual-as-object. And in so doing, we have gotten out of step with the most accurate descriptions of the world we have ever had—not just the messages of modern physics about the subatomic level—but the way of the world at the level of the living, the gross, the macroscopic, the world where homes and hospitals and clinics exist. At this level we continue to base our notions of health and illness, birth and death on visions of the world that have been transcended in our own time.

It is most ironic that we do so. For medicine, from which come many of our models, has always looked to physics for its own constructs; in the early days of science, medicine as a profession envied the precision and accuracy and reproducibility that was embodied in physics. The irony is, though, that the very physics that we look to has been modified in this century in all its major facets. Thus we find ourselves with models in medicine that are characterized not by accuracy, as we wished, but by obsolescence.

If we conceive of ourselves as objects floundering in a sea of objects, it is only natural, and perhaps inevitable, that we superimpose this object-type thinking onto our concepts of health and illness. Health and illness themselves become objects and events—atoms as it were, building blocks of experience—instead of the boundless processes about which Whitehead speaks. We lose the flowing unity of experience in an endless repetition of objects—whether these objects are physical examinations, laboratory tests, or specific diseases. We find ourselves adrift in an "either-or" world: either we are healthy or we are not; either the blood pressure is normal or it is not; either we will live another year or we will not. Life in a world of objects is a series of choices. It is a selection of options and alternatives. The experience of unity is not possible when all we see is units.

This is one of the characteristics of "the nature of evil" of which Whitehead spoke: "Alternatives exclude." One cannot choose everything; by selecting among alternatives, we exclude all the others and thereby sunder the wholeness that is life and health. Healthiness becomes the interlude between diseases, an experience that lasts until we contract some illness all over again. Life becomes a series of events of health *or* illness, a staccato-like process of one alternative excluding all others.

We are blind to the evil Whitehead spoke of that is inherent in this ordinary way of seeing and behaving about health, assuming that pain, suffering, successive periods of health and illness, decline, and eventual fall into death are part of the price we pay for being human. We *assume* the grotesqueness of life, the inevitability of grief, horror, and the unbearable. The most we can be thankful for is that "things" are not worse. We are oblivious to the fact that our habitual way of dissecting the world into unrelated things and events provides the womb for the incubation of this evil which envelops us like a shroud. Blinded by habit and impelled by common sense, we are living examples of the dichotomizing that pathologizes, and the pathology that dichotomizes.

HEALTH IN A TEMPORAL WORLD

In addition to the nature of evil that is epitomized in the fact that "alternatives exclude," Whitehead singles out the idea that "things fade" as also embodying the nature of evil. What does he mean by such an innocuous-sounding observation as the fading away of things? He is pointing to the notion of temporality, the idea of impermanence. Bluntly put, living things die. And the culprit is time—a *linear* time, one that flows, one that can be segmented into a past, present, and future. According to the Bhagavad Gita: "I am come as time, Waster of Peoples, Ready for the hour that ripens to their ruin."

We underestimate the profound role that our concept of time plays in our concepts of health. But in fact, it is not possible to have a philosophy of health without a philosophy of time. When we think about it, this fact becomes obvious, as illustrated in Cassell's observation:

> . . . suffering has a temporal element. In order for a situation to be a source of suffering, it must influence the person's perception of future events. ("If the pain continues like this, *I will be* overwhelmed;" "If the pain comes from cancer, *I will* die;" "If the pain cannot be controlled, *I will not* be able to take it.") At the moment when the patient is saying, "If the pain continues like this, I will be overwhelmed," he or she is not overwhelmed. Fear itself always involves the future.[4]

This is not just a philosophical problem—for the actual experience of pain and suffering is heightened if one feels that time flows. This relationship has made it possible to actually devise methods of relieving pain and suffering that, instead of directly annulling the pain itself as would an injection of morphine, annul the sense of time flow instead. Many therapies now exist which modify the time sense and which can, in proper subjects, profoundly diminish pain perception. Biofeedback, autogenic therapy, progressive relaxation, and hypnosis are examples. These are not just "fringe" therapies, but have found their way into mainstream medicine.

One such example is the pain management program that has been developed at the University of Massachusetts Medical School by Dr. Jon Kabat-Zinn. Patients are taught a process called "mindfulness meditation," or "the intentional self-regulation of attention from moment to moment."[5] This technique has its roots in Theravada and Mahayana Buddhism, as well as in the yogic traditions. Although it was not developed for the purpose of pain control, it is clear from the results that it is effective for such. And although it is not the time sense per se which the practitioner of the technique is attempting to modulate, it is obvious that the sense of time is involved in the process:

> By maintaining a perspective during periods of formal meditation . . . in which no mental event (including perceptions) is accorded any content value, the strong alarm reaction <the interpretation of the sensation as pain, i.e., "It's killing me," often accompanied *by future thinking*, i.e., the thought that *it will last for a long time or forever*> can lose considerable power and urgency. . . . The [pain signals] may be undiminished, but the emotional and cognitive components of the pain experience, the hurt, the suffering, are reduced. (italics added)[6]

It is no accident that a uniform characteristic of drugs that are effective in relieving pain is that they modify the sense of time passage. The patient receiving the drug is apt to say that time slows down or stops. What is admirable about the work of Kabat-Zinn and many other researchers and practitioners in this field is that they accomplish the same result without the use of drugs.

It is helpful at this point to return to Levi's observation with which we began this section: ". . . Things fade. . . . In the temporal world . . . the passage of time entails loss. . . ." The sense of doom, of extermination and obliteration, of impending nothingness and death which is part of the experience of pain and suffering are contingent on a sense of flowing time. "Loss" mandates linear time, implying the past and requiring a present and future for its very meaning. This is why temporality and suffering and grief are tied together experientially, and why a heightened sense of flowing time accentuates the experience of horror, pain, and hurt in all its forms.

There are those who say, "So what? Time is what it is. I know that it accentuates human suffering, but who can change time? The best we can do is to perhaps 'trick' ourselves through techniques such as meditation into temporarily viewing it differently. But that doesn't change the flowing nature of time, only the way we see it." This attitude reflects one of the real hallucinations of our day, the belief that we can objectively document an external, flowing time. If it comes as a shock to be told that there has *never* been any physical experiment to show that time flows,[7] we can only say that it has not been the business of most laymen to become informed about what modern physics says about the nature of time. The words of the physicist Thomas Gold are illustrative of the view of modern physics about time:

> The flow of time is clearly an inappropriate concept for the description of the physical world that has no past, present and future. It just is.[8]

And Bertrand Russell provides an affirmative description:

> A truer image of the world . . . is obtained by picturing things as entering into the stream of time from an external world outside, rather than from a view which regards time as the devouring tyrant of all that is.[9]

Russell's "devouring tyrant," a linear-flowing external "real" time, is for Whitehead the embodiment of the "nature of evil." It is the presumed, unquestioned, commonsensical event that causes things to fade, the process that engenders loss. *Without flowing time there is no loss.* Death, pain, and suffering manifest their vengeance in direct proportion to our felt sense of passing, external time.

If our most accurate view of the world, that offered by modern physics, does *not* affirm our commonly held notion that time does flow, what are we to say about the time-heavy experiences of pain, suffering, grief, and the expectancy of death? The statements of modern physicists have patently *not* banished these painful events from the lives of humans. Is there then not a near-total disjunction between what we can *prove* about the behavior of time and what we *experience* about it? Perhaps the modern concepts of time deserve to remain where they originated, in the laboratories of the physicists themselves. For when it comes to practical use they seem worthless in assuaging personal pain and suffering.

I do not believe there is an unbridgeable hiatus between modern phys-ics' view of time, and human experience. In fact, *it is the nature of humans to be able to experientially know and feel the time of the physicist*, the "eter-nal world outside" which Russell described. Entire cultures do so, as do contemporary segments within our own society. Our time-besotted, West-ern way of viewing the world is not natural for many other peoples. Alter-native ways of experiencing time *are* possible for us, ways affirmed not only by cultural records but by the descriptions of modern physical sci-ence as well.

A WAY OUT

There is, then, a way out—a potential escape from the self-inflicted, mor-bid sense of suffering, illness, pain, grief, and inexorable demise that we accept as a necessary ingredient of life. The way out will be one which entails new views of the universe, particularly with regard to the behavior of time and the idea of particularity. It will emphasize an "all-at-once" time and will discard the notion of noninteracting units that make up the world. The way out will not insist, as did the old view, on an endless subdivision of living things into nonliving units. It will cease to enforce an unending series of choices between mutually exclusive alternatives. It will empha-size process, interaction, and wholeness in place of isolation and disunity. And in so doing it will be infinitely more consistent with the ancient mes-sages of our race, and with the emerging scientific world view.

Pain, suffering, and grief will continue to be felt—but they will be at-tenuated, not magnified, by a new view of the world. We shall learn to par-ticipate in grief and pain from an utterly new perspective. It will be a per-spective that modifies the *meaning* we impart to the experience, without eliminating the experience itself. For we know that the emotional and cognitive components to experience are decidedly transmutable to other qualities, qualities which can transform sorrow, pain, and grief. In such a process the *fact* of the experience remains; the *event* is not destroyed—it is the *meaning* that is imparted to it that is everything. And the ultimate appeal of the "way out" is that the meanings we shall learn to impart to the morbid experiences of life will be truer to the intrinsic nature of things, to the way things are.

PROOF AND THE PROBLEM OF LANGUAGE

"Illness exists outside of time."
"To treat another is to treat one's self."

"Health, like disease, is shared."

"The body is not an object, it is not something localized to a specific time and space."

"Birth and death are not the ultimate poles of life—for, since time does not flow, final demarcations in time cannot be established."

These are typical expressions of health and illness that flow from the new ideas of space, time, health, illness, and body, and which have been examined extensively in *Space, Time and Medicine*.[10] The response they frequently elicit is, "Well, if they're true, prove it." Our rational mind rebels against them, protesting every step of the way.

While it is reasonable to ask for some kind of proof of these counter-intuitive claims, we ought to be careful about what kind of proof we demand. While in some cases it may be possible to establish an acceptable proof of these contentions, in other cases it may not be so easy. Take, for example, the principle that health and illness are shared phenomena. This can easily be shown to have importance at the actual *clinical* level. We know that our own illnesses have psychophysical "spinoffs" for those round us. For example, if our death evokes grief, depression, bereavement or anxiety in those close to us, their health suffers—as Schleifer and others have clearly shown.[11] Yet some of the new views of health and illness and body are more difficult to demonstrate—for instance, the idea that health events might exist outside of time. How could something which does such violence to common sense be true?

Much of the problem in discussing the truth or falsity of these wrenching new ideas is that we are forced to use a language which is unsuited for the purpose. Ours is a language designed to describe a world set in linear time: the tenses of the verbs we use reflect this fact. How then could we conceivably use a time-based language to describe a process that is outside of time?

The problem is not a new one, and has haunted physicists long before it began to cause problems for doctors. Consider the statement by a physicist, "No physical experiment has ever demonstrated the flow of time." The implication of the statement is that time does not flow, that it cannot be subdivided into past, present, and future. Yet the very language that is used to make this implication is at odds with it—for the phrase "has ever" implies flowing time. To try to fully describe phenomena of this sort may be difficult, if not impossible, using our everyday speech. Our language is drawn from an experience we believe to be embedded in linear time; and to expect it to adequately describe processes lying outside such is asking too much.

The main point, however, is *not* to give up on our demands for proof, but to learn what kinds of proofs to demand. Proving the validity of the time-transcendent qualities of health and illness through a proof that is tied to linear time would be as misguided as attempting to prove the value of the murals of the Sistine Chapel by chemically analyzing the pigments used.

We must learn to ask for proofs of the new concepts in a language suitable to the task of describing them—a language such as that used by Whitman, who, although he continued to use a time-based language, fully transcended its limitations:

> Space and Time! now I see it is true, what I guess'd at,
> What I guess'd when I loaf'd on the grass,
> What I guess'd while I lay alone in my bed,
> And again as I walk'd the beach under the paling stars of the morning.[12]

It is when our time-bound language escapes its bounds that it can arise to the task of describing something beyond time, and it is through the unabashed use of poetry and metaphor that such an escape can come about. Through imagery we reach the stillness of the eternal present, even though the imagery may be couched in the language of linear time:

> . . . I, turning, call to thee O soul, thou actual Me, . . . Thou matest Time, smilest content at Death, And fillest, swellest full the vastness of Space.[13]

We will also find that our ordinary language occasionally serves us quite well in describing the new views of health and illness. In the example we saw above, in which Schleifer demonstrated the nonlocal effects of illness, our language can fully describe this event. Using common language, we can adequately describe the facts that illness does "get around," that it is not localized in space, that it is indeed shared, and that bodies and minds do interact. But the language is suited for the description only because the picture we are trying to describe in this instance is not flagrantly bizarre. It is when we wrenchingly violate our view of reality, such as in postulating that we don't "become" well or "get" sick—in other words, when we give up linear time—that language miserably fails in its assigned task. Here our brow furrows, our spirit bridles, and our logic rebels. A new language, or the same language used in a different way through the full employment of metaphor, imagery, and poetry, is required.

We must continually remind ourselves that the "problem" of finding proof for these new views is made vastly easier if we stop insisting that there is only one valid form of knowing, only a single, exclusive way of describing reality. We can use the empirical-analytical methods of proof, couching them in ordinary language, so far as they take us; but we must be ready to employ alternative methods of knowing the world when ordinary modes limit us. The intuitive mode of probing the world, describable in the nonlogical language of poetry and metaphor, can exist alongside the linear forms of knowing that characterize traditional science. Used conjointly, the two modes can enrich, enliven, and broaden the description of the world we could achieve by using one method exclusively.

Those who resist the new ways of knowing and describing reality must be content with a limited view of what is meant by health and illness. For there is no way that ordinary language can paint the full picture.

When we demand, thus, proof of the new, overtly bizarre notions of health and illness that violate our ordinary ideas of space and time and object, we should remain aware of this important fact. If we insist that such proof be given in ordinary, time-based language in which the subject-object distinction is fundamental, we may have rendered proof impossible. Time-transcendent and object-transcendent truth cannot be easily given in a language whose basic structure denies their very existence. If we want proof of the new ideas, we must be willing to employ a language of a different kind—for example, the kind Whitman used in describing his own encounters with the world:

> O soul thou pleasest me, I thee,
> Sailing these seas or on the hills, or waking
>   in the night,
> Thoughts, silent thoughts, of Time and Space and
>   Death, like water flowing.[14]

NOTES

1. Albert William Levi, *Philosophy and the Modern World* (Bloomington: University of Indiana Press, 1959), p. 527.
2. Larry Dossey, *Space, Time and Medicine* (Boulder, Colo.: Shambhala Press, 1982).
3. Levi, *Philosophy*, p. 494.
4. Eric Cassell, "The Nature of Suffering and the Goals of Medicine, *The New England Journal of Medicine* 306 (1982): p. 639.
5. Jon Kabat-Zinn, "An Outpatient Program in Behavioral Medicine for Chronic Pain Patients Based on the Practice of Mindfulness Meditation: Theoretical Considerations and Preliminary Results," *General Hospital Psychiatry* 4 (1982): pp. 33–47.

6. *Ibid.*, p. 35.

7. Dossey, *Space, Time and Medicine*, p. 151.

8. *Ibid.*, p. 31.

9. *Ibid.*, p. 34.

10. *Ibid.*

11. Schleifer et al., "Suppression of Lymphocyte Stimulation Following Bereavement," *Journal of the American Medical Association* 250 (1983): p. 374.

12. Walt Whitman, "Song of Myself," *A Choice of Whitman's Verse*, Donald Hall, ed. (London: Faber and Faber, 1968), p. 54.

13. Walt Whitman, "Passage to India," *A Choice of Whitman's Verse*, p. 167.

14. *Ibid.*, p. 166.

V

The Distant View of Health and Illness

Every proposition proposing a fact must, in the complete analysis, propose the general character of the universe required for that fact. There are no self-sustained facts, floating in non-entity.

—Alfred North Whitehead

The objective world simply is, it does not happen. Only to the gaze of my consciousness, crawling upward along the life line of my body, does a section of this world come to life as a fleeting image in space which continually changes in time.

—Hermann Weyl
Philosophy of Mathematics and Natural Science

The defense of [the] "panoramic" view of life led the 18th century German poet, Goethe, to lament the invention of the microscope. He was, to be sure, scientist and naturalist enough to understand the increasing observational potential the microscope offered: allowing us to see the heretofore invisible, a world formerly the domain of magic and mystic speculation. But Goethe feared the reduction of life into the narrowed field of vision the focusing powers of the microscope introduced, and his prophecy was fulfilled. The eye would now surrender its sense of reality to this magical new instrument and the new, constricted but enlarged, reality which the instrument offered. The problem is not what the microscope as tool allows us to include, but what it allows us to exclude from the domain of relevant data. The problem is not the instrument, but the world view which determines how we use that instrument.

—Howard F. Stein

Thus the individual's mind-and-body may be in pain, or humiliation, or fear, but as long as he consents to simply abide as the witness of these affairs, as if from on high, they no longer threaten *him*, and thus he need no longer manipulate them, wrestle with them, subdue them, or try to "understand" them. Because he is willing to witness them, to look at them impartially, he is thereby able to transcend them. As St. Thomas put it, "Whatever knows certain things cannot have any of them in its own nature."

Every time we become exclusively identified with or attached to the persona, ego, [or]body . . . , then anything which threatens their existence . . . seems to threaten our very Self. Every attachment to thoughts, sensations, feelings, or experiences is merely another link in the chain of our own self-enslavement.

—Ken Wilber

The main obstacle to seeing the interconnectedness and oneness of health and illness, how one depends for its meaning on the other, is primarily psychological. Once we think about it there are enormous logical difficulties in keeping these two entities neatly separated in crisp categories. This idea is illustrated in a Sufi tale of a poor man whose only horse ran away. He was woeful, for because of his poverty he could not replace it. But the next day the horse returned, bringing with it a beautiful wild stallion. The poor man was exuberant! Then the man's only son tried to tame the horse but was thrown from it, breaking his leg. Now the old man was distraught. How could they survive without the labor of his son? The next day representatives of the governor of the province came to the old man's house, drafting conscripts into the army to fight a war. When they saw the old man's only son lying in bed with a broken leg they passed him by and did not return. This time the old man was joyful at his good fortune.

This Sufi tale could go on endlessly, reverberating with events which initially seem tragic but which blend into good fortune. Sufi tales are, in fact, quite famous for this quality, that of taking the mind off guard, of cutting through assumptions and expectations of how things ought to be. The point here is that any attempt to designate a life-event as either good or bad is bound to fail. There is a connection and fluidity to the events of life, not isolation and stasis, and these qualities make it impossible to superficially inspect a single happening and ascertain its goodness or badness.

THE DISTANT VIEW IN HEALTH AND ILLNESS

It is obvious that the conclusions we make about the overtly tragic events in life depend on the focal length of our observations. That is, how far back do we stand in observing them? It is possible to adopt a stance that is very close, so that only a single thing is witnessed. When only single events meet our eye, it is then that we categorize them in decisive ways, as either good or bad, for we have deceived ourselves into thinking we have observed all there is to know. In moments of anguish and pain involving ourselves or those we love, we narrow our field of vision to encompass only the obvious—the actual experience of suffering, illness, grief, and hurt. It is at these times that we resort to firm categorizations and easy classifications.

But through the more distant and larger perspective we begin to appreciate the sheer interpenetration of all things and events, the most grotesque as well as the most sublime. Through the distant view we perceive the webs of relationships that tie us together in the fabric that is never rent. We can focus narrowly and only observe single threads of the cloth, thinking that we have seen its totality, but it is never so. Only the larger view can tell us what we need to know.

Whitehead knew about this perspective, and said, "In the modern concept . . . there is no possibility of a detached, self-contained existence."[1] And the great English astronomer-physicist Sir Arthur Eddington knew it too, and poetically stated, "When the electron vibrates, the universe shakes."

But these connections are not limited to the remote domains of nature such as the realms of the subatomic particle and the distant galaxy; they pervade the in-between realm of living beings such as ourselves. Indeed, this is the *raison d'etre*, the very meaning of the discipline of ecology, whose task it is to describe the intricate, intermingled relationships between the organism and the environment. The message from ecology is that living things cannot be extracted from the world around them or from all other living things about them and be understood. Only from the distant perspective can the whole be seen; and only through attention to the whole can life processes be deciphered. It may be tempting to take the short view, to scrutinize life-events by restricting one's attention; but we do this only by sacrificing something much more important: the knowledge that the universe is a whole.

THE DISTANT VIEW AND THE EXPERIENCE OF PAIN

One of the deadliest ways of reinforcing pain and suffering and a sense of tragedy is to take the narrow, limited, close-on view. By simply restricting one's attention to pain it is heightened; by excluding all else from one's field of awareness suffering is accentuated. This is a simple observation, one that anyone can try for himself. The next time a headache arises, first, try as hard as possible to focus your attention on the pain, excluding all other sensory input possible. Let the pain be all there is for you at the moment. Make a mental note of its severity. Then adopt, after a few minutes, a perspective in which you see yourself standing far away from the you who is hurting. Notice that the head that is hurting is part of a body, which itself is embedded in a larger space: a house, a block, a community, a city, and so on. Enlarge this perspective, distancing eventually away from the earth itself, seeing it from afar as if you were stationed on a satellite in space. Finally let the earth merge into the galaxy, and let the galaxy blend into the entire universe itself. Hold these interconnections in your mind as vividly as possible, finally returning to the sense of pain. Then compare mentally the degree of pain to its intensity before you performed the exercise. Most persons find that the pain has diminished significantly. Through taking the larger view one can actually defuse the ugliness of life's painful moments. And this is not done through self-deception, but by seeing the event as part of a larger event.

LIFE ITSELF: THE ONLY HEALTH EVENT

This simple experiment demonstrates that the view which we decide to take—whether the short or the long view—is intimately connected with what we call good or bad. Put another way, *there is nothing absolute about the goodness or badness of health and illness.* Einstein once said of space and time that they are not conditions in which we live, but modes by which we think. The same is true with health and illness. They are not rigid categories of experience but dynamic, fluid phenomena interlaced in the entire structure of the world in which they occur. As Sir James Jeans said,

> There is no scientific justification for dividing the happenings of the world into detached events, and still less for supposing that they are strung in pairs, like rows of dominoes, each being the cause of the event which follows and at the same time the effect of that which precedes. The changes in the world are too continuous in their nature, and also too closely interwoven, for any such procedure to be valid.[2]

There is only one health-event, and that is life itself. All the dissecting we engage in, all the carving of life into bit-pieces of health and illness, creates an illusion that destroys the seamless existence of life.

Select any health-event—for example, your blood pressure reading the last time you visited your doctor's office. Suppose it was higher than usual, elevated perhaps for the first time. You might typically go through a convoluted process of trying to explain why it was up. Patients in this situation frequently say, "I'm sure it's up because I rushed to get here on time. The traffic was really bad on the way to your office, and I couldn't find a parking place." The emotional harassment is erected as the cause of the elevated blood pressure. Yet a moment's reflection tells us that the chain of causality has more than two links. Perhaps the traffic was bad because of a wreck on the expressway. Perhaps the wreck was caused by a driver who dozed from sleep deprivation, his boss compelling him to work overtime for three days in a row. Perhaps the boss was striving to meet a production schedule in his company due to increased buyers' demands which were unanticipated. This, in turn, was caused by an upswing in the economy, which resulted in greater spending power for the consumer in this business's particular line of products. The economy, in turn, was helped by greater wheat harvests in the Midwest, which were made possible by greater rainfall than in the previous drought-ridden years. The greater rainfall was due to modifications in climatic behavior, which was affected by several volcanic eruptions worldwide in the preceding year, and on and on. There is, then, no *single* cause for the elevation of the blood pressure in the physician's office, which the distant view makes clear.

THE DISTANT VIEW: EXAMPLES FROM CHEMOTHERAPY

The tendency to impart to health and illness a quality of sheer objectivity is nothing more than a bad habit which all of us learn early on but which is *not* unchangeable. We *can* learn to sense health and illness in different ways. And if we do so we should remember that we are most decidedly *not* engaging in hallucinations or distortions of "reality," for that would imply an external, objective set of "things" that we were deceiving ourselves "about." When it comes to health and illness, nothing we know of their inner nature justifies the idea that they are events which are "out there," just waiting around for us to apply our perceptions to them. The following examples illustrate how this principle operates in "actual life" situations.

Among the difficulties associated with chemotherapy, the administration of anticancer drugs, are nausea and vomiting. One in four cancer patients experiences this effect and, although a host of drugs are used to control it, they are usually incompletely effective. The problem is a serious one. Not only does it cause enormous discomfort for those who experience it, in severe cases it may necessitate aborting the use of chemotherapy altogether.

It is known that in certain patients the nausea and vomiting precede the administration of the drug itself. Typically these persons report that the nausea begins the day before the chemotherapeutic drugs are to be given, with increasing intensity the evening before, during breakfast of the treatment day, and while driving to the clinic for treatment. In terms of the observations we have been making above, it is as if these patients have adopted a very short view, a very narrow perspective: They are narrowly focused on an event which they judge to be overwhelmingly dominant in their life, the administration of the anticancer medication. So keen is this focus that they begin to live out this so-called "anticipatory" nausea and vomiting even before the drugs are given.

At the University of Rochester, Morrow and Morrell studied a group of such patients.[3] In effect, those patients with anticipatory nausea and vomiting were asked to restructure their experience of chemotherapy and were taught to see the event in a different way. They were instructed in a technique called Jacobsonian progressive relaxation in which they would visualize the serial relaxation of parts of their bodies—forearms, hand, eyes, forehead, mouth, tongue, upper back, shoulders, chest, stomach, legs, etc. They learned to associate the word "relax" with actual sensations of relaxation in these body parts. Then, after learning this technique, they would imagine themselves in the situations leading up to the administration of the drug itself—the day and night before, the breakfast of the day of treatment, and the drive to the clinic. The result? Those patients who learned to take a different perspective of chemotherapy had a significant reduction in the frequency, severity, and duration of their anticipatory nausea.

While we do not know the actual perceptions of these patients, it seems likely, based on the reports of other patients who undergo chemotherapy, that they learned to dissociate, or "back away," from the belief that nausea was an omnipresent, inevitable, and dominating part of the experience of chemotherapy. They took a larger view, focusing not only on what they believed to be unchangeable and inevitable, but on other things—the parts of their body and on sensations other than nausea, such as the sensation of relaxation. They expanded their repertoire of possible experiences during the chemotherapy process—which included the possibility that they might *not* become nauseated. As a result, the problems associated with their treatment diminished.

In another study, another disagreeable side effect of chemotherapy, that of hair loss, was investigated.[4] It is well-known that loss of hair, or alopecia, frequently accompanies the use of anticancer drugs. In this study some patients were not given the chemotherapy drug which they expected but instead received a placebo (an inert substance of no known pharmacological effect). The result was that one-fourth of those patients who expected to receive an anticancer drug but who received a placebo instead *still* lost their hair. So focused were they on the narrow view, the expectation and certainty of hair loss, that they actually brought the "reality" into existence.

These kinds of clinical examples in medicine could be multiplied endlessly. They show that we tend to live out our expectations. If an event such as receiving chemotherapy is narrowly judged as tragic—for example, if it is thought to inevitably cause hair loss or nausea—it is highly likely that it will be so. If, on the other hand, it is felt to possibly *not* do such, it is much less likely to cause these regrettable problems. The lesson we meet again and again in these clinical examples is that there is nothing invariable, absolute, and objective about health and illness. They are not conditions in which we live, but modes by which we think.

GREAT TRAGEDY: CAN THE DISTANT VIEW HELP?

Or are they? It is one thing to speak about the nausea and hair loss which chemotherapy patients experience, but what about the tragedy felt by a mother of a stillborn child? What about the infant born with mental retardation or without limbs or with hydrocephaly? What about children who die minute by minute on this planet from hunger, or those who are needlessly killed in wars? Surely these events are not similar in kind to the clinical examples mentioned.

At the risk of sounding calloused, I must state that I deeply believe that they *are* similar in kind. That is not to say that they do not evoke from us a degree of suffering and grief that can at times seem almost unbearable, or a sense of pain that is so intense it seems to foreclose even life itself. We have all experienced times when we shrank from life's darkest moments. But those moments do not annihilate the principle of interconnectedness of one event with all others, for the fabric of wholeness cannot be sundered.

At these times it may seem little consolation to speak of larger perspectives and broader views. But some persons *are* able to comprehend larger meanings even in the midst of the most enormous tragedies and while experiencing the most profound grief. Just as black clouds do not annul the fact that the sun shines bright above them, the fact of tragedy cannot destroy the fact that all events, tragic ones included, are part of a larger whole, regardless of their immediate and local impact.

How tenaciously we cling to ideas such as the *uniqueness* of individual suffering, the *necessity* of grief! To some, to suggest that these are not absolute events or concepts is to suggest that all of life becomes a sort of smudged canvas in which one experience cannot be differentiated from any other. Life becomes a blur if we admit that there is some diaphanous "whole" that envelops birth and death, health and illness, ecstasy and suffering. If the boundaries of experience are not kept crisp, life loses its meaning for the very reason that individual experiences cannot be distinguished. Life in such a situation would be like living in a snowstorm—featureless, directionless, inchoate. So even though tragedy and illness may necessitate pain, at least they prevent life from degenerating into an experiental goo, regardless of whether the goo is called wholeness, interaction, interpenetration, oneness, unity, or any other of the mystical appellations that have been given it.

But surely it is a curious quality of human nature that prompts us to cling to misery in the name of individuality and meaning. We fear the unfamiliar and will do anything to escape it, even to the extent of choosing in favor of horror and tragedy. This inner fear is part of the reason we have so much difficulty in adopting the larger perspectives that encompass the opposites of life, such as health and illness, birth and death, and grief and happiness. We need to "keep our edges straight," we need to preserve our definitions and boundaries out of fear of being overwhelmed should we let go of the familiar—even if the familiar is tragedy, death, illness, and suffering.

AN ALTERNATIVE APPROACH

The need to cling to the familiar in order to ensure certainty is not new. One of the goals of the Buddhist masters has always been to guide the seeker to an understanding of what this void, this emptiness, actually is, in which all distinctions begin to blur. Many of the great stories with which Zen Buddhism abounds are permeated with the concepts of the unfamiliar—emptiness, nothingness, no-thought, tranquility, and other similar notions, which, as acknowledged by the great scholar of Buddhism, D. T. Suzuki, ". . . we may regard as nihilistic or as advocating a negative quietism."[5] But far from being nihilistic or inhumane, the empty and the void are seen to be the origin of fullness, indeed of everything there is. This great paradox is revealed in the following selection from a classic of Buddhist literature, the Prajnaparamita Sutra.

Thus, Sariputra, all things have the character of emptiness, they have no beginning, no end, they are faultless and not faultless, they are not perfect and not imperfect. Therefore, O Sariputra, here in this emptiness there is no form, no perception, no name, no concepts, no knowledge. No eye, no ear, no nose, no tongue, no body, no mind. No form, no sound, no smell, no taste, no touch, no objects. . . . There is no knowledge, no ignorance, no destruction of ignorance. . . . There is no decay nor death; there are no four truths, viz., there is no pain, no origin of pain, no stoppage of pain, and path to the stoppage of pain. There is no knowledge of Nirvana, no obtaining of it, no not-obtaining of it. Therefore, O Sariputra, as there is no obtaining of Nirvana, a man who has approached the Prajnaparamita . . . , dwells unimpeded in consciousness. When the impediments of consciousness are annihilated, then he becomes free of all fear, is beyond the reach of change, enjoying final Nirvana.[6]

This way of speaking appears as nonsense when first encountered, and is difficult to comprehend even by those who expend the most diligent effort to do so, such as the Zen adepts and monks who study it. For now it is enough to note that in the history of our species, methods *have* been devised to try to understand the problem at hand: how opposites, such as health and illness, grief and happiness, can be complementarily included in something that goes beyond each. This is the search to understand the distant view—the Whole, the One, the Unity that has always been the quest of the great spiritual traditions of mankind.

Oddly, medicine has run into the same problem, that of understanding the whole. As the above clinical examples suggest the particulate event—health, illness, disease—cannot be comprehended (and indeed, clinical medicine cannot be accurately practiced) without grasping, at least in some degree, the principle of Oneness.

NOTES

1. Alfred North Whitehead, *Nature and Life* (London: Cambridge University Press, 1934), p. 30.
2. Sir James Jeans, *Physics and Philosophy* (New York: Doer, 1981), p. 103.
3. G. R. Morrow and C. Morrell, "Behavioral Treatment for the Anticipatory Nausea

and Vomiting Induced by Cancer Chemotherapy," *New England Journal of Medicine* 307 (9 Dec. 1982): pp. 1476-1480.

4. J. W. L. Fielding et al., "An Interim Report of a Prospective Randomized, Controlled Study of Adjuvant Chemotherapy in Operable, Gastric Cancer, British Stomach Cancer Group," *World Journal of Surgery* 7, (1983): pp. 390–399.

5. D. T. Suzuki, *The Essentials of Zen Buddhism* (New York: E. P. Dutton, 1962), p. 31.

6. *Ibid.*, pp. 31–33.

VI

Mind or Matter?:
The Wrong Question

So long as we adhere to the conventional notions of mind and matter, we are condemned to a view of perception which is miraculous. We suppose that a physical process starts from a visible object, travels to the eye, there changes into another physical process, causes yet another physical process in the optic nerve, and finally produces some effect in the brain, simultaneously with which we see the object from which the process started, the seeing being something "mental," totally different in character from the physical processes which precede and accompany it. This view is so queer that metaphysicians have invented all sorts of theories designed to substitute something less incredible. . .

Everything that we can directly observe of the physical world happens inside our heads, and consists of *mental* events in at least one sense of the word *mental*. It also consists of events which form part of the physical world. [This leads] to the conclusion that the distinction between mind and matter is illusory. The stuff of the world may be called physical or mental or both or neither as we please; in fact the words serve no purpose.

—Bertrand Russell

The world is far too rich to be described in a single language. Music does not exhaust itself in a sequence of styles. Equally, the essential aspects of our experience can never be condensed into a single description. We have to use many descriptions which are irreducible to each other, but which are connected by precise rules of translations. . . . Scientific work consists of selective exploration and not of the discovery of a given reality. It consists of the choice of questions which have to be posed.

—Ilya Prigogine

. . . a consequence of quantum mechanics [is the] . . . inseparability . . . of . . . particles which originated in the same event. . . . a principle seems to be evoked here which stipulates a basic connectedness of dynamic phenomena in a universe which, after all, originated in all of its parts in the big bang. . . . The linking backward to the origin presents the possibility of a new start. It is therefore not surprising that hopes of eschatological dimensions are nourished, for example, by influencing the biological evolution of mankind by pursuing consciousness down to the levels of cells, molecules and atoms . . .

—Erich Jantsch
The Self-Organizing Universe

. . . we have no indication where precisely psyche leaves off and only reflexes and neurophysiological events remain.

—Ludwig von Bertalanffy

"Do not say that the Cartesian dualism is a dead horse or a straw man erected to be knocked down, as nowadays we have "unitary concepts" and conceive of man as a "psychophysical whole." These are nice ways of speaking, but as a matter of fact, the Cartesian dualism is still with us and is at the basis of our thinking in neurophysiology, psychology, psychiatry, and related fields."[1]

These words were written two decades ago by the great biologist and philosopher, Ludwig von Bertalanffy, and they are as applicable today as then. In spite of all we have heard in recent times of "holistic" approaches to health that emphasize the importance of man's psyche as well as soma, no one who has recently participated in the health care system—either as physician or as patient—can have any doubt that the usual emphasis is overwhelmingly on the physical, not the psychological. The plain fact is that in the *practice* of medicine by physicians, and in the *experience* of medical practice by patients, it is the *body* that we value most. The psyche, mind or consciousness is usually left to fend for itself.

What is so bad about the emphasis on the body? After all, it has given us cures and therapies that were only fantasies a few decades ago. It is frequently said that we should be grateful for the physicalistic approach; if only for its track record, it deserves continued emphasis. It is physically oriented modern medicine that has given us our present triumphs over disease, and it is from this quarter that future balms will come.

But it would take the most entrenched devotee of the current approach to deny its shortcomings. What *are* the failures of the present methodologies? Here it is interesting to ask *patients*, not physicians. One must go to those who actually "take the cure," not to those who provide it, for answers. What do patients say?

The problem is that they say *all* things. Some see in modern medicine something of the miraculous—the person whose chronic and incapacitating chest pain from heart disease is abolished through coronary artery bypass surgery; or the person with cancer, the early discovery of which allowed curative surgery and chemotherapy. But for others modern medicine is worse than worthless—as for the person who awaits death from infection because all his white blood cells have been destroyed due to a side effect of a common drug. One simply cannot get from patients a uniform response about the state of modern medicine.

But patterns do emerge. We know, for example, that recent polls have shown that the physician is generally less respected than in times past. Clamor for alternative forms of health care is at an all-time high. Self-help healing groups abound. Many persons look to medicine now as a last resort rather than a first approach. Unorthodox healers and nontraditional therapists of every stripe enjoy a booming business. While these trends certainly do not show that patients wish to abandon modern forms of health care, they do reveal that they are not uncritically in love with modern medicine.

What is going on? If the wonders and benefits of modern medicine are as self-evident as most bioscientists and physicians claim, why the groundswell of dissent from the health care consumer? Why does one side, proud of its accomplishments, view the other side as ungrateful and naive? Why do disaffected consumer groups decry the cold, technological, physically oriented thrust of modern medicine? Why do they continually refer to the narrow physicalism, dehumanization, and escalating costs?

For all that is said, neither side is seldom specific in its objections. One gets the idea from the proponents of modern medicine that it is *uniformly* effective; and one hears from the doomsdayers that it is *roundly* a failure and that even the apparent successes of the "system" are temporary or could have been arrived at by other means. Both stances seem more vitriolic than accurate.

What *is* the success of modern medicine? What *can* it do? These are the questions in need of answers in the debate. If we can go beyond the extreme positions of both sides, we can get a clearer picture of what happens in actual practice.

The fact is that for the majority of patients who see physicians, the likeliest diagnosis is some type of psychosomatic or stress disorder.[2] And regrettably, it is in this area—the area from which most patients suffer—that modern medicine is *not* at its best. This fact is underscored by a late respected figure in American medicine, Franz J. Ingelfinger, M.D., who for years edited the prestigious *New England Journal of Medicine*:

> Let us assume that 80 per cent of patients have either self-limited disorders or conditions not improvable, even by modern medicine. . . . In slightly over 10 per cent of cases, however, medical intervention is dramatically successful. . . . But, alas, in the other 9 per cent, give or take a point or two, the doctor may diagnose or treat inadequately, or he may just have had bad luck.[3]

Ingelfinger's estimates have been corroborated by actual studies that show that three-fourths of all illnesses brought to physicians are self-limiting. And of the remaining one-fourth, in only about half of the cases is medicine dramatically helpful.

It is difficult to prove such an assertion, but I suspect that most of the adherents of modern medical techniques actually believe the "10 per cent of cases" where medicine is truly successful is actually greater than it is. It is easy to inflate our opinion of ourselves. Furthermore, I suspect that those who would pillory modern medicine believe the 10 percent of cases is much less than it is. And it is frequently forgotten that if one is a *patient* in the 10 percent category where medicine *is* spectacularly successful, the statistics become meaningless. For when one's own self is concerned, when one's *own* life is at stake, the 10 percent figure magically transforms into *100* percent.

But what of the 80 percent of persons for whom modern medicine is not very helpful? It is largely from the needs of this group that the so-called holistic health movement has evolved. Its emphasis, unlike the orthodox approach, is on the psyche, not the soma—and, according to some advocates, on the spiritual as well. Wholes, not parts, are said to be most important. There is great importance attached to the health-creating effects of lifestyle, exercise, nutrition, and self-regulatory techniques designed to annul the noxious effects of stress on the body.

The belief that these approaches are valuable has led to the founding of the American Holistic Medical Association in May, 1978. Grass-roots organizations have emerged elsewhere, attracting an array of both professionals and lay persons both within and without medical circles. What is particularly regrettable is the extreme polarization of opinion that these developments evoke from traditional medical sources. A typical example is an editorial appearing in the official organ of the American Medical Association with the defiant title, "Holistic Health or Holistic Hoax?" It provides the flavor of what seems to be the mainstream reaction of the profession to the holistic effort and is thus quoted at length.

Holistic health, a term increasingly bandied about with reserve or reverence depending on one's perspective, is an uncharted or at least fuzzy area for many physicians. Its proponents, a curious axis of faith healers, chiropractors, clergymen, and Ph.D.s, along with M.D.s, R.N.s, D.O.s, and others without visible signs of qualifications, preach a message as old as the Bible and as American as apple pie: personal growth through self-actualization and maximum functioning of mind, body, and spirit. Their methods of achieving such laudable goals run the full gamut from laying on of hands and kinesiology through internal purging or external application of castor oil, to meditation, unusual diets, and some of the most recent scientific developments, including biofeedback.

Holistic practitioners profess to treat the whole person, not simply disease. They claim traditional Western or scientific medicine is too disease oriented and splits mind from body. They not only integrate both but go one better by including the spirit as well. Some say that disease comes from sin and cure from God. Others are more secular; they do not discount God but say cure comes from within the person from the self, that the spirit has the power to heal.

The holistic self includes not only a person's physical body but also the surrounding environment, like an invisible yard tacked onto a house. Eastern-oriented holistics base their philosophy on the Yin-Yang teeter-totter of balancing positive with the negative. Some domestic-leaning holistics accept the American Indian concept that disease is due to disharmony with nature. In this instance, nature includes family, friends, and environment. Diverging and converging forces may not sound too distant from classic psychoanalysis, where mental illness is viewed as an ego unbalanced by pressures from the id and superego.

. . . more recently, holism has flourished on the West Coast, fanned by the flames of the "Me," self-centered, generation and is spreading inland. Like an uncontrolled nuclear reaction, a myriad of hypothetical institutes for this, academies for that, organizations for integration of East and West, and advocates for touching, thinking, and trotting has erupted.

Holistic medicine (also called wholistic, humanistic, alternative, and new age or consciousness medicine) attempts to practice a kind of superhealing. Practitioners do not stop at the simple idea of illness (they say that is not health), but they advocate "complete wellness," insisting that there is a distinct difference between the two. Perhaps there is, but it might be difficult to demonstrate a difference by objective, scientific means. However, few can quarrel with holistic medicine's avowed philosophy: complete personal fulfillment, no matter how unrealistic or grandiose this goal may seem.[4]

One gets the idea from the overall hostile tone of the editorial that the last sentence was allowed begrudgingly, an example of "condemnation through faint praise." Yet many of the objections to the holistic philosophy come from physicians who, although they may violently disagree, are unmistakably humane and well-meaning in their devotion to caring for sick persons. Such a response follows:

. . . Where in the name of everything holy does it say that a physician is to be more than a healer of sickness? And why have we as a profession allowed ourselves to be placed in such a defensive posture when "accused" of limiting our activities to attempting to diagnose and treat illness? Lord knows it is a worthwhle cause, a most difficult and demanding task, and an honorable living. Why in the world are we expected to be all things to all people and take care of all of everyone's problems? And why, worst of all, do we as a profession go about in sackcloth and ashes, beating our breast, and crying "mea culpa" whenever we are accused of not being involved with "all of man?"

Certainly, no one expects a clergyman to do appendectomies or a sociologist to treat acute glomerulonephritis. For some strange reason, it is perfectly acceptable for these and other professionals involved with helping humans to limit themselves to certain areas of expertise. It is high time that we physicians tell the holy, the holistic, and the wholistic in our society to "do their thing." We, in turn, should stand proudly and shout from the rooftops: "We are sick and tired of being lambasted by every politician and guru. We have a most complex, difficult, and demanding task to perform and only one—the diagnosis and management of illness."

Needless to say, we need to do the task well and always strive for excellence in our field. We must be considerate of our patient and his many needs.

We have our hands full, and then some, just taking care of illness to the best of our ability.[5]

The majority of physicians I know would agree in principle with such a statement. They are high-minded, highly motivated practitioners who are intensely devoted to patient care. Their skills in many cases are awesome—as are their workloads. My point is not to extoll the qualifications and work ethic of physicians but to assert that, from the point of view of highly trained, hard-working doctors, philosophical disenchantment about "the system" is hard to tolerate for many of them. When one is "in the trenches" taking care of the "10 per cent" who are ill, the figure seems like 90 percent. After laboring through a sleepless day and night to save the life of a patient with diabetic ketoacidosis only to have three more days and nights on call, one isn't kindly disposed toward charges of not having treated the "whole patient." That even a *part* of the patient should have survived sometimes seems a miracle.

Proponents of "the system" also have a point—which is justified, I believe—about some of the more obvious failings of certain "holistic" endeavors. Take for example the case of several deaths occurring in a "holistic" clinic which promoted enema therapy ("colon cleansing"), a popular "alternative" health care technique.[6] Due to failure to properly disinfect the enema equipment, a deadly microorganism was spread from patient to patient—*Entamoeba histolytica*, an intestinal parasite that can spread throughout the body and infect, even, the brain. Of the persons infected, six died—all from a technique, opponents would say, for which there was no justification in the first place—and adding, in derision, that it is no better to die "holistically" than any other way.

The charges flow back and forth. Nagelberg-Gerhard, a registered nurse and an insider of modern health care, wrote of her experience of illness in a New York City teaching hospital in an essay entitled, "The Sign above the Bed Read 'Please Touch Me': A Personal Account."

I did not pass "go" . . . I went "directly to jail"—the hospital bed.

Each physical examination left me in worse shape—all that pressing and poking wasn't helping my pain or my mind very much. . . . it was also evident the attending physician wasn't too sure what was going on either.

The hospitalization experience has allowed me to be at the receiving end of the health care system, rather than at the giving end. No matter how many learning labs you practice in, you can't understand how helpless one can feel when stuck between the siderails of a narrow stretcher with no call button in sight; or how nasty and painful one feels after the fifth "accidental" bumping of a bed by the very same "helpful?" nurse![7]

The same problems of depersonalization are described by a respected figure in American medicine, Harvard's Bernard Lown, M.D. In speaking of the treatment of patients following a heart attack, he says: "[An] important principle is the laying-on of hands—a practice that is rapidly atrophying because physicians are too busy with the laying-on of tools."[8]

But again there is no simple, clear-cut reaction of physicians to the questions raised by the holistic approach. This is illustrated in an essay, "Must Physicians Treat the 'Whole Man' for Proper Medical Care?" by Peter Black, M.D. Dr. Black contends that the proper goal of physicians has never been to make their patients virtuous or to restore them to some ideal state:

Twentieth century medicine deals with illness, not health. I believe this emphasis results from the significant development of 19th century classification and pathophysiologic mechanisms. . . . It is this emphasis on specificity, on subdividing man into his organs and tissues, that seems to me to have given medicine its greatest capacities for cure in this century. By ignoring the "whole man" it has been able to give maximum freedom with minimum general discomfort.[9]

These kinds of illustrations for both positions—for and against the idea of treating the "whole" man in ways that go beyond ordinary medicine—could be multiplied endlessly. What can we learn from them?

Some people see in them an emergence of a new view of "the patient"—a whole man, not one dissected endlessly through the limitless process of subspecialization in medicine. Others foresee a return to older values, and claim there is nothing new in the evolving changes. We are merely rediscovering what we have forgotten. There is a yearning in this view, it seems, for simpler times—times in which persons *were* more whole and were perceived as whole by their physicians. What we shall see is a re-emergence of *caring* that will complement the technological *care* of our time, this view has it. This is a return to old principles such as those espoused by many great figures throughout the development of American medicine, such as Dr. Francis Peabody. Peabody's words seem a touchstone for this point of view:

> The practice of medicine in its broadest sense includes the whole relationship of the physician with his patient. Good practice presupposes an understanding of modern medicine, but it is obvious that sound professional training should include a much broader equipment.[10]

And it is the "much broader equipment" that holists see lacking in the modern physician, and it is the "whole relationship" which they would re-create.

WHERE ARE WE HEADED?

An examination of the arguments over the state of affairs in medicine suggests strongly that both sides are polarized. Emotionally charged rhetoric, as we have seen, flows from both camps, occasionally leaving reason waiting in the wings.

In the midst of this polemic an important fact has been obscured: *both the holists and the traditionalists are reasoning from a dualistic point of view*, a position no longer tenable when viewed from many perspectives in modern science. It makes no essential difference that holists argue for a dominant role for mind and consciousness in the evolution of health and illness, nor that the traditionalists in medicine hold for a primary role for matter. As long as the debate hinges on the issue of *dominance*, both sides will fail for the same reason: in the emerging view of man, domination of one part of ourselves over all the other parts is an archaic, improper, and indefensible concept. For matter does not dominate mind, nor does mind dominate the body.

The failure to recognize this fact has led well-intended holists to misplaced therapies that imply mind-as-all—just as traditional medicine has followed the opposite extreme, regarding matter-as-all. These mistakes will continue to be unavoidable as long as we build into our thinking the view that some part of our being predominates *over* some other part.

The view that *mind* is dominant leads to therapies that are as grotesque and inhumane as the view that *matter* is dominant. Such views ignore the physical aspect of being, just as the physicalistic views have ignored the mental and spiritual parts of ourselves. Neither side has a monopoly on conceptual error. Blunders abound, and on both sides.

The mental and spiritual qualities of man will never be dignified through debasing the physical, and vice versa. This understanding is crucial to the maturation of a holistic theory of health that is sorely needed by contemporary medicine. Until this understanding emerges, the holistic endeavor will be condemned to reenact many of the errors it has sought to expel from modern forms of health care.

We are faced with new conceptualizations of mind and matter, the implications of which neither side—holists *nor* traditionalists—have yet to grasp. Von Bertalanffy describes this situation:

> In science, the antithesis of "matter" and "mind" is a conceptualization characteristic of the mechanistic model and world-view of physics. "Mind" and "matter" are reifying conceptualizations that become increasingly inadequate in modern science. The concept of "matter" in the classical sense is abandoned in modern physics. Similarly, the concept of "mind" is a reification of what actually is a dynamic process. This concept no longer holds in present science.[11]

Both the traditional and holistic approaches reify their "candidate quality" of man—matter and mind, respectively—and, in so doing, commit to an outmoded dualistic concept of how human beings are comprised, and how they relate to the world. New ways of thinking about mind and matter—ways that are superordinate to the mind-matter dichotomy that modern medicine has taken for granted—are required. Any view of health and illness that would elevate the role of mind and consciousness *at the cost of devaluing the role of matter—or vice versa*—is doubly flawed: it is both bad science, and bad humanism as well.

NOTES

1. Ludwig von Bertalanffy, "The Mind-Body Problem: A New View," *Psychosomatic Medicine* 26:1 (1964): p. 31.
2. C. N. Shealy, letter to the editor, *Journal of the American Medical Association*, 5 Oct. 1979: pp. 1489–1490.
3. Franz J. Ingelfinger, "Health: A Matter of Statistics of Feeling," *New England Journal of Medicine* 296 (1977): pp. 448–449.
4. John B. Callan, "Holistic Health or Holistic Hoax?" *Journal of the American Medical Association* 241:11 (16 March 1979): p. 1156.
5. P. P. Friedlieb, letter to the editor, *Journal of the American Medical Association* 242:14 (5 Oct. 1979): p. 1490.

6. G. R. Istre et al., "An outbreak of amebiasis spread by colonic irrigation at a chiropractic clinic," *New England Journal of Medicine* 307: 339–342, 1982.

7. Marianne D. Borelli and Patricia Heidt, eds., *Therapeutic Touch* (New York: Springer, 1981), pp. 155–159.

8. B. Lown and J. Segal, "Post-M.I. Care: How to Manage Your Patients' Arrhythmias," *Modern Medicine* (30 Sept. 1978): pp. 60–77.

9. P. McL. Black, "Must Physicians Treat the 'Whole Man' for Proper Medical Care?" *Pharos* 39 (1976): pp. 8–11.

10. F. W. Peabody, "The Care of the Patient," *Journal of the American Medical Association* 88 (1927): pp. 877–882.

11. von Bertalanffy, *"The Mind-Body Problem."*

VII

Rhythms of Life: Health and Illness, Birth and Death

rhythm. n. 1. The recurrence of repetition or stress, beat, sound, accent, motion, etc., usually occurring in a regular or harmonious pattern or manner.

—Funk and Wagnall's *Standard Desk Dictionary*

"The detail of the pattern is movement."

—T. S. Eliot

Modern physics has shown that the rhythm of creation and destruction is not only manifest in the turn of the seasons and in the birth and death of all living creatures, but is also the very essence of inorganic matter. . . . the dance of creation and destruction is the basis of the very existence of matter.

—Fritjof Capra *The Tao of Physics*

This suggests . . . rhythm as the causal counterpart of life: namely, that wherever there is some rhythm, there is some life, only perceptible to us when the analogies are sufficiently close. The rhythm is then the life, in the sense in which it can be said to be included with nature. . . . The essence of rhythm is the fusion of sameness and novelty; so that the whole never loses the essential unity of the pattern, while the parts exhibit the contrast arising from the novelty of their detail. A mere recurrence kills rhythm as surely as does a mere confusion of differences. A

crystal lacks rhythm from excess of pattern, while a fog is unrhythmic in
that it exhibits a patternless confusion of detail.

—Alfred North Whitehead
An Enquiry Concerning the Principles of Natural Knowledge

The contrapuntal arrangement of health and illness in our life is necessary if we are to ever hear the music of wellness. Indeed, like counterpoint
in music, sickness and health exist as two melodic parts to life intended to
be heard simultaneously. One enduring note does not constitute a musical
score. Neither does enduring health constitute wellness.

Yet most of us do not recognize this principle when it comes to our own
health, and we strive for a continuous, unblemished record of healthiness—a goal as foolish as a composer setting out to compose a symphony
by using only a single, sonorous note. Such a composition would be unrecognizable as music, just as an unchanging physical state would be imper-
ceptible as healthiness.

THE IMPORTANCE OF DIFFERENCE

As we have frequently observed, without a sense of difference, without
illness-events to counterpose health, health becomes nonexistent. Without
the fact of standing apart there can be no difference, no recognition, and
thus no existence. Bertrand Russell was aware of this epistemological necessity when he remarked that, although we do not know who discovered
water, we can be sure it was not a fish. Analogously, we can be certain that
if our fantasies for an unsullied record of health actually occurred, we
would be oblivious to the fact. For without illness the "fact" of health is a
contradiction in terms. For facts to be facts at all they first must be recognized. And, to be recognizable, they must stand out—here against a back-
drop of periodic nonhealth, or illness.

THE IMPORTANCE OF CLOSENESS

Whitehead tells us that where there is some rhythm there is some life—but
that this phenomenon is perceptible to us *only* if the analogies (which are
the counterposed events) are "sufficiently close." And they need to be
close in at least two fundamental ways: first, they need to be temporally
close; and, secondly, there needs to be a close enough resemblance in the
events that we can at least make a mental connection between them.

The importance of temporal closeness of the counterposed events of health and illness is obvious in the lives of children. Most children have little concern about health and little preoccupation with staying well. The infatuation with wellness simply does not begin early in life. Why? Not because children are never sick—most *are* ill from time to time—but because partly these contrasting events are not temporally close enough to form a sufficient contrast. Recovery from extremely sporadic illnesses usually comes quickly for children; once a strep throat is over, it is swept aside and forgotten. There is little contrast, for the next bout of illness is usually far into the future, and by the time it arrives the last one has been relatively forgotten. A lack of temporal proximity is at work here, creating rhythms that are so distantly spaced as to be incomprehensible.

Moreover, the sense of time is different in young children than in adults. It requires years for children to develop a fully formed sense of linear time. The notion of a past, present, and future is acquired gradually. Children have an innate ability to live in the present, a capacity which seems gradually to diminish with maturity. Thus, by living in the "now," if children are healthy at the moment, the experience of having been sick is effectively annulled. It is not surprising, then, that children seldom dwell on whether they are sick or well.

This is not so, however, for children who are chronically ill or who suffer from recurrent, closely spaced medical problems. Children with chronic or acute leukemia who must visit the doctor for periodic examinations, blood analysis, or treatment; or children with chronic renal failure who live from one episode of dialysis to another, are keenly aware of the contrasts of health and illness. They may impart other names to these periodic experiences, imprecise terms such as "feeling good" or "feeling bad," but the rhythms come through to them sharply. They have an internal sensitivity about health that their healthier peers know nothing about.

The knowledge of the rhythms of health and illness in these children is sometimes so keenly developed that dealing with them becomes a challenge. Most doctors and nurses who care for chronically sick children are healthy themselves, they know little about the life-rhythms of health and illness in their own lives. Because it is only an observed phenomenon for them, something they see only in their patients, it is disarming to have one's ignorance about the mutual interrelatedness of birth and death, health and illness, blindingly reflected from the countenance of a terminally ill child. What business does my patient have knowing more about birth and death than I, when he or she is only six years old? Why am I shocked at hearing the wisdom of life pour from the mouth of this chronically ill, illiterate four-year-old who knows she won't be alive a month from now? Why am I being defensive about hearing recondite child-talk concerning the before, the now, and the hereafter from this kid who is aware that he will never experience another birthday?

TIM'S STORY

In her poignant and penetrating book, *The Human Patient*,[1] pediatrician Dr. Naomi Remen describes many of her reactions in situations such as these. And in her lectures she has also beautifully described the rhythms of life that sick children learn, which are sometimes incomprehensible even to the professionals who care for them. She tells of seven-year-old Tim, who had terminal leukemia, which he had suffered from for most of his life. Although he had experienced remissions early on in the course of his treatments, and had had a year or two that was punctuated with weeks of "feeling good," now he lay in his hospital bed, emaciated. Tim was too weak to walk to the bathroom, his body a patchwork of bruises from having had blood periodically drawn and not being able to stop the bleeding that followed. The walls of his room were adorned with the paraphernalia of seven-year-olds which usually finds its way into the hospital rooms of kids who experience extensive hospital stays—posters of TV and movie heroes, balloons, cut-outs, drawings. Personal messages from friends crudely scribbled were everywhere, while he lay amid a pile of his favorite stuffed animals. The room was hardly recognizable as a hospital room except for the stark bed and its white sheets, and the I.V. device with its tubing which trailed down to a point in the scant tissue of an arm.

Dr. Remen arrived one morning to make her hospital rounds to find the ward personnel in an uproar. Doctors, nurses, and aides were embroiled in a heated discussion at the nurses' station. The problem, she discovered, was that Tim—by now too weak to eat or walk and almost unable to speak— had announced that today he was going home. He had had enough of the hospital. He was tired of it all—food, medicines, I.V.'s. The interns, residents, and nurses alike were angry: who could possibly have told this poor child with terminal leukemia that he could go home? They were at each others' throats to find the culprit—who, it had been decided, was to be the one to perform the very disagreeable task of telling this beloved child that he could *not* go home as he had apparently been told.

Dr. Remen, the Chief of the Pediatrics Service, saw this melee was going nowhere. She announced she would sort out the misunderstanding with Tim and went directly to his room, alone.

Tim's eyes met her at the door. Pale and wan, yet alert, he seemed totally composed and peaceful. How, Dr. Remen thought, could any of her staff have made such a grievous error as to tell this angelic skeleton of a child he could leave the hospital today?

She began. "Tim, I hear you're leaving the hospital today. Is that right?"

Tim replied, almost too weak to hear, "No, Doctor Remen. I'm not leaving the hospital."

"But one of the other doctors told me you were going home."

"Well," said Tim, patiently attempting to correct his physician's obvious confusion, "I'm not leaving the hospital. But I am going Home." With that he was quiet. He'd said enough. The rest was up to her to figure out, it seemed. So he closed his eyes to rest a bit, for the talking had exhausted him.

Dr. Remen, sitting by him on his bed and holding the hand of the arm that was free of the I.V., began to weep silently. She felt the Fool in the White Coat. And so were they all—the interns, residents, and nurses down the hall who were awaiting her return even now. She knew now that no one had told Tim he could go home, but that he was going nonetheless. He had made the decision, not they.

She arose quietly, placing a stuffed animal where she had been sitting so Tim would be less alone. At the door to his room she turned again to look at him. He was completely serene and silent, breathing easily and quietly, totally without pain. She could do no more; she need do no more. Walking back to the nurses' station she continued her crying.

"Well, what happened in there?" one of the interns on Tim's case wanted to know. "Did you tell him he couldn't go home?"

The group was somber and concluded from her red eyes, still filled with tears, that her job had been a painful one. They were shocked when she replied, "No. I did not tell him he could not go home. In fact, that's just what he's going to do today." With that, she explained what had happened.

No one said much. The assembly of doctors and nurses scattered gradually, each finding something that needed doing, or else seeking a more private place to cry.

Dr. Remen knew it was time for her to return to Tim's room. She wanted this visit, unlike the last trip down this same long hall. She knew what she would find: as she entered his room, she saw that Tim had gone Home.

It is not just temporal closeness that is required for us to make mental connections between events of health and illness; there must be at least some closeness in kind between these events. As an example, it is much easier to conceive how a tension headache might contribute to our sense of healthiness than a distinctly morbid event. Tension headaches alert us to the fact that we are exposing ourselves to needless stress, for instance, and thus serve a positive function. They provide a contrast, usually not too se-verely painful, between the sensations of pain and pleasure. They heighten our sense of *not* having a headache and thus deepen our experience of wellness.

But when a child is born with birth defects; or a family of five is killed in an auto accident; or when a son is killed at war—what then? How do we conceivably profit from these perceptions? For most of us these contrasts are too stark to deal with in the way we might deal with a tension head-ache. They are the agonizing, insufferable events of life, the events whose horror we feel we cannot bear. They are unspeakable in their unfairness, their ugliness, and the pain they evoke.

The association of the dark elements of life with its brighter moments is perceptible only when the analogies between the rhythmic components are sufficiently close, as Whitehead tells us. And for the unspeakably un-bearable events such as those above, we sense no closeness at all between them and the positive periods of life. The rhythm does not come through, and life itself seems to stop.

Yet it may not be that the rhythm fails or ceases to exist, but that it be-comes more complex. We prefer simple rhythmic messages from life and shrink from complicated cadences. We prefer tension headaches to cata-strophic calamities. Thus, it may be that in the dark moments when the painful events of life become counterposed with the balmier ones, that if we can sharpen our rhythmic senses, we *can* hear the beat, and we can hear "the fusion of sameness and novelty" about which Whitehead spoke, so that "the whole [of life] never loses the essential unity of the pattern." Life then ceases to be a disjunct sequence of the good and the bad, but becomes a unitary phenomenon.

HEALTH AND WHOLENESS

The words "health" and "wholeness" are derived from the same source, and the search for health is a search for wholeness. The struggle for health is a struggle against fragmentation and disunity. Health in its fullest form involves the capacity to accept the whole—in the certain knowledge that *all* the experiences of life cohere in a locked interdependence, connected to each other for their very meaning. Again, Whitehead's metaphysics is helpful:

> The [parts of an experience] contribute to the massive feeling of the whole, and the whole contributes to the intensity of feeling of the parts.[2]

We *can* truncate life into a few acceptable experiences when it comes to health and manage to get by. We can restrict "the acceptable" to a certain range of blood pressure, body weight, physical performance, even psychological attitudes. We can roundly prohibit the intrusion into our lives of sore throats, arthritis, strokes and heart attacks, ingrown toenails and dandruff—but in so doing we create what for Whitehead is the chief barrier to all types of perfection: the "mutual inhibition" of certain of the elements that make up an experience.[3] The process of cutting off certain elements of life-experience he calls "anaesthesia"—a particularly appropriate term because in eliminating certain parts of life-events we indeed dull our senses, sometimes to the extent of total unawareness.

What might our ability to handle life's vicissitudes have been if we had not committed "anesthesia"—if we had not begun to limit our full emotional apprehension of all the happenings which constitute the Whole? At what point did we begin to guard ourselves against the intrusion of "that which we cannot bear"? What were our capacities before overwhelming grief and horror set in and we began to rebel at the unfairness and ugliness of life? The narrower our ability to incorporate the difficult experiences in life as a natural part of the whole, the earlier the sense of evil asserts itself and the more contaminated life seems with evil things.

REPETITION AS DEATH AND DECAY

The philosopher Albert William Levi tells us:

> Still, it must be remembered that the intermingling of Beauty and Evil lies in the nature of things. . . . Progress is founded upon the experience of discordant feelings. The disease fatal . . . is that perfection once attained, the inspiration withers, repetition sets in, and freshness gradually withers.[4]

This process affects entire societies, not just individuals:

> . . . societies [suffer] from the tedium of infinite repetition, and of insufficient contrasts in the character of their component parts. They demonstrate how the demand for Harmony must be supplemented by a recognition of the necessity for Adventure.[5]

These observations hold true, too, for our experiences of health. Endless repetition of health-events, as attractive as they may sound, are actually a death knell to wellness. An enduring, unchanging state of healthiness is not health. It is a figment of the imagination.

A recognition of the necessity for Adventure (that no static maintenance of perfection is possible) is the foundation of all theories of man and of society. In art it requires that conventional training be supplemented by novel experiment; in sociology it requires the Hellenic mentality rather than the Byzantine; in the learned world it requires the precedence of speculation over scholarship. But ultimately it too is based upon a meta-physical principle: the principle of process. *Each actual thing can be understood only in terms of its becoming and its perishing. There is no halt in which the actuality is just its static self.* . . . no culmination can maintain itself long at its height. Without fresh experimentation the minor variations are exhausted. *There is a lowering of the vividness of experience in individuals.*[6] (italics added)

Illness, then, leads health onward, makes it perceptible, is its progeni-tor, its guarantor, the silver behind the mirror without which the mirror is nothing more than a transparent sheet of glass.

Yet what of tragic events in life, those discordant feelings that occur when the hoped-for is juxtaposed with that which is real—when, for example, health *does* fail, and fails painfully and tragically? Whitehead answers:

Each tragedy is the disclosure of an ideal:—What might have been, and was not: What can be. The tragedy was not in vain.[7]

And,

This survival power in motive force, by reason of appeal to reserves of Beauty, marks the difference between the tragic evil and the gross evil. *The inner feeling belonging to this grasp of the service of tragedy is peace—the purification of the emotions.* (italics added)[8]

Whitman too enunciated the vision of the oneness of contraries, which has always occupied a focal point in the expression of the poet:

Out of the dimness opposite equals advance, always substance and increase, . . .
Always a knit of identity, always distinction, always a breed of life.[9]

And the same vision was recognized by Jung:

> There must always be high and low, hot and cold, etc., so that the equili-
> brating process—which is energy—can take place. . . . The point is not
> conversion into the opposite but conservation of previous values to-
> gether with recognition of their opposites.[10]

Without the high and the low, the hot and cold, life would be a seamless, undifferentiated experience of sameness. Without the rhythms of health and illness and birth and death we would fall heir not to a state of pristine perfection but to one of experiential anesthesia. Our health strategy must always be supplemented with this awareness. For if we ever achieved our goal of total health we would find not fulfillment but emptiness. Health, if seen as wholeness, guards against this dreadful error; for the whole contains all—even, we must always recall, the opposites of birth and death, pain and pleasure, illness and health.

NOTES

1. Naomi Remen, *The Human Patient* (New York: Anchor Press, 1980).
2. Albert William Levi, *Philosophy and the Modern World* (Bloomington, Ind.: Indiana University Press, 1959), p. 525.
3. *Ibid.*
4. *Ibid.*
5. *Ibid.*
6. *Ibid.*, p. 526.
7. *Ibid.*, p. 527.
8. *Ibid.*
9. Walt Whitman, "Song of Myself," in *Leaves of Grass* (N.Y.: Modern Library, n.d.), p. 26.
10. Jolande Jacobi, *The Psychology of C. G. Jung* (New Haven and London: Yale University Press, 1962), p. 61.

VIII

Conscious Choice and Health: A New View

. . . law is helpful in our struggle to be free, because if things were not constant in their qualities, we would not know how to behave. The law helps us to find our way in our lives.

—Lama Govinda

For most of the founders of classical science—even for Einstein—science was an attempt to go beyond the world of appearances, to reach a timeless world of supreme rationality—the world of Spinoza. But perhaps there is a more subtle form of reality that involves *both laws and games*, time and eternity. (italics added)

—Ilya Prigogine
From Being to Becoming: Time and Complexity in the
Physical Sciences

If something determines [our] choice, we are back to determinism; if nothing, [we act] from pure caprice, and this leads to a free-will which is neither of the kind we want to find nor of the kind we feel we do find.

Neither does a capricious indeterminism give us a free-will at all resembling that of our experience or imagined experience. If every event were not determined by a sufficient reason, the whole world would, as Leibniz remarked, be a chaos. A mind endowed with free-will of the capricious variety would be a prey to spontaneous and wholly irrational impulses; we should describe it as the mind of a madman, although in actual fact no madman's mind is ever quite so crazy.

—Sir James Jeans
Physics and Philosophy

In a process-oriented view, the evolution of specific structures is not predetermined. But then are functions—processes which may realize themselves in a multitude of structures—predetermined? In other words, does the evolution of mind follow a predetermined pattern? Or does such an assumption again lead to a wrong conclusion already prefigured in process thinking, just as the predetermination of structures has been prefigured by mechanistic, structure-oriented thinking? Is the formula of Eastern mysticism that the universe is made to become self-reflexive, only the expression of an inherent limitation of Eastern process philosophy?

Perhaps it is not that important to find answers to these questions at all. Our search is ultimately devoted not to a precise knowledge of the universe, but to a grasp of the role which we play in it—to the meaning of our life. The . . . dimensions of connectedness between all forms of unfolding of a natural dynamics . . . is about to deepen the recognition of such a meaning.

—Erich Jantsch
The Self-Organizing Universe

One of our most persistent habits of thought is in thinking in terms of opposites: freedom versus enslavement, mind versus body, reason versus intuition, health versus illness, birth versus death, etc. Our way of carving up our reality into these either/or categories is so natural we seldom question the validity of doing so.

Whether or not the world can be thought of in these terms surfaces in medicine in a particularly acute way. We want to know whether or not conscious decision-making about our health makes any difference *or* if health and illness are only a matter of fate—our sense of opposites in action. Is health a matter of consciousness *or* chemistry? Can our choices make us healthier? *Or* are we under the sway of our genes, our anatomy, and physiology? Are we deluded into thinking that our thoughts count for something, when in reality they only reflect the basic laws of chemistry and physics? These, of course, are ancient questions with which many generations have struggled. The question today is the same as it has been for centuries: is there free will or determinism at work in our health?

Implicit in the question is the assumption that it can only be approached in terms of opposites: free will and the power of consciousness are unalterably set against determinism and blind law. It is one way or the other in the world, for it obviously cannot be both. The primacy of consciousness simply cannot exist alongside determinism, just as black cannot simultaneously coexist with white.

The problem is particularly important in the holistic health care movement, for its credo is anchored in the concept of self-responsibility. And self-responsibility is an empty principle in a physically determined universe. The holistic health care movement, then, should rise or fall on how the ancient problem of free will versus determinism is answered.

THE CODE AND THE STRATEGY

Other alternatives in approaching the "either/or" nature of the problem of free will and determinism have arisen in recent years, one of the most intriguing of which is that offered by Koestler.[1] He has proposed the notion of "code" and "strategy" to distinguish between, but also to unite, the concepts of determinism and freedom. The code, says Koestler, is the possible boundaries between which events can happen. An example is the limits imposed on us by our genes, or our genetic code, which constrains our anatomy and physiology in certain ways. For example, it is unlikely that a person who is an achondroplastic dwarf will ever become an Olympic power weightlifter, just as it is unlikely that a fullback on a professional football team will ever become an accomplished ballet performer. On the other hand, there are "strategies" which can be consciously willed *within* the code. There is freedom, but with constraints. For example, the professional football player might choose to utilize his athletic prowess in any number of ways besides playing football. His "code" does not determine his precise destiny in any rigid way. Options still exist, provided the code is not violated.

The code, then, defines all possible choices, and the strategy is the way those possible choices are enacted. It is here that consciousness enters in the form of choice and volition.

It seems a mistake to consider this form of choice to be a watered-down version of free will. For without constraints, without a code of some sort, the power of consciousness—what we here call free will—simply makes no sense. As a way of understanding the interplay between conscious choice and constraint, and why free will, to be meaningful, demands constraint, let us consider the grandest code of all—the so-called laws of nature, among which we can include the phenomenon of gravity. The fact of gravity allows a constant set of events to unfold in our lives. When we set a glass down, we assume it will stay put. If we toss a ball into the air, we do not doubt that it will come down. It is against this dependable background or code that consciousness must work if choices are to have predictable outcomes. For if gravity were inconstant we would never know if the glass which we set on the table would be there or not. Consequently the "choice" to pick it up would be senseless, for we would have no way of knowing whether it would be on the table to pick up, or whether it would be floating in midair somewhere else. The complete absence of constraint—here the force of gravity—would make a mockery of the concept of freedom of choice. Total chaos would follow from a complete absence of some constraining code which provides a context for choice. Freedom, from this perspective, is possible only as a corollary of constraint.

This is the meaning of Lama Govinda's comments at the beginning of this section. There is no conflict between law and freedom. It is the law that helps us to be free, not something which enslaves us, as we generally think. It is the background against which choices come alive. Seen from this perspective, conscious choice-making in matters of health takes on a new liveliness.

Opponents of choice-making in medicine often point to the impossibility of altering such genetically linked facts as the color of our eyes, our stature, or the size of our ears or nose. And those who take the extreme reductionist view aver that, not only are our external features controlled by our genetic constitution, but our thoughts are too. According to this view the constraints of chemistry in our bodies effectively annuls the potency of choice-making. But seen from the point of view offered by Koestler and Govinda, it is these very constraints which makes choice meaningful. Far from neutralizing the power of consciousness, the "laws" of our inner nature—expressed in terms of anatomy, physiology, chemistry—make possible this very power. Like the invariable law of gravity against which thoughts can be applied in some predictable, reliable way, our genetic constraints provide an assurance that conscious choice-making will result in constant, predictable outcomes. Were it not so, I would have no way of being sure that certain obvious actions would have any effect on my health at all: that a bullet through my brain would be harmful; or that smoking cigarettes would pose a hazard to my cardiopulmonary health; or that placing my hand in an open fire would cause a third degree burn. In the absence of some sort of code, some set of anatomic-physiological-biochemical constraints, the world of health care would be topsy turvy—not only for those who champion the cause of holistic medicine ("Mind matters!") but *also* for those who espouse a rigid, undying physicalism ("Mind *is* matter!"). As Lama Govinda put it, "The law helps us to find our way in our lives."

All this is just another way of describing the interdependence of opposites, the unity of apparent contradictions. In this view there is no contradiction between the fact of the code—be it genetic or otherwise—and the concept of the strategy that is enacted within the constraints of the code. For the strategy is impossible without the code, and the code is defined by the strategy (without something to confine, the confining entity is meaningless). Both can be seen as the "moving principles" of each other, each dependent on the other for its very meaning.

Suppose, as traditionalists in medicine assume, I indeed cannot "think my cancer away." Suppose I cannot purposely regrow a severed limb or restore sight to eyes blinded by severe corneal scarring. Suppose I cannot eradicate my diabetes mellitus or replace the scarred tissue in my heart following a heart attack. Should we then assume that the body has the upper hand in health, and that consciousness doesn't matter? Do such apparently unalterable physiological situations serve as proof that the physicalists are right and the mentalists wrong? Of course not—for the reasons we have been examining. For just as the code and the strategy are interdependent, just as law and freedom are interrelated, the cases of the physicalist and the mentalist are inseparably linked. Neither can exclude the other without destroying itself in the process.

It is important to bear this relationship in mind. For the drift in thinking in many circles in medicine is that if genetic influences can be shown to hold sway over *certain* physiologic functions (as they do, of course), then it is axiomatic and only a matter of time until it will be shown that they control, inexorably, *all* human functions. Presto! Mind, in all its expressions, is effectively neutralized. Volition, choice, and conscious decision-making become illusory. The record from certain lines of clinical research— for example, from biofeedback, whose central assumption is that one *can* consciously bring certain physiological events under control— are dismissed as naive at best and unscientific at worst. But seen from the perspective we have been examining, it does not have to be a case of either/or, of *all* genetic control or *no* genetic control. Consciousness can still hold sway, it can still exert a potency, but within limits. The concept of the mind as a factor in health need not be abandoned simply because genetic events are demonstrated to be inexorable in certain situations. Mind and matter can coexist—and the truce between them need not necessarily be uneasy.

Rather than taking the conventional view that our chemistry, anatomy, physiology, and genes determine our health and illness, perhaps a more modified view is possible. Our physical properties provide a stable ground against which choices can be made, against which consciousness can work. They are an antidote to chaos and afford a certain stability to things. Like the force of gravity, they are there, always at work, pervasive in their action but not enslaving. Gravity benevolently assures us that our coffee will stay in our cups at the breakfast table and will not leap out and soil our shirt, but it does not compel us to drink the coffee. It is an ordering principle, but not an iron dictator. So with our physical nature that allows, for example, for us to digest a sirloin steak or bean sprouts, but does not force us to be a carnivore or a vegetarian. Without physical constraints, we would experience physiological chaos. Anarchy would pervade the body, and, indeed, there might be no body at all. Freedom from physical constraint would be a hellish nightmare.

This perspective denies that physical law is ironclad and enslaving, as we have been habituated to believing. On the contrary, law contains the mutual properties of constraint *and* freedom. There is a dynamic, interdependent interplay between limitation and choice within this perspective. Complete, unrestrained choice-making in matters of health is a contradiction in terms, more akin to chaos than freedom.

Law is not something we need to escape *from*, but something we function *within*. It is the vivifying principle which imparts meaning to freedom. It provides the code which, instead of banishing our various strategies for freedom, contains them and makes them possible.

NOTES

1. Arthur Koestler, *Janus: A Summing Up* (New York: Random House, 1978), p. 38.

IX

The Living Force: Toward a New Model of Healing

It is conceivable that life may have a larger role to play than we have yet imagined. Life may succeed against all the odds in moulding the universe to its own purposes. And the design of the inanimate universe may not be as detached from the potentialities of life and intelligence as scientists of the 20th century have tended to suppose.

—Freeman J. Dyson

From a Platonic point of view, it can rightfully be argued that a lack of health is a lack of wholeness. . . .

The most fundamental of these [holistic] principles is the claim that there is but *one* reality. This strict non-dualistic basis for the entire cosmos is the starting-point for any explanation of healing. It postulates an organic unity beneath the multiplicity evident to our senses, a unity that is primary and causal compared with the derivative and secondary status of the manifested things in the world (i.e., the objects of our sense-perceptions). . . . that being the case, matter and consciousness are but two expressions of the one unbroken reality. They differ at best in degree and in function but not in kind. On the surface, this position may also sound reductionistic and hence reminiscent of the very behaviorism rejected earlier. . . . In fact, the present view is diametrically distinct from the Cartesian-Skinnerian one, since the interconnected oneness proclaimed here is a living force that unites all beings *through integration, not reduction.* Any apparent "reductionism" found here favors consciousness as the primary nature of reality, a consciousness in which the universe becomes unified.[1]

—Reneé Weber

We know that the belief in the autonomy of these two parts [mind and body] is an illusion; there are not in man two distinct parts, but only two distinct aspects of a single being; man is in reality an *individual* artificially divided by an erroneous interpretation of his analytic observation. The error of our dualistic conception does not lie in the discrimination between two aspects in us—for there are indeed two aspects—but in concluding that these two aspects are two different entities.

To tell the truth, our observation does not show us that there are two parts in us; it only shows us that everything happens in us as though there were two parts separated by a hiatus. It is our ignorant intellect that takes the illusory leap from the statement "everything happens as though" to the erroneous affirmation that there are in us two parts separated by a hiatus.

—H. Benoit
The Supreme Doctrine

Disease, it seems, is inevitable, and death will come to all of us sooner or later. These self-evident facts suggest that life is basically characterized by disorganization, dissolution, decay, and ultimate chaos. To propose that, in fact, the opposite situation exists seems absurd.

But what if the universe were characterized by oneness and wholeness instead of disorganization and particularity? What if the apparent disjunctions in our physical function were no more than local eddies in the current which go this way or that, but which do not deflect the main course of the river? What if the world were an unbroken reality impossible to disrupt, even in principle?

Suppose for a moment that it is so. What would the consequences for health and healing be?

THE CONSEQUENCES OF WHOLENESS FOR HEALING

1. Healing becomes impossible. What is not broken cannot be fixed. If the fundamental reality is the whole, then the apparent molecular malfunctions which we term "disease" are in a deep sense subsumed by a larger reality. This greater realm is the primary state of things, the true face of the universe that includes all things in it (otherwise it would not be the whole)—including, it must be said, disease, the "local eddies" in the larger current. The local turbulences which we call illness, grief, and misfortune

are not primary. Coexistent with them is a more fundamental and perfect wholeness which cannot be sundered, even by the most catastrophic occurrence.

2. Healers cannot bring about wholeness, for it already exists. If it did not already exist, it would not be the whole. *The proper goal of healing is to facilitate this awareness in the person needing to be healed.* But it is to be constantly borne in mind that at the deepest level the sick person has no sickness and is in no need of healing, because the wholeness which cannot be broken envelops and includes him.

3. Healing is not a matter of setting the molecules straight. It is a matter of helping the one in need of healing into an awareness of wholeness. It is in assisting the realization that the natural state of the world is one of unbroken oneness and perfection, and that, therefore, all illness, in some basic sense, is an illusion. Healing in its most fundamental character has less to do with "doing"—that is, employing physicalistic techniques—than in assisting with the "being" and the "knowing" of the patient.

4. The perspective of wholeness is not the only point of view from which to view illness and health. Indeed, as the current models of illness attest, the exact opposite perspective can be elected, that of entropic decline and disorganization. This perspective works in certain contexts: surgery *can* cure appendicitis, immunizations *do* prevent disease, and antihypertensive medications *do* lower blood pressure and prevent strokes and heart attacks. The perspective which one chooses depends on the goal one wishes to accomplish.

5. There is, thus, a hierarchy of healing strategies. At one end is the strategy that emphasizes wholeness. This view, as Weber states, emphasizes that "the interconnected oneness . . . is a living force that unites all beings," and that "consciousness [is] the primary nature of reality, a consciousness in which the universe becomes unified." The perspective of wholeness emphasizes the power of consciousness in affecting health. Indeed, the realization and experience of the proclaimed wholeness requires consciousness.

At the other end of the hierarchy, the mechanistically oriented perspective de-emphasizes consciousness. As a factor in healing, its role is minimal. Material interventions are required for effecting change in the state of the physical world, the world of the body. Consciousness is too diaphanous an entity to make much difference in healing.

6. The perspective of wholeness invokes a different world view than does the mechanistic mode of healing. In the holistic view, time is seen as nondurational. This is the time of being, not the time of becoming. There

are no strict separations between the domains of matter and consciousness, and thus no insuperable distinctions between the living and the nonliving. "There is but one reality," as Weber puts it—not separate realms for the living and the dead or for the conscious and the unconscious. Strict separations between energy and matter, space and time, the material and the void also break down in the new view.

In contrast, the mechanistic approach emphasizes the opposite and traditional facets of the world view: time is linear, divisible into a past, present, and future. It is the time of becoming, not of being. In this time, nothing happens without a cause. Strict divisions are assumed separating consciousness and matter, the living and nonliving, and the material and the void.

7. The goals of healing are different from the perspective of wholeness as opposed to the mechanistic point of view. In the current mechanistic philosophy, length of life is of paramount importance. This follows from the view that time is linear, that death is final and is to be delayed as long as possible. The mechanistic view emphasizes the elimination of pain and suffering also, and for the same reason: they are harbingers of death, demise, and extermination. They are preludes to the end—again, a perspective evolving from the fact of an inexorably flowing, linear time.

The strategy of wholeness emphasizes *none* of these goals as being of ultimate importance—a fact which follows from employing a different world view. For in nondurational time there are no finalities such as death. Thus, length of life is of no ultimate importance. Pain and suffering are not seen as precursors to death, either, and for the same reason: death has no status as an ultimate end in a nonlinear time which has no past, present, or future. Yet the perspective of wholeness does not *de*-emphasize these ordinary goals of health care, for one may act to promote longevity and relief of pain and suffering as vigorously from this perspective as any other. But there is no grim imperative implicit in the effort.

8. These two therapeutic points of departure can be used jointly, therefore. One can achieve the goals of the mechanistic strategy while operating from the holistic perspective.

9. All illness can be explained in terms of the philosophy of wholeness, but not in terms of the philosophy of mechanism. Thus the holistic perspective is more comprehensive and inclusive a model of health and illness than is the current mechanistic viewpoint.

The limitations of the mechanistic strategy flow in large measure from its tendency to relegate consciousness to an effete status. It is the molecules, not mind, that are important. Therefore, many "limiting cases" arise in medicine—clinical observations that show the limitations of the theory of mechanism and which can only be explained by imputing potency to consciousness. When the cholesterol level falls as persons meditate; when immune activity in the body slows during grief and bereavement; when fatal or near-fatal cardiac arrhythmias arise during emotional upheavals, we witness cases which the mechanistic theory cannot explain. These limitations are transcended by the philosophy of wholeness, which sees consciousness as a fundamental, irreducible entity in the universe. As such, it is not dogged by clinical observations such as those above. It is not compelled to dismiss them as irrelevant, because it can account for the occurrences—not because it can *explain* what consciousness *is*, but because it acknowledges its power.

10. The holistic perspective of healing may potentiate the mechanistic perspective, and vice versa. Consider, for example, the case of a sufferer of a heart attack who is brought unconscious to the emergency room in overt heart failure with lungs filled with fluid, no blood pressure, and a chaotic heart rhythm. It is senseless to appeal to that person's consciousness at such a time, attempting to facilitate his understanding of the intrinsic wholeness that permeates the world. Better, perhaps, to first perform the most mechanistic of all therapies, CPR (cardiopulmonary resuscitation), to use oxygen and diuretics and other drugs to reestablish his psychophysiologic integrity—and to *then* attempt to work in broader ways. Here we see the complementary approach in action. Neither perspective, either that of wholeness or that of mechanism, need be seen as an exclusive mode of healing. Even though the holistic view is judged as more comprehensive, inclusive, and fundamental than the mechanistic view, it need not supplant it entirely as a medical strategy.

Yet, that is. Whether we shall evolve healing capacities in the future or awaken latent potentials that we presently have, which shall entirely eliminate the need for current mechanistic therapies, we cannot now say. My hunch is that this will indeed prove possible, and that we shall come to rely less on current therapies that we now think indispensable. In the meantime, what do we do? My belief is that we should proceed to use *both* modalities of healing, the strategy that emphasizes wholeness as well as that which stresses mechanism—drugs, surgery, diet, etc. These forms of therapy can be used *with the simultaneous knowledge* that they are limited approaches, that there is something more, something incipient in the nature of the world that transcends the need for these specific actions. One can participate in the sense of the whole and can invoke the primacy of consciousness while *still* utilizing mechanistic forms of treatment.

11. Concrete change in the state of the physical world can be brought about by the sure knowledge of the intrinsic wholeness of the universe. It

is patently *not* mandatory to solely employ mechanistically oriented therapies in order to change the body. For when a sense of oneness is achieved, physiological changes follow—a startling fact demonstrated in numerous laboratories investigating the physical changes during meditation, biofeedback, and numerous other states of mind-body integration. Thus, to achieve the goal of healing (that of facilitating the awareness of the whole) is to set in motion a diverse variety of body changes that can be measured at will. It is from the fact that physiological change flows from the integration of mind, body, and world that *the realization of wholeness can be viewed as a medicine*—as a technique that evokes physical change as substantial as that following the use of drugs or surgery.

The realization of wholeness does not stay in the mind. It permeates the body, causing changes that we have heretofore only guessed at. The formulation of a healing model that incorporates this effect, therefore, seems *mandated*.

The features of such a model will evolve as we learn more about the intrinsic connections of mind, body, and universe. Those offered above are a start, a skeleton of a new model. They should be seen as only an early attempt to ground healing in a way of perceiving the world that is far less limited than the visions to which we are currently wedded.

NOTES

1. Reneé Weber, "Philosophical Foundations and Frameworks for Healing," *ReVision* (Summer/Fall 1979), 66–67.

X

Three Patients

When we view ourselves in space and time, our consciousnesses are obviously the separate individuals of a particle-picture, but when we pass beyond space and time, they may perhaps form ingredients of a single continuous stream of life. As it is with light and electricity, so it may be with life; the phenomena may be individuals carrying on separate existences in space and time, while in the deeper reality beyond space and time we may all be members of one body.

—Sir James Jeans
Physics and Philosophy

Martha G.: Cancer

Through my
Invisible new veil
Of finity, I see
November's world——
Low scud, slick street, three giggling girls——
As, oddly, not as sombre
As December,
But as green
As anything:
As spring.

—L. E. Sissman
(after discovering he was dying of cancer)

That birth and death alternate, that winter and summer repeatedly succeed each other, and that all things move on like a current is an ordinary belief of men. But I think it is not the case.

—Seng-Chao

In the immediacy of existence, linear and irreversible time becomes
suspended. The experienced processes of the past and the visions of an
anticipated open evolution are directly grasped in a four-dimensional
present. Poetic reality breaks into the profane reality of everyday life.

—Erich Jantsch
The Self-Organizing Universe

The ceaseless struggle for health and well-being is a hopeless one. We
suppose that if we pursue this task tenaciously enough, if we discover and
apply diligently the correct "rules of health," we shall have our wish, that of
an unblemished, disease-free life. This way of thinking is typically Western,
suggesting that by dint of effort and intellect no task is too great. If only we
expend the effort, we can attain the goal of healthiness.

Not all cultures have thought in this way, of course. The ancient Chinese
suggested that implicit in every condition in life, such as health and illness,
lay its opposite. Life's qualities do not exist in isolation. They are contained
in, and give rise to, their opposites. This is not a view that is arrived at by
merely toying with words, but a universal principle which each person was
asked to affirm by his own observations.

Lao Tzu (circa 480–390 B.C.), who condensed and recorded the basic
tenets of Taoism, expressed this basic oneness of the opposing experiences of life in his classic *Tao Te Ching*:

Only when man recognizes beauty as such does ugliness become reality. Only when man recognizes goodness as such does evil become
reality.

Because: being and nothingness began as one. Weight and weight-
lessness cannot exist alone. Distance and brevity prove each other and
so do height and depth. Tune and voice abound together and past and
present flow into one.

Having realized this principle, Lao Tzu tells us that it affects the way we
experience life itself:

Therefore the Sage remains in serenity whatever happens. . . .
As matters proceed, the Sage is not irritated.[2]

How does one actually develop an understanding of how health and illness fit together? The idea is so foreign to ordinary experience that it
seems absurd to suppose that these opposites, as well as others, begin as
one and meld into unity. This problem was thoroughly recognized by
those who proposed it in the earliest developmental stages of Taoistic philosophy. The first realization is that, when viewed from the perspective of
everyday thought, the notion of the fusion of opposites *is* absurd. It is paradoxical and mysterious when approached with ordinary logic, yet clear
and nonesoteric when seen intuitively. Again the words of Lao Tzu express
the point:

> We search for it yet see it not;
> it is the invisible.
> We listen for it, yet hear it not;
> it is the inaudible.
> We grasp for it, yet touch it not;
> it is the untouchable.
> Its trinity is inseparable.
> We recognize it only as *One*, innerbound.
> Its distance is incomprehensible,
> Its depth can not be fathomed.
> Eternally creative, it can not be defined.
> It goes back to Nothingness.
> It can be called: The form of the formless, the
>   face of the faceless.
> It can be called: The incomprehensible Mysterious.
> You walk towards it and find not even its Beginning.
> You follow it and there is no End.
> Who understands the Spirit of the old Sages masters
>   his own time, and thru them the very root of all
>   time.
> Such is the continuum of the Spirit.[3]

The understanding of how opposites unite is, then, ungraspable yet
knowable. It is formless and faceless and mysterious, yet it can be understood. Its true nature cannot be characterized by words, even though those
who know it ceaselessly employ words to do what they cannot do. To know

this "innerbound" oneness and unity is the goal of true wisdom, the ulti-mate attainment by which one could be called a Sage.

There is the recurrent impulse to keep the opposites of life cleanly sep-arated. We *know* health and illness are different, and no amount of esoteric Taoistic chichanery will convince us otherwise. And to propose that true health cannot be attained, worked at, developed, or otherwise apprehended is heretical. Yet no matter how stridently we wish to dismiss the notion that opposites are one, there are moments in the experiences of all of us that affirm the formless, faceless, and incomprehensibly mysterious fact that health and illness *are* one.

The knowledge never surfaces more forcefully than in the experience of dire illness. In the face of the possibility of losing one's life a clarity of vision occasionally arises. These moments provide a substrate for wisdom and understanding that we seldom sense when healthy. And these ex-periences are not rare. If we look for them, I suspect that most persons could recall friends who touched on this wisdom during illness; and I am convinced that in the experiences of physicians these instances are commonplace.

MARTHA'S STORY

Martha G. was brought to the office by her son, who petulantly insisted that she relent and see a physician: she was a sixty-five-year-old widow who lived in a small town some distance away. Fiercely independent, she did not take kindly to the suggestion that she see a doctor in spite of the fact that the pains in her abdomen had become so intense she could not sleep.

She sat across the desk from me, her son behind her. She related her history begrudgingly, and had it not been for her son's frequent comments I would have had few facts with which to understand her problem.

"Martha, why did you decide to come?" I asked her.

"Because I can't work in my garden anymore," she replied.

I discovered that her vegetable garden occupied a central focus in her life. She was known throughout her community as something of a magi-cian with plants. Her methods were thoroughly organic, for she eschewed the use of chemical additives of any kind to either soil or food. She fed not only herself from her garden, but a considerable number of neighbors as well. I asked her numerous questions about it, and she radiated enthusi-asm in describing, with vivid imagery, her plants. She was quick to sense my genuine interest as a fellow-gardener, and began to ask me questions, reversing the history-taking process. Her son was smiling quietly in the background, for as the conversation proceeded he knew his mother was glad she came, although he also knew she would never admit it.

Her story unfolded. Weeks before, she had begun to notice some swelling in her abdomen. She attributed this to "fluid accumulation," and invoked her own special organic remedy, straight from the garden, to correct the problem. But the remedy didn't work. The swelling increased to the point where clothes would no longer fit. Then a dull pain appeared in the lower abdomen. At first it was intermittent, but became constant and more severe. Again more remedies were tried, and again they failed. The pain was at times excruciating. She tried to "work it off," by which she meant doing hard labor in the midday Texas heat in her garden. It was at such a time that her son found her—after stopping by for an impromptu visit— holding onto a garden fence post, perspiring from both pain and the heat, struggling to keep from passing out. After helping her inside the house he put her to bed, and for the first time noticed the remarkable swelling in her entire abdomen. The next day, her own devices exhausted, she was in my office.

Her physical examination disclosed massive ascites—an accumulation of fluid within the abdominal cavity—and rock-hard masses that filled her mid- and lower abdomen. I was astonished that she could have endured this state for so long. Months had elapsed since the problem first appeared, during which most of her nights had been both sleepless and agonizing.

At first I thought that she was employing a massive kind of denial, a psychological ploy frequently used by persons to avoid the fact of illness. But for Martha, as I began to realize, this didn't fit. She had the fullest awareness of the problem. Indeed, it was precisely because she did recognize its existence that she was able to call forth her own repertoire of remedies from her organic garden. Denial wasn't an explanation. Martha was "doing" something else.

Her evaluation was undertaken, leading eventually to an exploratory laparatomy in which the diagnosis of cancer of the ovary was made at the time of surgery. Her attitude to the diagnostic tests and to the surgical procedure was unusual. There was none of the expected dread, nor did she want to get on with the studies. There was no despair in her attitude, nor was there any feisty aggressiveness that many cancer patients show. There was, instead, a kind of dispassionate perspective. She seemed to be someone—as strange as it may sound—who both had, and did not have, an illness. She was not brought down by the disease, nor did she seem oblivious to it. Somehow, it just "was." At no time did she give any hint that she saw it as either good or bad. And never did she display what could be called a nihilistic or fatalistic posture, nor did she ever demonstrate any overtly hopeful or positive comments about her state.

Following surgery, during the recovery phase she began to be concerned about my tomatoes. How were they doing? Did I use fertilizer and pesticides, or did I know how to grow them the "natural" way? Such questions were by no means superficial. Behind them there was a genuine interest in my plants, which in no way seemed to her an odd thing to express. Tomatoes were some of the most important facts of life, whether they were hers or mine. She even had her son bring me several large reference books from her library of organic gardening when she disappointedly began to glean that her physician was not the gardening purist that she was.

I asked one of my associates to become involved in her care as her oncologist, or cancer treatment specialist. After one visit to her room he abruptly entered my office and blurted, "What's *with* this woman? Why, she's hard as nails!" I had described her to him as "an elderly female with ovarian carcinoma," being deliberately vague, wanting him to experience all that she was in an unbiased way.

Oncologists are frequently felt to be rather strange medical specialists—aloof and dispassionate, dealing daily with death and dying, yet seemingly oblivious and enduring through it all. This reputation, which borders on the uncaring and the inhumane, is almost always inaccurate, I believe. By and large, they are very generous and loving physicians who do more than most to relieve human misery—even though they are blamed by many as doing exactly the opposite. (It may sound odd to imply that physicians need love, too, but "doctoring" always works best when caring flows in both directions—when the physician cares for the patient, and when the patient cares for the physician.)

My oncology associate developed a sense of awe for this "hard as nails" woman. He always spoke to me about her in admiring superlatives. He developed a keen awareness of her attitude toward her illness. And he could characterize it no better than I, even though we spoke frequently of it.

Martha affected his life through her contact with him, just as he changed hers through the administration of his skills. I could always tell when he had just seen her, for he always had a telltale smile on his face seldom evoked during the course of his day.

Her cancer had been widespread—from ovary to liver, spleen, peritoneum, and lymph nodes—and it was impossible to remove it all at the time of surgery. But she recovered from her operation without a hitch, and proved to be a magnificent "responder" to the chemotherapy drugs which she and her oncologist eventually chose. After discharge from the hospital she made occasional visits to his office as an outpatient.

One day I knew she had been in my office: there was a basket of tomatoes on my desk. Not the kind I grew or that are sold in super-markets—but tomatoes that were otherworldy in their size, hue, and taste. I knew they were Martha's tomatoes even before I read the terse, hand-scribbled note:

"Chemotherapy works. So do tomatoes. Thanks.—Martha G."

Martha is still alive as of this writing. She is not disease-free, for evidence of her tumor remains. But she is pain-free, and feeling energetic and vital. She still putters in her garden. And she still manifests her enigmatic, inscrutable attitude toward health and illness.

I do not wish to say that her course following the diagnosis of cancer was profoundly influenced by her transcendent approach to the fact of illness, although I believe it to be so. I do not want to imply a causal link between her marvelous clinical course and her mental state, because I have no sure way to prove it. In fact, I do not even believe it is important in any ultimate sense whether she "did well" or "did poorly" following diagnosis—for she herself was beyond such concerns. She had begun to employ a way of viewing life and death that had nothing to do with the presence or absence of disease. She had gone beyond, I feel, the "conditionalities" of health and illness to some ground state distal to both. This posture she adopted not out of resignation or a sense of giving up, but from a sure awareness of "how things are." If her attitude was enigmatic and mysterious, I suspect it is because the Oneness which she realized is itself "faceless" and "formless," as Lao Tzu put it.

Martha G., like many other persons, discovered a kind of health that is the "no-health" that we have spoken of, the "suchness" of existence that does not depend on whether or not the cancer is cured, whether the myocardial infarction occurs, or whether the stroke is prevented through control of the blood pressure. It may *include* these problems, or worse ones. It is an unconditional state, it is not dependent on the vicissitudes and flux of health- and illness-events for its final status. Thus it is, and is not, health. It is Health in the sense of the etymological meaning of the word: wholeness, oneness. But it is not our ordinary habit of health, defined by carving it into individual events and particularities.

I emphatically believe that Martha did not arrive at her transcendent perspective by asking herself the question, "Now what is the psychological strategy I should adopt if I want to 'beat' my cancer?" In this case she would have arrived at some outlook that would have been strictly utilitarian, having a fixed goal in mind, that of effecting a cure of her disease. This was patently not her objective. Indeed, she did not have an objective. She was "merely" dwelling in the unconditioned "suchness" and the "innerbound" and "incomprehensible Mysterious," which has no place for strategies to become healthier, no matter what their type. She had entered the domain of Highest Health, the realm of no-health, the health-beyond-health. The payoff? Not being healthier in any ordinary sense, but the certainty of living in the One, the "invisible," "inaudible," and "untouchable" state which medicine does not describe.

There are, of course, many forms of cancer treatment which have emerged in recent years which rightly recognize the relationship between the psyche and the immune process. The handwriting is on the wall in medicine today: not only cancer, but all the major diseases of our day have intimate connections with the psyche. Attitude, emotion, and feelings enter in vital ways into the process of disease. We can say of the techniques which employ this new understanding in the treatment of disease that they are consistent with our best knowledge. But we can say, too, that they stop short.

Persons who enter programs which seek to maximize the positive use of mental states in treating illness may indeed experience a better result than if ordinary, non-psychologically oriented forms of treatment are employed. Pain may be diminished, extent of disease may be attenuated, and longevity may be increased. A sense of "being in control" of the disease itself can be developed, a goal which should be applauded. But these results are not to be confused with the "ploy" of Martha G. in the above case, for the plain fact is that she did not have a ploy. She did not intentionally invoke a mental state of a particular type out of a desire to improve her physical status. Even though the disease proved to remit in a striking way, she would have been, I feel, relatively unmoved had it not responded. Her goals were beyond "remission," "response rate," and "cure." She was not trying to "become" anything, not attempting to "gain" something. Such concepts imply time; they are anchored in a durational, flowing past, present, and future. Martha was beyond durational time in her perspective. There was nothing to be gained, nothing to become. In the "isness" and "suchness" which she experienced, there was only the present moment.

Future forms of therapy that emphasize the potency of the mind in the origin and course of human illness will recognize this fact. They will utilize psychological interventions to more effectively and humanely treat illness, but with the added understanding that there is something yet more important for the patient to learn. They will rightly acknowledge a state of health that transcends the problem at hand or any illness that might develop in the future. They will proclaim that the highest use of the psyche in the course of human illness is not for cure, but for transcendence of the conditional events we call health and disease, birth and death.

The irony will prove to be, I feel, that through this "giving up" patients will *then* be able to use their mental life in their own behalf in ways that are astonishingly more effective than anything we now know. By "giving up," by going beyond the relevancy of pain and suffering and illness, the most potent health strategies will be discovered; but at that point they will no longer be called "strategies," for they will spring to life not in response *to* the fact of illness, but from the transcendence of it.

> Who can as they [the great sages of antiquity] interpret
>   the turbulent thru serenity?
> Who can as they thru their own lives revive the dead
>   souls?
> Who is filled with serene thoughts desires no other
>   fulfillment,
> Who desires no other fulfillment is not attacked by
>   novelties of the day.
> Such man can be of simple status yet reach perfection.
>
> Who ascends the peak of Emptiness
> Will reach serenity.
> And thus the ephemerality of the body can not harm us.[4]

The state of Highest Health is beyond harm, beyond the touch of the "ephemerality of the body." It is the goal of all enlightened therapies. It is not a modern task, nor is it old—for it is beyond time. It is the "suchness," the "isness" of this very moment, of all present moments, the Now, which is the only time there is.

Ted: Bronchial Asthma

> Whatsoever therefore makes the blood to boyl, or raises it into an effer-
> vescence, as violent motion of the body or minde . . . doth cause asth-
> matical assaults to such as are predisposed.
>
> —Thomas Willis, 1679
> "Of An Asthma"

My asthma is part of me. I can't *force* it out, so I'm taking a more playful attitude toward it. I'm attempting to integrate myself with the world.

—Ted Frank, asthmatic

Ted Frank was at the peak of his profession, a forty-eight-year-old attorney with a prestigious law firm. His office was where respectable attorneys in Dallas are *supposed* to have offices, in a downtown high rise—the prestige of the practice being proportionate to the height of the floor one occupied. Ted was a star in his firm, but he was unhappy with his work—bored with tasks, little gratified even when things went his way, and, worst of all, disgruntled with the way his associates directed the firm. He implemented his "grin and bear it" philosophy with quiet boredom and silent hostility for years, functioning with clear competence professionally yet becoming increasingly disenchanted with his lot.

Then he developed asthma for the first time in his life—totally unexpected, without any history in childhood of asthma or allergies of any kind, and without any family history of such. At first he tried to ignore the problem. But the wheezing and shortness of breath grew worse, and he began to limit his activity. He could not talk to clients without wheezing audibly, and daytime wheezing gradually turned into nighttime wheezing. When he found himself unable to sleep, he gave in. For one of the few times in his life he went to a doctor.

His physician could find nothing wrong. Indeed, he seemed in peak physical condition aside from the asthma. He was put on a variety of asthma medications and was referred to an allergy specialist, where he underwent testing for a battery of offending agents or allergens that are known to trigger asthma. The tests proved to be of no help; and, although his medications were juggled, the asthma persisted, albeit at a lesser intensity. For six months various medications were started, then stopped when they failed to work. As each medication dosage was adjusted upward to tolerance, all he experienced was the noxious side effects—nervousness, anxiety, insomnia—without any obvious benefit. Finally, when he found himself taking sizeable doses of a hydrocortisone-like drug, he decided to take another direction.

He had learned of a specially designed hospital which focused on allergy problems. Patients were hospitalized for extensive periods, sometimes for months, and were painstakingly isolated from all environmental chemicals such as those in water and foods. Even bed sheets and clothing were scrutinized (no synthetic fibers allowed), as well as the wall coverings, floors, and ceilings for fear that organic solvents used in the manufacturing process were the asthma-causing culprits. Special organic foods were used, all chemical-free. Nurses were not allowed to wear cosmetics or perfume while working in the isolation area, and even the air entering the rooms was filtered through great charcoal canisters to remove impurities.

The goal of the program was to achieve "complete ecological control and environmental isolation." Then, when the asthma had faded, various known common substances would be introduced, one at a time. When the asthma flared following the introduction of a specific food, soap, or clothing of a particular type, it could be concluded that this was the offending agent. If this substance or article was then eliminated from one's exposure, it was expected that the asthma would not return.

The entire logic and rationale of the program infatuated Ted Frank, and he enthusiastically checked himself into the hospital-based unit. He followed every instruction the way he practiced law—attending to every detail—and was delighted when the physicians in charge predicted total success.

There was only one problem: it didn't work. A month later Ted was discharged from the hospital back into the real world of impure air, tainted food, and chemically treated water—several thousand dollars poorer and still wheezing. The compelling logic of the isolation program now seemed spurious, and he felt as if he had been misled. He had begun to develop a logic of his own about why this approach had failed, an idea that he shared with no one, not even the well-intended physicians who had attempted to cure him. Ted began to conclude that the approach of the ecological and environmental program was naive because it conceived of "ecology" and "environment" as something physical, something external, something "out there." No attention was paid to inner states, to emotions, attitudes, feelings—the world of consciousness. He had reluctantly concluded that there were *two* environments, an inward and an outer one—and that in his own case it was the ecology of his inner environment, his consciousness, that was of greater importance than the outer world in affecting his asthma. His proof?—mainly an intuition, but a string of failures, as well, of approaches that focused on his asthma as the result of an assault from the external world. Ted felt deeply that this approach was wrong.

He saw it as no accident that his official diagnosis, "adult-onset asthma," had befallen him at a time of emotional turmoil related to his increasing disaffection with his work and peers. He simply could not agree with the conclusions of his various physicians that the total origin of his ailment was some external source. Perhaps, he reasoned, there was *some* validity to an objectively caused illness, but this was not, for him, the whole story. He felt his anxiety and inner chaos were factors also—maybe not a total explanation, but important nonetheless. It seemed simplistic to do what the various approaches had attempted—to treat his *body*, or to isolate him physically from some offending agent. He was astonished that at no time had any physician, nurse, or respiratory therapist inquired as to the state of his psyche.

Ted Frank sensed a relatedness of body and mind to which his physicians had been oblivious. He felt that if this relatedness had been sundered, and if it were not repaired, his efforts at controlling his asthma would continue to be fruitless. He set out in his usual analytical, logical way in his own investigation of this ineluctable connection, and began to read various books dealing with psychosomatic concepts and the mind-body relationships in various forms of disease.

By the time he appeared in my office he had become a lay authority on his own illness. He even brought a reading list demonstrating the sincerity of his pursuit and the depth of his beliefs. His compendium was far more extensive than what could be found on required reading lists in medical school courses dealing with psychosomatic medicine. His intensity and sincerity convinced me that this man was extraordinarily committed to becoming well, and was willing to expend an enormous personal energy in the process. From that time forward he always appeared in my office with a new book or two which he brought along to peruse in the waiting room. I found myself wondering what he would bring next, and what I could learn from his latest selections.

He had resigned from his firm, and had hung out his shingle in a small town thirty miles from the metropolis. Resolving to come to terms with the emotional upheavals caused by his work, he saw the move as necessary and as therapeutic as the drugs he was still taking for his asthma. He specified in our initial visit that he wanted to learn biofeedback, a decision he had arrived at after probing several books on the subject. He was infatuated with the possibility of learning to control or abort his asthmatic attacks willfully and consciously. With his characteristic energy and enthusiasm he seemed completely convinced he could do so.

I reveled in our conversations. He had no inflexible belief system to break through, no "Doctor, *you* make me well" philosophy to deal with. He felt convinced he had a hand in the appearance of his asthma, and was even surer he could have a hand in its control. Furthermore, his grasp of psychophysiological principles was basic and accurate. There was an instant rapport and cohesion between us, the felt magic that lends an experiential wonder to the doctor-patient relationship.

Following a thorough history and physical examination we reviewed his current medications and made some modifications. Then we talked about his reason for wanting to enroll as a subject in my biofeedback laboratory. I reminded him what he already knew: the record of biofeedback in the treatment of asthma is not uniform, the results are mixed, and the most rigorous sorts of studies have yet to be done. Yes, anecdotal and uncontrolled series of cases abound wherein success has been seen, but across-the-board proof of efficacy is lacking. True, we have known for years that emotions can play a key role in asthma, and we know too that asthma is not a homogeneous disease. There are surely several sub-types of asthma, some of which are undoubtedly influenced by emotions in varying degrees. I felt a full disclosure of the present state of the art was important to dispel any illusions and false hopes he might have about the effectiveness of biofeedback. He had been given plenty of inaccurate expectations about treatments in the past, and didn't need more.

We both decided that he was a fit candidate to begin biofeedback training. The biofeedback therapist with whom he worked, interestingly, was also a registered respiratory therapist, and knew well the physiological processes underlying his disease. She was marvelously adept at evoking in her patients an awareness of mind-body relatedness. They were a good match, and he learned the rudiments of biofeedback training quickly.

He learned to recognize inner tension, what emotional stress felt like in his body, and developed a surer conviction that his psychological state affected his asthmatic wheezing. His asthma began to abate.

But not completely. Although his skills at learning to deeply relax his body were enviable in the lab, he, like almost all biofeedback subjects early in their training, had difficulty in maintaining this state outside the laboratory environment in the "real world." Ted's asthma would still flare at predictable times, usually associated with emotional tension. But his improvement was unmistakable, and he felt he was on the correct path. He affirmed time and again his belief in the body-mind connection that propelled him toward biofeedback in the first place.

He continued to practice his skills at home and in the lab with an admirable discipline. His reading list, which he continued to share with me, became increasingly sophisticated. He gradually developed a calm which reflected an underlying wisdom about his illness. Ted's logical-intellectual probes and his experiential excursions into body-mind domains via his adventures in biofeedback combined in some unfathomable way to emerge as what only can be described as a spiritual approach to the problem.

Illness for him came to take on a new meaning. "My asthma is part of me," he said, and he and I talked frequently about the approaches to his problem that had led him to this formulation. His early ventures in treatment emphasized disease as a malevolent external intruder, a thief in the night who catches one unaware. These views fit poorly with his own inner observations about how his emotions affected his symptoms. He simply could not affirm the notion that disease was "out there." Indeed, the therapeutic approaches that had totally emphasized this philosophy had failed. His statement, "I can't *force* it out" reflected an understanding that illness can never be vengefully exterminated by any technique, for the reason that it *is* part of oneself. To hate one's illness is to disdain oneself, he knew. Because of the interrelatedness of body and mind, one cannot focus merely on the physiology without evoking simultaneous repercussions of the psyche; and it was this connectedness that had been ignored by the purely physical approaches he had originally elected. His understanding that *he* was not different from his asthma led him to a new therapeutic strategy: "I'm taking a more playful attitude toward it." In recognizing the relationship between self and illness, he transcended the grim imperative to "conquer" his problem, to drive it into oblivion, to purge himself of it. Finally a new ontologic understanding emerged: "I'm attempting to integrate myself with the world."

BODY-MIND ONENESS: BEYOND METAPHOR

Ted Frank's awareness grew from a confrontation with illness. His experience epitomizes the fact that adversity, even dreadful physical diseases, can culminate in breakthroughs in awareness. This is an ancient observation, but one we forget in our blind categorization of illness as enemy. We do not often realize that disease can represent real opportunity for growth and transcendence, and that if we *do* categorically war against disease, there is an element of ourselves that we also combat.

These observations go beyond metaphor. The understanding of inner connection, of body-mind unity, are demonstrable events whose reality can be demonstrated in the physiologist's laboratory. In particular, asthma is an illness that vividly demonstrates the inaccuracy of regarding a disease as if it were some disembodied entity, as if it had no connection with the psyche. The very name of the illness is derived from the Greek word *azein*, meaning "breathe hard." The word implies a *smothering*, an apt description of the experience of acute asthma.

Hinshaw, an authority on diseases of the chest, expressed the interconnectedness of psyche and soma in asthma:

Fear is both a cause and consequence of asthma. Treatment that serves to quiet fear, be it pharmacologic or psychologic, is good treatment.[1]

Not only is fear capable of triggering asthma, a simple *belief* can do the same. Several experiments in adults and children have shown that the mere suggestion to an asthmatic subject that he is inhaling an allergic agent (although not, in fact, true) can provoke an attack.[2]

The unity of body and mind illustrated in cases of asthma such as Ted Frank's is not some mystical fabrication, as statements of "oneness" are frequently regarded in medicine. Although much of the mechanism undoubtedly remains to be worked out, it has been suggested that emotions, acting via the autonomic nervous system, cause changes in the lining of the bronchial tubes that make them more sensitive to both infectious and allergic agents.[3] In addition to the effects of the emotions on the lungs, emotions in turn are affected *by* the asthmatic process once it begins—a vicious cycle. Fear and apprehension, as Hinshaw points out, are part of asthma.

Ted Frank had learned empirically these associations, and set out to change them. He had reasoned in the footsteps of many researchers that since so many physiological variables can be modified significantly with a variety of relaxation techniques (e.g., blood pressure, heart rate, galvanic skin response, muscle tension, and certain aspects of the respiratory cycle),[4] it only made sense to try to apply relaxation techniques to the treatment of asthma. The result? Ted himself had begun to replicate the results of many experimenters: Both with and without biofeedback, the use of relaxation training in asthmatic persons can result in both immediate and long-term improvement of lung function. In his attempts to voluntarily improve his asthma, Ted was on firm ground.

Ted Frank's asthma illustrates the folly of attempting to understand disease in terms of simple cause-and-effect. The more we learn about the intricate interplay of mind and body, how a psychological event may follow *or* precede a cascade of physiological events, the more we become mired in an endless reverberating chain of happenings in human illness. Because of this complexity, simple causal explanations for most human diseases have lost much of the authority they once had.[5]

The ecological-environmental approach to which Ted was drawn early in his course committed this simplistic error in judgment. It regarded allergic substances in simple causal terms. "To be allergic" to a substance expressed purely objective phenomena which could then be capitalized upon therapeutically, so it was presumed: eliminate the allergic substance, and the asthma will be cured. Such simplistic thinking disregarded the fact that *non*allergic persons, under suggestion, may begin to wheeze if told they are allergic to an innocuous substance; and that *allergic* individuals, also under suggestion, can significantly eliminate wheezing in response to substances to which they *are* allergic.

Not that this understanding is new. As early as 1930, Hill observed that a picture of a hay field could evoke hay fever attacks in very sensitive subjects.[6] And in 1933, Smith and Salinger described an earlier clinical observation of Sir William Osler, the most towering figure in the history of American medicine, of a patient who experienced an asthmatic attack when presented with an artificial rose.[7] Such examples are by no means rare, as Ader has pointed out.[8] They stand in stark contrast to the prevailing, extremist views that disease is *either* subjective (all "in the mind") *or* objective (all "out there"). Only by considering illness as part of the *whole* world, including the inner as well as the outer landscapes, will we be able to accommodate the clinical complexities involved in problems such as asthma.

Ted Frank had served as his own body-mind research laboratory. His insight, "My asthma is part of me," seemed an understated expression of the unity of psyche and soma that pervades not just asthma, but all the major diseases of our day.

Anne: Anorexia Nervosa

It is all right to be sick. Seeing sickness as a calamity and misfortune directed at oneself for some particular reason is all too easy, but it is not compatible with the view that illness is the necessary complement to health. . . .

. . . it is fine to regard relative sickness as undesired and to work with all effort and intelligence toward reducing its severity and duration. We must not reject it as something that should not happen, however, nor interpret it as any sort of statement about our worth as human beings. Sickness does not mean; it just is.

Sickness is the way to the next relative period of health, and one state cannot exist without the other, any more than day can exist without night. Anger and guilt about falling sick not only go together with impossible dreams about attaining perfect health, they also *interfere* with the process of reaching a new equilibrium.

—Andrew Weil
Health and Healing

The mask, given time, comes to be the face itself.

—Marguerite Yourcenar
Memoirs of Hadrian

One of the strangest illnesses of our day is anorexia nervosa. It is a lesson in how disunity and disruption of the relatedness of mind and body can lead not only to overt illness but to death as well.

Anorexia nervosa is a disease that remains an enigma for modern medicine. It is

. . . a self-imposed state of cachexia and malnutrition and may at times be life-threatening. It is accompanied by severe psychologic disturbances which lead to an abnormal desire to lose weight.[1]

It is frustrating that therapy for persons with anorexia nervosa is not uniformly successful. The profound irony of the illness is that fatal weight loss may occur, and the patient may die without any other evidence of demonstrable physical abnormalities. And frequently, even until the time of death, the person with anorexia nervosa will deny vehemently that there is something wrong with his health.

Peculiar behaviors may occur, which are interpreted by the anorexia nervosa patient as being totally rational. In order to avoid gaining weight, self-induced vomiting after eating is frequently engaged in. Food may be surreptitiously hidden or disposed of; laxatives may be taken to eliminate food before it can be absorbed; or vigorous, excessive exercise may be engaged in after eating to "burn up calories" before weight gain can occur. As the disease progresses, persons with this illness may develop a distorted body image, coming to view their emaciated, wasted body as completely normal.

Because of the severely wasted, malnourished state, various physical problems eventually become apparent. Menstruation may stop; the skin may become dry and scaly; and body temperature may be subnormal. Various vitamin deficiency syndromes may occur. Tooth decay is common because with repeated vomiting the enamel of the teeth is eroded: hydrochloric acid from the stomach, which normally digests food, can digest the teeth as well.

Although there can be underlying problems such as severe depression, obsession, withdrawal, and occasionally psychiatric delusions, outwardly the anorexia nervosa patient is cooperative, alert, and intelligent. This persona is frequently accompanied by a "What's all the fuss about?" attitude toward concerned family and friends.

The mortality in this illness is shocking: from 20 to 30 percent of those afflicted die. With increasing weight loss and starvation, the potassium level in the blood may fall to life-threatening levels. Potassium is an ion in body fluids and cells necessary for maintenance of a normal heartbeat. At critically low levels the heart's electrical stability is threatened, and extra beats begin to occur. Death usually occurs when the heartbeat degenerates into a chaotic, ineffective runaway rhythm called ventricular fibrillation.

ANNE

She entered my office with profuse protestations. This twenty-nine-year-old woman was there, she said, at the behest of her mother, who, along with her husband, was worried about her health. She was sure nothing was wrong. For reasons she could not fathom, they—parents, husband, friends—were continually plaguing her about her weight. At five feet, six inches tall, she weighed seventy-two pounds—a perfectly reasonable weight for her height, she said. Her cachectic state hidden by a long dress and wrist-long sleeves, Anne was a lovely girl with angular facial features that were cosmetically perfect. She was precise in her speech and charming in her demeanor. She related her history willingly.

She had always been slim, she said, but never as thin as she wished. She despised obesity but could not say why, and had had a fear of becoming obese for as long as she could remember. Her maximum weight had been 110 pounds on graduation from high school, a level she maintained until three years ago when her weight began to fall.

She had become infatuated with physical exercise at that time, and attributed her weight loss to a vigorous conditioning program. She had taken up jogging, and ran on the average of thirty miles a week—until recently, that is, when she began to develop unexplained fatigue and easy tiring. Although she could not explain these new symptoms, she was sure they were meaningless and would prove to be transient.

Her physical examination demonstrated severe emaciation. Skin hung on bone. The nurse assisting me in the examination was generally unflappable, but, I noticed from the corner of my eye, was aghast at Anne's appearance. Anne looked as if she were going to die.

Following the examination we entered my private office again to discuss my findings. I told her of my concern for her life, and I encouraged her to enter the hospital for nutritional support and psychological evaluation. At this suggestion Anne feigned shock and disbelief and looked at me as if I had gone mad. She reminded me she had come reluctantly in the first place, to prove to her worried mother and husband that nothing was wrong. Entering the hospital was out of the question, since she wasn't sick. I was accusing her of what she was already hearing from friends and family—that she was "too thin." Her body was *hers*, she said, and if she wanted to weigh seventy-two pounds it was her choice, not mine.

At this point she opened her purse and withdrew three Polaroid color snapshots, thrusting them angrily toward me across the desk. "If you don't believe I'm beautiful, look at these!" she stammered, now almost in tears. The pictures revealed a smiling Anne posing upright in her living room, totally nude—front, back, and profile. For her, these amateurish photos constituted unassailable proof of her slim beauty. She evidently felt that now there could be no argument, that I could not possibly disagree. I asked if I could make the pictures a part of her file, and she agreed, perhaps thinking that if they were a permanent part of her record her position would be documented and validated.

The laboratory technician arrived with the report of her blood studies, all normal except for the potassium level, which was dangerously low. I inquired how it could have fallen to such a drastic level. Did she vomit or take laxatives frequently, or did she use diuretic medications?—all common ways of losing potassium from the body. No, she assured me she did none of these things. Her only way of "keeping thin" was to vigorously exercise. She seemed affronted that I had even suggested other possibilities.

It was only when I told her of the life-threatening potassium level that she consented to come into the hospital for treatment. The terms of her admission were firmly dictated by her: a private room; oral—not intravenous—potassium replacement; and *no* psychiatrists. She would leave when the potassium replacement was finished. But there were no private rooms in the hospital. Reluctantly she consented to occupy a semiprivate room after being told her "roommate" would be a woman her own age.

That evening following office hours I made hospital rounds. The night meals had already been served to the patients. I entered Anne's room and observed that her food had hardly been touched. And, interestingly, she was clad not in the usual hospital-issue patient gown, but in a designer-styled *jogging suit* that covered her totally to neck, wrists, and ankles. Her body habitus was cleverly concealed. Anne was even wearing running shoes.

We chatted, and her previous hostility to me seemed to have abated. Again we discussed the immediate goal of her hospital stay, that of restoring the potassium in her blood. I reminded her also that the diet I had ordered her was high in potassium content and that we could accomplish our goal faster if she ate her food as well as taking her medication.

Two days later her potassium level had not changed. This was difficult to understand, since she had begun to eat all her food, and since she was witnessed by the nurses who administered them to be taking all her potassium tablets. The potassium had to be going *somewhere*. Unexpectedly, it was her roommate who solved the mystery.

As I left Anne's room the next morning, her roommate followed me down the hall. "Doctor, there's something I should tell you. It's about Anne." This woman, knowing nothing about the clinical illness of anorexia nervosa, could nonetheless recognize bizarre behavior when she saw it. Still, she was reluctant to reveal what was going on because she and Anne had become friends. Please, I was to understand that she was telling me these things only because she was concerned for Anne's health.

We stepped into an empty examination room just off the main nurses' station, and her roommate began her revelations. From the time she began to share the room with Anne, her behavior had been peculiar. After eating she would lock herself in the bathroom, from whence would emanate the unmistakable sounds of vomiting. Then Anne would emerge, denying when asked if she had been sick. She would then disappear from the room for up to an hour at a time, and when she returned in her jogging suit and running shoes she would be breathless and perspiring. The roommate was mystified why she should be *exercising* if she was sick enough to be hospitalized. Anyway, where could she possibly be exercising on a hospital ward? None of these things made any sense to her. I thanked her for her information, and she returned to her room.

The next clues came from the nurses on the floor. The head nurse approached me before I could finish writing an entry into Anne's chart, with a string of complaints. She was livid: "Your patient has got to get her act together, or she's got to go!" She went on to disclose how Anne had been apprehended by the night nurse on the "11 to 7" shift, going from room to room, talking with patients she had never met before. She would introduce herself, enjoin them in conversation at this odd hour, and would manipulate the exchange into the same message to each of them: "Can't you see how overweight you are? Don't you see your obesity isn't good for your health?" The first complaint came at 2 in the morning from a patient Anne accused of obesity. The woman, whose "obesity" was due to being in her eighth month of pregnancy, called the night nurse and complained.

The head nurse had more complaints for me. The night security guard had seen Anne for two consecutive nights running up and down the stairs of the hospital. He stopped her the first time, wondering what this cachectic patient was doing in the middle of the night clad in jogging togs running up and down the stairwell. "Just trying to build up my strength," he was told. This bluffed him the first night; but his second exposure to Anne's routine exceeded his gullibility. He followed her at a distance, discovered what floor she was on, and reported her strange behavior to the nurse in charge.

Later that day when her potassium level registered even lower than before, I confronted Anne with my new knowledge, having thought about what the most effective approach might be all day long. As usual, she denied any wrongdoing. "There must be some mistake." Why would she vomit or exercise when her potassium level was dangerously low? Her roommate (who had been discharged earlier in the day) was merely trying to cause trouble. I was not to worry, she said, for she was already feeling better.

I responded that we were going to begin an intravenous infusion of potassium, since the oral approach hadn't worked, and that I had asked a psychiatric consultant to talk with her. The problems were too profound to ignore any longer. Our present approach was inadequate, and we needed help, I told her. Anne did not say no to the suggestion of the intravenous potassium or to the psychiatrist. Indeed, she said nothing at all. Interpreting her silence as agreement, I left her room.

"She's gone. Can't find her anywhere, not even her bag!" With this comment from the night nurse on the other end of the phone, I knew I had been naive, even stupid, about Anne's compliance. She had left the hospital A.M.A.—"against medical advice"—shortly after I had called her hand on her behavior and had suggested psychiatric intervention. I phoned her husband and her mother: no one had seen her. I told her husband what had happened, and that she was seriously ill. I suggested that when she arrived home that he bring her immediately to the emergency room.

Anne never returned home. She was found dead, on a sidewalk a mile from the hospital, carrying her bag and dressed, as always, in her beloved jogging outfit. She died, I am sure, just as many persons with anorexia nervosa die—a cardiac death from ventricular fibrillation due to depletion of the body's potassium stores. An autopsy, required legally, revealed nothing, a fact that the examining pathologist could hardly believe in this emaciated young woman.

MORE THAN PHILOSOPHY

I rethought Anne's case for months, pondering what I should have done differently. Would earlier psychiatric care have made a difference? Should she have been involuntarily restrained and the potassium administered intravenously against her will? How could I have dealt more effectively with her artifice and denial? I still have no sure answers.

Since then I have seen other Annes, other persons with anorexia nervosa of varying degrees of severity. Some have done well and some have not. None of the psychiatrists who have assisted me in these cases are eager to work with these persons, for in spite of all that has been written about the intricate psychodynamics of the problem, "cure" remains an altogether too infrequent occurrence. Many approaches have been tried, as the psychiatric literature attests. Most of them work—only some of the time.

What can be said of anorexia nervosa from the perspective of body-mind unity that is our concern here? Anorexia nervosa is an illness that represents a well-nigh total dismemberment of body-mind oneness, a complete disjunction of psychophysiological integration. Anne's pathetic Polaroids said it well: the body is an "it"—an idea, an image, an object. It is some*thing* I choose to feed or starve or exercise. I can manipulate it into leanness or obesity at will. I can purge it, I can make it vomit. I can even kill it.

Much has been written about the obvious distortion of the body image in the anorexia nervosa patient. The body is for some arcane psychological reason (it is said) rejected and abused. As the abuse and starvation increase, the anorexia nervosa patient professes a love of the distorted, cachectic body. But it is more a hatred than a love, because it is a "love" that frequently ends in a death that is patently suicidal.

According to our best reckoning, the incidence of anorexia nervosa in modern society is increasing at a rapid rate. There is an infatuation with image, with body-as-object. And the image that is loved is the lithe, svelte look of youth. It has been suggested that an entire spectrum of the anorexia cult exists; while extreme cases such as Anne's exist, milder cases are much more numerous and rarely go detected.

It is not the image that we should take issue with here, but the tendency to elevate the image over the "felt I," the valuation of object over experience. It is the disjunction of psyche and soma, of mind and body, that is a concern, not the particular form the patient's notion of loveliness may take. Without an understanding of this rift, no therapy is likely to be successful; for it is the sense of body-mind unity that must be restored if healing is to occur. All other therapies—restoration of the blood potassium level, cessation of vomiting, etc.—are important but are only adjunctive measures.

When we chronically separate ourself from the object of our knowledge, the path to disease is paved. The anorexia nervosa patient is a living embodiment of the physical devastations that can come about through this mode of being. In this disease, "I" becomes utterly remote from "body," and it is likely impossible for this illness to occur if the sense of oneness of body and mind is intact.

Anorexia nervosa is a spectacular example that the concept of body-mind unity is more than pious, poetic musings. When the interrelatedness of psyche and soma is ignored to an exaggerated degree, catastrophe frequently results. This issue transcends the level of the philosophical. As Anne's case demonstrates, it is a matter of life and death.

NOTES

Martha G.: Cancer

1. Wade Baskin, ed., *Classics in Chinese Philosophy* (Totawa, N.J.: Littlefield, Adams & Co., 1974), p. 55.
2. *Ibid.*
3. *Ibid.*, pp. 58–59.
4. *Ibid.*, pp. 59–60.

Ted: Bronchial Asthma

1. H. C. Hinshaw, *Diseases of the Chest*, 3rd ed. (Philadelphia: W. B. Saunders, 1969), p. 332.
2. R. L. Phillip, G. J. S. Wilde, and J. H. Day, "Suggestion and Relaxation in Asthmatics," *Journal of Psychosomatic Research* 16 (1972): pp. 193–204; M. J. Weiss, C. Martin, and J. Riley, "Effects of Suggestion on Respiration in Asthmatic Children," *Psychosomatic Medicine* 32 (1970): pp. 409–415; T. Luparello, et al., "Influence of Suggestion in Airway Reactivity in Asthmatic Subjects," *Psychosomatic Medicine* 30 (1968): pp. 819–825; E. Dekker, H. E. Pelser, and J. Groen, "Conditioning as a Cause of Asthmatic Attacks," *Journal of Psychosomatic Research* 2 (1957): p. 97; and E. R. McFadden, Jr. et al., "The Mechanism of Action of Suggestion in the Induction of Acute Asthma Attacks," *Psychosomatic Medicine* 31 (1969): pp. 134–143.
3. C. W. Moorefield, "The Use of Hypnosis and Behavior Therapy in Asthma," *American Journal of Clinical Hypnosis* 13 (1970): pp. 162–168.
4. M. Spevack, "Behavior Therapy Treatment of Bronchial Asthma: A Critical Overview," *Canadian Psychological Review* 19 (1978): p. 322.
5. S. Vaisrub, "Groping for Causation," *Journal of the American Medical Association* 241:8 (1979): p. 830.
6. L. E. Hill, *Philosophy of a Biologist* (London: Arnold, 1930); and Patricia D. Higgins, "Classical Conditioning of the Immune System," paper presented to East Texas State University, Commerce, Texas, March, 1984.
7. G. H. Smith and R. Salinger, "Hypersensitiveness and the Conditioned Reflex," *Yale Journal of Biological Medicine* 5 (1933): pp. 387–402.

8. R. Ader, "A Historical Account of Conditioned Immunobiologic Responses," in *Psychoneuroimmunology*, ed. R. Ader, (New York.: Academic Press, 1981), pp. 321–352.

Anne: Anorexia Nervosa

1. K. J. Isselbacher and J. B. Shumaker, "Anorexia, Nausea, and Vomiting," in *Harrison's Principles of Internal Medicine,* 7th ed. (New York: McGraw-Hill, 1974), p. 211.

XI

Holistic Health: A Critique

Science is held in such awe in our culture that every scientist has a special responsibility to make clear to the lay audience where his expert knowledge actually yields scientifically verifiable results and where he is guessing, indulging in sheer speculation, or expressing his own personal hopes about the success of his research. This is an important task because the lay audience is in no position to make these distinctions.

—Noam Chomsky

An integration of our intellectual and spiritual tendencies, or of science and religion . . . is essential for the healing of the whole culture.
When science does serve as a spiritual path, then there are moments when one is bathed in the wonder of it all. One stays in front of the mystery in amazement. It is a mystery that broadens and deepens with contemplation. One comes to the mystery of oneself and the mystery of it all. One knows somewhere that one must do science, just as others must write poetry or make music. All this is man. . . . It seems we must theorize to go beyond theory, we must intellectualize to come to a stillness of the mind, and we must make music to come to the silence.

—Ravi Ravindra

A forest of facts unordered by concepts and constructive relations may be cherished for its existential appeal, its vividness, its pleasure or its nausea yet it is meaningless, insignificant, and usually uninteresting unless it is organized by reason.

—Henry Margenau

Thus in practical activities the American love for novelty and their lack of circumspection has led to great achievements which are too well known to call for enumeration. In contrast, dire results have ensued from the operation of the same bias in domains where there are no immanent mechanisms for eliminating error: where correctness and falsehood are normally a matter of degree, and truth can only be partially gleaned by a laborious crawl over dangerous ground between attractively camouflaged traps, and where every step calls for a suspicious examination and often a suspended judgement; and to top it all, where excessive incredulity can be just as misleading as gullibility.

—Stanslav Andreski
Social Sciences as Sorcery

Everybody wants to change the world, but nobody wants to change his mind.

—Seaborn Blair

The following critique is a harsh one. It is rendered, however, out of a deep sense of care and love for the philosophy of holism which at last is beginning to penetrate medicine.

If a respectful dialogue ever develops between traditional and holistic medicine it will be necessary for holists to speak in clear, reasonably unambiguous terms about what holism is all about. A disciplined voice is required if holists are to be listened to. Not that they all must speak with a common view, but that the speech at least be intelligible and conform to certain constructs.

A philosophy of holism is not a luxury idea—it is an essential requirement for the sustenance of medicine itself. It is toward the furtherance of this necessary fusion that this critique is offered.

Our goal is to answer the question: How can we live in the worlds of traditional *and* holistic medicine? How can we bring together the best of both into a form of health care that might provide us with something grander than either? Or are they qualitatively so different that miscibility is impossible? Are they worlds apart and impossible to fuse?

First, let's look at the fundamental propositions of each.

TRADITIONAL AND HOLISTIC MEDICINE: STRENGTHS AND WEAKNESSES

The traditional medical model hinges on what has been called the "molecular theory of disease causation." This theory states that the origin of all human illness—with no exception—is rooted in matter. When certain ab-normalities occur at the level of molecules, a reverberation occurs which is eventually felt at the level of the body. It is there that the human percep-tion of "illness" takes place.

For example, to use a common medical problem, if too many choles-terol molecules exist in the blood, a condition called hypercholesterol-emia—a major risk factor for heart attack—is said to exist. These molecules form deposits called atheromas in the lining of arteries in the heart and elsewhere in the body, a process called atherosclerosis, or "hardening of the arteries." This process leads directly to forms of therapy pitted against the cholesterol molecule—a low cholesterol diet, weight loss and exer-cise, and drugs (other molecules) designed to decrease the concentration of cholesterol in the blood.

The emphasis from the traditional approach is squarely on the material. Mind or psyche ordinarily does not enter as an important factor in the process.

Holistic medicine, on the other hand, asserts that illness cannot be un-derstood only in terms of material processes. For humans are best seen as wholes, not as parts, and part of the whole is the mind and the spirit, as well as the body. Focusing on the material facets of illness is shortsighted and incomplete. Consequently, therapy itself need not be physical. The point of therapeutic entry in any problem does not have to be via drugs or surgery but can utilize the effect of consciousness on the body—since the holistic position implicitly accepts that mind *does* act on the material, and that it is not merely affected *by* material happenings.

Each side, the traditional and holistic, has its unmistakable strengths. The molecular theory is patently demonstrable in the laboratory and in the clinical arena: cholesterol molecules *do* block arteries; if the blood con-centration of cholesterol is high, persons *do* develop heart attacks at alarm-ing rates; and other molecules, i.e. drugs, *can* lower the cholesterol level.

The appeal of the holistic position is also compelling. After all, it *seems* right to propose that mind and spirit count for something, a feeling which resonates through the inner experience of each of us. How could the holis-tic postulate be false if it is so uniformly consistent with human experience?

Each side, too, has its weaknesses. The molecular approach of tradi-tional medicine, continuing with the example of high cholesterol levels in the blood, is unable to account for the fact that the problem *does* have a psychological element. What the molecules do *is* affected, quite apparently, by mind. For example, as I have stated, the cholesterol level in certified public accountants, under pressure to finish income tax returns, may rise as much as 50 percent without any change in diet; abrupt rises are seen also in medical students before examinations. And, conversely, if men with high cholesterol levels are taught to sit quietly and clear the mind twice daily for short periods of time, the cholesterol level falls. Even the position that the genes are the ultimate materialistic determinant of illness and health does not seem to be the whole picture. In identical twins (who therefore have identical genes), it is invariably the one who has the greater degree of job stress who develops atherosclerosis. Clearly, then, mind seems to matter, and molecules, apparently, are not the sole cause.

(This conclusion can easily be brushed aside and the molecular theory be preserved, of course, by saying that mind itself is nothing more than the result of molecular behavior. This is the famous identity theory of the origin of mind, in which mind is said to have no fundamental status of its own. It is only the molecules behind the scene that count, expressing themselves in terms of anatomy, physiology, and biochemistry. According to this view, the above examples do not demonstrate any action of mind on matter, but merely matter interacting *with* matter.)

The weakness of the holistic school of thought is also glaring. Try as it may to ignore it, the sheer weight of the evidence showing that there *is* an enormous material component in all illness will simply not go away. For example, the genetic predisposition toward high cholesterol levels is plainly associated with a greater death rate from heart disease. While they may not tell the whole story, nonetheless, the numbers do not entirely lie: matter *does* matter. Moreover, while we can only speculate what the science of the future will reveal about the power of mind to influence health and illness, to date the movement of holistic medicine does not even come close to competing with traditional molecular medicine in demonstrating empirical-analytical proofs of its own contentions.

Both sides, traditional and holistic medical models alike, are incomplete. They have their compelling strengths, as well as their individual Achilles' heels. This fact alone, that neither model tells the whole picture, would suggest that a complementary approach might be wise. And the incompleteness of each should make us wary of anyone who would advise us to abandon one system in total acceptance of the other.

TRADITIONAL AND HOLISTIC MEDICINE: WHAT ARE THE GOALS?

Much of the confusion between these two systems comes from the fact that they have different goals. This may seem surprising—for do not both strive to bring about a cure, to make patients well? Overtly, yes, but what is meant by "health" is so different that the goals of the two systems can hardly be equated.

Consider the following advertisement from a holistic health care magazine for chelation therapy, a popular "alternative treatment" for atherosclerotic vascular disease, arthritis, and various other illnesses, wherein certain chemicals are injected into the bloodstream to remove injurious deposits from the blood vessel walls (the accuracy of this claim is not our concern here):

Chelation therapy removes harmful accumulations from your body's blood vessels. It restores natural blood flow to starved organs, restoring the energy balance and vitality to body and mind. Without good blood flow our energy fields are diminished. Chelation therapy reestablishes this balance, leading to proper functioning of body, mind, and spirit.

From the holistic perspective, this description is perfectly reasonable; it speaks to the "whole person," emphasizing the right relation of soma, psyche, and spirit. No matter that the chelating agent involved is a chemical; it purportedly transcends the actual material domain by evoking energy balance and, ultimately, spiritual harmony. For that reason, it is "holistic"—unlike, for example, surgery to bypass the same clogged arteries, a technique which simply focuses on the material.

Contrast this ad for chelation therapy with ads for two different drugs recently advertised in reputable medical journals. The caption for one says, "Feeling cured is one thing. Being cured is another," followed by the name of the drug in question. And, "Counseling may help her concerns, but (drug name) helps her condition."

The message implicit in these two drug ads is that the feelings, emotions, and concerns of the patient are for naught; it is the actual physical state of the body that counts. The mind is no index to cure, nor to health. It is the objective world of matter that is real, and it is this domain that is to be manipulated with drugs. There is no talk of "energy," "fields," nor "spirit" here. What really counts is what can be quantified and measured, which by definition is physical and not mental.

These comparisons could be multiplied endlessly but should be sufficient to prove a point. Traditionalists and holists live in two different worlds. They do not use the same concepts. Even though they may use the same words, such as "cure" or "health," they mean different things.

It is necessary to recognize and acknowledge these vast differences early on if one wants to extract the best of both systems. One *cannot* visit a traditional and holistic doctor and come away satisfied if the words used carry different meanings. What one physician means by "health" will likely be entirely different from the other. It is when patients or clients overlook these issues that confusion occurs. Aside from the obvious problem that these two types of healers frequently disagree about what causes the disease in the first place, or what to do about it, the most proximal and fundamental problem is that they are in different worlds as to what, even, disease *is*.

TRADITIONAL AND HOLISTIC MEDICINE: A CONSUMER'S GUIDE

In sorting out the claims made by the traditionalists and the holists—why the holists evoke the ire of the traditionalists for being scientifically undisciplined and why the holists rebuke the traditionalists for being spiritually desiccated—let's look at how each actually looks at the world.

To begin with, for purposes of this analysis, let us assume that the world around us can be divided into three levels—matter, mind, and spirit. This structure is by no means a scientific statement and would, in fact, be rejected by most scientists. But it will, I trust, be heuristically useful for our purpose here. It is essentially the same cartography that has been developed and used by Ken Wilber in his discussion of the "New Age Paradigm."[1] All the world's great religions are uniform in describing these basic strata in reality, although many, like the Hindu tradition (which describes seven levels), include many more.

As Wilber states, these general realms of matter, mind, and spirit are variously translated into other terms:

Subconscious, self-conscious, and superconscious, or instinct, reason, intuition, and so on. These three realms, for instance, have been explicitly mentioned by Hegel, Berdyaev, and Aurobindo.[2]

It is crucial to note that these formulations which bridge many spiritual and cultural traditions contain the idea of *hierarchy*—that is, these three levels of matter, mind, and spirit are not strictly equivalent. Higher levels cannot be fully explained in terms of lower levels. Matter, for example, is insufficient to completely explain mind, and spirit is somehow anterior to both.

All the lower is in the higher but not all the higher is in the lower. A three-dimensional cube contains two-dimensional squares, but not vice versa. And it is that "not vice versa" that creates hierarchy.[3]

Each level in our three-level scheme of reality stands on its own as a somewhat unified totality. Although it contains the levels below it (bodies contain minerals, for example), it does not contain nor subsume the levels above it (minerals do not contain bodies). But lower levels do *serve* higher levels and are part of them (water molecules are necessary to form bodies; mitochrondia are necessary parts of cells, etc.).

This kind of hierarchical structure, while it can be traced to many great religious traditions, is also thoroughly modern. Although the level of spirit might be deleted, this basic idea of hierarchical relatedness in the entire natural world, from subatomic particles to the biosphere, lies at the heart of general systems theory. This body of knowledge grew from the work of von Bertalanffy and others out of an attempt to understand the biological world and includes the same essential notion of patterning, layering, and relationship in a hierarchical mode.[4] It has recently been popularized by Arthur Koestler, who has proposed the word "holon" to describe the individual units that comprise each level.[5] The subcomponents, like the Roman god, Janus (who had a double face, front and back) look simultaneously upward and downward, being served by the function of "lower," less complex units, while serving in turn the more complex holons which lie "above." And Fritjof Capra has recently rendered a highly readable synthesis of systems theory, revealing clearly that the essential concepts of hierarchy extend beyond the biological world to the domain of the sociocultural.[6]

Importantly then, the levels of matter, mind, and spirit interact, *but are not equivalent*. This point cannot be stressed too emphatically and will emerge again in our discussion. There is nothing we know about the natural world that justifies our equating one level with others. Relatedness is *not* sameness. Matter is not mind, and neither is mind spirit. Minerals are *not* the "Mona Lisa," although paintings contain minerals and pigments. Without maintaining these distinctions the entire notion of hierarchy becomes meaningless. If the distinctions between levels are forgotten, "the hierarchy collapses," as Wilber aptly puts it, resulting in "pure pop mysticism" wherein everything is declared to be an undifferentiated, Jello-like blob, the "wow!/one!" vision. While this insight may give momentary bliss, it is a distorted one at worst and incomplete at best. It is inconsistent with the great mystical-religious visions of "the way things are," as the philosopher of religion Huston Smith puts it, and with certain modern views such as natural systems theory as well.

We come, then, to a view of the world in which at least three different strata can be seen—matter, mind, and spirit. Each layer is subsumed by those above it, and each higher level (with spirit here conceived as the highest) including all below it—*while not being the same as* those levels inferior to it.

Again, still following Wilber, we can observe that we have different ways of gaining knowledge of these three levels. When we want to know about the material world, the ways of logic and linear thinking, which science knows well, work best—the empirical-analytical frameworks of thought and analysis that have led to the technical prowess which allows us to probe this domain. But if we want to study the level of the mind or the psyche, microscopes and linear accelerators are not very helpful. Another mode of knowing is needed here—a knowledge of symbols and their meanings, an appreciation of all that is contained in the world of the inter-subjective discourse between humans. Here we are involved with meanings that go far beyond descriptions of the physical level. We can describe the behavior of humans and of electrons and can even use similar words— we can say, for example, that neither can be ultimately viewed in "isolation"—but eventually we must admit that such similarities do not identify humans and electrons as one and the same entities. If we try to describe ourselves in the technical language of science, which is wonderfully adapted for the material world, something gets left out. And that "something" is the ineffable essence that makes another mode of description mandatory when we talk about mind.

In the same way, another mode of knowing is appropriate for the level of spirit. Here not even the symbolic descriptions appropriate for the level of mind work very well. Here all words fail. Why? Somehow spirit seems ultimate, final, the highest realm of the hierarchy, all there is. And problems arise when we try to attach any description to the ultimate, because in so doing we automatically set something apart from it. By attaching attributes to the ultimate, we immediately create *opposite* qualities which it does not contain. But if it does not contain all, it is no longer the absolute nor the ultimate. In this way all attempts at describing the absolute ultimately fail; they come crashing in on us as a pile of word-rubble, visible for what they really are: *words*, not the real thing.

In spite of these difficulties, we still continue to struggle with the absolute, continually trying to define it with words. Who has not agonized as a child with such dilemmas as "Where did God come from?" or "Who made God?" All verbal attempts to grasp the ungraspable, however, lead to paradox—so that, in the end, we conclude nonsensically that God is both graspable *and* ungraspable, characterizable *and* uncharacterizable, seen and unseen, the one and the many. The attempt to shatter the reliance on symbols and verbal construction in trying to comprehend the level of spirit led, for example, the Buddhist master, when asked "What is the Tao?" to reply "A rotten head of cabbage!"

The problem with all characterizations of spirit is so acute that we can say with certainty that if we *have* used words to capture this level, we can rest assured we are describing something else. The confusion about the spirit is generated by our dogged insistence that, if we are simply clever enough and persistent enough, we *can* eventually find some verbal or symbolic key. Yet the only result can be a paradox—ingenious though it may be, it is a paradox nonetheless. But not even the most clever paradox is an apt description of spirit, for it too is mere words.

As Wilber states, "Spirit is not paradoxical. It is not characterizable at all."[7] Paradox is a quality belonging to the realm of language, therefore, and is not a quality of the spiritual domain itself.

We must rely, then, on a transverbal mode of gaining knowledge about the spiritual level of the world. This mode has been called by many names—contemplation, meditation, prayer, intuition. The point is that this is a different level of the world that requires a different mode of knowing—and that when empirical analysis or even words are used, what is being described is a *lower* level, and not the level of spirit.

Just as each lower level of being is included by each higher level (matter is included by mind, and mind is included by spirit), the corresponding ways of knowing are similarly related: intuition transcends but includes the symbolic, and the symbolic transcends but includes the empirical-analytical. The hierarchical quality applies, then, to the modes of knowing, as well as to the levels they describe.

We have dwelled at some length on these distinctions because, without some type of map, the territory of traditional and holistic medicine is hopelessly confusing. With a guide, it is easier to make sense of the debate.

THE MUTUAL ERROR OF HIERARCHY COLLAPSE

The most egregious mistake made in the debate between holistic and traditional medicine is that *both* sides "collapse the hierarchy," as Wilber puts it. The divisions of the world into the domains of matter, mind, and spirit are ignored by both sides—traditionalists and holists alike—and the appropriate ways of knowing about each level are all but forgotten. The problem, although it is calamitous in its consequences, is nonetheless subtle—for the collapse is in different directions: the traditionalists forcing the hierarchy to collapse "downward," so that everything becomes material, and the holists pushing it "upward," so that all becomes spirit or mind. The former mistake results in reductionism, the latter in some sort of therapeutic pan-psychism wherein mind or spirit is expected to be the Big Medicine in the Sky.

Each mistake is as naive as the other. Each system deals with the world primarily in either/or, black vs. white, terms. Each is oblivious to the delicate complexities that constitute the fabric of reality. Each tries to stake out the world according to its own special geometry, imposing its own grid on a world that cannot be forced into a one-dimensional conceptual mold. Each ignores the value of the other, trying to discredit its opposite as if engaged in an Armageddon of principles.

How does traditional medicine "collapse the hierarchy"? It does so by insisting that the origins of all disease lie deep within matter—and that, consequently, therapeutic strategies ought best to originate there, through matter acting on matter. Even psychiatric illness is largely a misnomer according to this way of thinking, since mind is merely an expression of chemistry, anatomy, and physiology. Thus, "talk therapy" for psychiatric problems, while certainly still in vogue, is frequently supplemented by an array of psychotropic drugs to "make it work better." And the thrust of modern psychiatry seems clearly in the direction of developing new drugs that are specific treatments for all mental disorders, just as lithium carbonate has proved to be invaluable as a treatment for manic-depression.

It isn't that this approach doesn't work. It is, in fact, astonishingly effective, as is attested to by open heart surgical techniques, chemotherapeutic cures of cancer, and immunizations with near-100 percent effectiveness. But it is incomplete. By collapsing the hierarchy, by forcing spirit and mind into the lowest level, that of the material, it denies not only the existence of man's highest qualities, but *it limits its own therapeutic effectiveness*.

For instance, by denying the legitimacy of the mental level, certain potent therapies are passed by as if they were nonexistent. Not only, for example, can men with elevated cholesterol blood levels lower them, as we saw above, by merely sitting quietly twice a day for brief periods, but the clotting of the blood can also be altered by mental means.[8] And the ability of the body's immune system to resist invasion by microorganisms and to combat cancerous changes is known to be affected by psychological events.[9] These kinds of observations are taken generally by traditionalists to be either meaningless or inconsequential, or they are ignored altogether. When they *are* recognized, they are frequently dismissed by saying that they are not manifestations of mind at all but are *physiological* events masquerading *as* mental.

As an example of the collapse of the hierarchy in action, consider the following excerpt from an interview with the great contemporary immunologist, Baruj Benacerraf, who shared the Nobel Prize in physiology and medicine in 1980.

> Interviewer: "A paper presented to the American Psychiatric Association offered preliminary evidence that the immune system of recent widowers showed marked reduction in function."
>
> Benacerraf: "Well, there are so many different things happening to a person at such a time. It is known that people who lose a mate tend to die earlier than those who have not suffered such a loss. But that could be for a variety of reasons. Their food intake may change. They may expose themselves to more colds. There may be nobody to give them love. I mean, what do we really know?" [10]

The purpose of pointing to Benacerraf's comment is not to disparage this great scientist but to illustrate how key observations from one level (here, the mental) are collapsed or reduced to a lower one (the material). To say that the shutdown of the immune system in widowers is due to poor eating habits or to exposure to more colds does not eliminate mind as a factor. It merely inserts another variable—here, nutrition or infections—in the mind-matter chain of connections. For one has to eventually ask, *why* did the widowers stop eating? *Why* did they change their behavior in a way that compromised their immune status? A mechanism is not the same thing as an explanation, for the reason that a "how" is not a "why." To insert more "hows" into the mind-body continuum merely makes the phenomenon of immune shutdown more complex but does *not* eliminate the psychological variable itself.

This way of reasoning, the way of reductionism, is not without benefit, as we acknowledged earlier. And the holists who wish to abandon "reductionism," as if it were some sort of evil, in favor of a type of "elevationism"—that is, reverse reductionism, are downright naive. Conceivably, poor nutrition and exposure to more respiratory infections *could* be eliminated in bereaved widowers to their benefit and increased longevity. In other words, one can usually, in any clinical situation, discover a therapeutic approach based along reductionistic lines that does have merit.

But still the problem of grief would remain—and *this* is the kind of problem overlooked in the reductionistic approach. For grief is patently more than colds and poor eating habits. It is a problem *at a different level of the hierarchy*, a level where traditional medicine is not used to looking, and where it feels ill at ease. When it does cast an eye at this level it is likely to follow a familiar strategy: grief is depression or anxiety—both of which have known chemical correlates in the brain. So—the hierarchy collapsed—let us prescribe antidepressant or tranquilizing medications.

If traditional medicine tends to structure solutions according to the lowest known realm, the material, the holists tend to structure it in the highest, that of spirit. The mistake is made in the other extreme. Physical problems become problems of spirit. When medicines are used, they should be "natural," if possible, for natural substances contain the "energy essences" that "resonate" with man's "spiritual energy patterns," whereas crass, synthetic drugs do not. *Non*material forms of healing become important—massage, music, words, meditation—because they help connect us with "the highest centers," which are "the source of all true healing." Since these approaches are hard to quantify in the empirical-analytical language of science, scientific analysis frequently becomes eschewed, even offensive; and in some circles it has become a sign of moral weakness to submit to ordinary medical methods.

If what has been said up to now has been followed, it requires only the slightest scrutiny to see some of the problems with the holistic scenario. The hierarchial levels of matter, mind, and spirit are allowed to melt into each other as if there were no distinctions whatsoever separating them. "Spirit"—which is not characterizable with words—becomes the equivalent of energy, vibrations, and the healing source. It can be apprehended not only through nonverbal intuition, but through material techniques (massage, for example) and, even, ingestion of roots, herbs, and other natural substances. As spirit melts into mind and mind into matter, the entire hodgepodge is then shoved into our conceptual refrigerator to emerge as a homogeneous, holistic Jell-o called "healing." And, if challenged, the adherents to such beliefs frequently respond with banalities, such as "What's wrong? Man is a continuum of body-mind-spirit. We are a 'whole.' That's what holistic medicine is all about!"

I have a reverence for the holistic philosophy, just as many wise holists have a deep respect for the best of traditional medicine. I do not know which is more offensive to the human spirit—the pop holism described above, or sterile reductionism. Both are distortions. Both are anemic versions of reality, an illegible shorthand of what humans are about.

SPIRITUAL HEALING

Is there any room in the hierarchical scheme for such an event as spiritual healing to occur? Or do the proposed levels rule out such a phenomenon?

First, let us recall a central concept of the matter-mind-spirit hierarchy. The lowest level, matter, is contained in mind, and the middle level, mind, is contained in the highest level, that of spirit. Each higher level influences what lies below and can be influenced by it, although it ultimately transcends the levels below it. In this view, since spirit is ultimately transcendent over matter and mind, we would expect it to "leave its tracks" in the mind, as Wilber puts it. And, similarly, we should expect mind to leave its tracks in matter, to influence the material. In fact, clinical medicine verifies this expectation. For example, mind *can* act on matter, as anyone can ascertain for himself by visiting a modern biofeedback laboratory where subjects routinely perform feats such as modifying heart rate, blood pressure, skin temperature, and skin conductance. Cardiac arrhythmias can be extinguished, regional blood flow can be radically affected, and brain wave patterns can be manipulated at will. But even though mind can influence what lies "under" it—i.e., the material domain—can spirit do the same for mind and matter, the levels which lie distal to it? The blunt question for health is: Is spiritual healing possible?

Even as I pose the question, I feel myself about to be investigated by the Committee for the Scientific Investigation of Claims of the Paranormal. This is a murky area in medicine, and I would be the first to admit it. My own way of thinking about it, as a physician, begins with St. Augustine's reminder: "Miracles do not happen in contradiction of nature, but in contradiction of what we know about nature."

From this point of view, "miracles" such as spiritual healing are not miracles at all. They are simply events that lie in the gaps of our understanding of the world.

Many of the therapeutic ploys we use today would at one time have appeared to be miracles. Consider immunizations. If someone in smallpox-infested Europe in the 1400s had suggested that this scourge could have been prevented by actually inoculating a susceptible human being with a similar disease from a cow, such a proposal would have been called a miracle had it worked. But work it did. It is no longer considered a miracle today, of course, because we have supplemented our knowledge with facts about antibodies, antigens, and the workings of our own immune system. Our sense of the miraculous seems to be inversely related to our knowledge about the world.

Spiritual healing then, if it exists (and I believe it does), may reflect a perfectly acceptable way for the world to behave. Its uniqueness may lie in direct proportion to our ignorance about "the way things are." My own inclination as a physician is to acknowledge it as a special form of healing, for I cannot dismiss as deranged all the persons who have written about this phenomenon and who have claimed to experience it themselves. I have little patience with the scientific critic who must condemn what he cannot explain, even though I respect the need to guard against the fatuous. We need to constantly remind ourselves that the best scientific minds also rejected the belief in meteorites and embraced the notion of the ether. It seems to me rank arrogance to suppose that we have exhausted nature's inventory of how healing occurs, and we ought to expect some surprises. Moreover, I suspect the "surprises" are all around us—masquerading as unexpected turns in the course of illness; the person with cancer who should have died but didn't; or, the person who should not have died but who did (if spiritual *healing* exists, spiritual *sickness* is to be expected). There are those who have written wisely on the subject of spiritual healing, such as Weber, Kunz, and LeShan. My purpose in raising the issue of spiritual healing here is to suggest that it is an event not only expected by the hierarchical way of looking at the world, but is *demanded* by that very structure.

Some persons will object to the use of an hierarchical scheme, such as the one proposed here, to explore healing. The reductionistic objection will be that it introduces what is unnecessary—mind, to say nothing of spirit. After all, only the molecules are needed to explain human health and illness. However, many of the wisest founders of modern reductionistic science have believed otherwise, such as the great Rudolf Virchow, the founder of the science of pathology, who said, "Much illness is a conflict in values sailing under a psychological flag."[11]

The holists, on the other hand, may object that the insertion of levels may sunder man's "oneness and unity." I suggest that what is most likely to be sundered by a rational map of the territory of reality is not man's oneness and unity with the cosmos but the undisciplined, sloppy metaphysics that have defiled the perfectly legitimate philosophy of holism, and which has greatly distorted the disciplined thinking that has always lain at the heart of the great mystical paths. Without a clearer vision of what holistic medicine is all about, we will end up reinforcing the chasm separating the traditional physicians who today are struggling to fashion a more humanistic and encompassing model of health, and those holists who understand not only the deep tenets of holism but who sense the best of materialistic medicine as well.

Alan Watts once spoke of using psychedelic drugs, "When you get the message, you hang up the phone." In holistic medicine we have had our blissful "Oh, Wow!" phone message. It's time to hang up the phone. It's time to make a map, a model, a path; it's time to chart the territory. It's time to go to work—not by expending more energy foolishly, but by fashioning a discipline of right thinking and right doing. And we do not have to start anew: there is an enormous reservoir of value in traditional medicine on the one hand, and there is the wisdom of the great religious and spiritual traditions to draw from on the other.

SPIRIT: BEYOND HEALTH AND ILLNESS

What is frequently ignored by the pop holism movement is that, in the "body-mind-spirit" composite that is used to refer to man, spirit is radically *beyond* health. It includes all qualities, because it is subject to no dualisms. It is, thus, healthy *and* unhealthy, and is, paradoxically, all other sets of contrasts we can devise.

One gets the idea from the lofty "spiritualese" language of many holistically oriented persons that man's spirit sits on top of the body-mind-spirit triad in benevolent concern for our health. "It" always sets things right (if only mind and body are not too obstreperous to listen), for its natural state is healthiness. "Spirit" in this view is antithetical to illness, disease, and death. It eschews peptic ulcers, high blood pressure, herpes, and cancer. If only we can "get in touch" with our "higher center," we can lay claim to not only spiritual bliss but perfect health as well. I believe the perennial philosophy is uniform in rejecting such an idea.* To say that spirit contains all things is not the same as saying that it adores health. When we dress spirit in such garb we are merely making it a puppet of mind—injecting mental and anthropomorphic concerns where they simply do not belong. For it is the mind, not spirit, which prefers clean coronary arteries to clogged ones, and to talk about physical health and spiritual enlightenment in the same breath is to collapse the hierarchy again, so that meaningful distinctions between psyche, soma, and spirit become blurred beyond recognition.

After all, there are distinct clues that an ideal state of health is *not* an inevitable accompaniment to spiritual enlightenment. If one reads, for example, Evelyn Underhill's great treatise, *Mysticism*,[12] which deals with the

*The perennial philosophy, as Aldous Huxley described, is a remarkably consistent body of spiritual wisdom appearing repeatedly in many cultures throughout history. (See Aldous Huxley, *The Perennial Philosophy*. N.Y.: Harper, 1970.)

perennial philosophy of the West, one is struck by the fact that the mystics are frequently a sickly lot—their physical health sometimes appearing in direct *dis*proportion to their spiritual health. And even today, when health care is more readily available and nutrition is far better than in the medieval times about which Underhill wrote, well-known mystics still seem to garner their share of maladies. Presumably, if perfect enlightenment and perfect health were to go together, the enlightened mystic should never die. If we pair this observation with the obvious fact that many spiritually bankrupt persons seem to live enormously long and illness-free lives, it seems that we face on every hand an incontrovertible lesson: It is not the business of spirit to supervise our physical health, and spiritual health is no guarantee of physical well-being.

Obviously, though, many persons do experience a sense of vitality, energy, and psychophysical enhancement on traversing their spiritual paths, and I have no doubt that major physical problems do occasionally fall away in the course of one's spiritual progress. Yet these wonderful events seem almost an aside—a grace, as it were—to the ultimate goal of spiritual enlightenment. If one scrutinizes the disregard which many great mystics demonstrate for health, it seems that, at some point on the spiritual path, pressing concerns about physical health are discarded and health care in the ordinary sense becomes irrelevant. Yes, health may indeed flower at such times—but what is more likely is that a *sense* of healthiness supervenes which goes beyond the presence or absence of pain or suffering, disease or infirmity. Ordinary indices of health—whether heart disease, cancer, or high blood pressure—simply fall into no consequence. *This* is the healthiness of the spirit, and it *includes* both illness and death as crucial parts of it.

This view of how spiritual health and physical health are related is altogether different from the "holistic" insistence that perfect spiritual awareness leads to the discarding of crutches, the abandonment of hearing aids, and the melting away of cancers. Such a view is actually not holistic at all—because it sets certain qualities such as illness, disease, and infirmity apart from the ultimate, creating dualisms that are contrary to wholeness.

Actually, even to characterize the ultimate as "ultimate" or "whole" commits the same error, let us admit—for it suggests that there are qualities not possessed by the ultimate. Having recognized this linguistic booby trap, however, we can continue to use language to talk about the ultimate and about spirit, hopefully being wise enough to avoid being deceived in the process.

There is another fallacy hidden in the desire to link spiritual and physical well-being. When some things are done purposefully or from a desire for gain, they simply do not work. For example, the best way to frustrate one's efforts in meditation is to meditate for a reason. Meditation becomes fruitful partly when one gives up purpose and desire, even the desire to meditate well. Like the attempt at pulling oneself up by one's bootstraps, sometimes active effort backfires; it is only through "letting go" that results come about. This is nowhere truer than in biofeedback laboratories where the active attempt to "make it happen" on the biofeedback monitor instruments dooms one to poor performance, and where simply not trying, or a state of "passive volition," works best. This is the "doing by not doing" philosophy that bedevils the ordinary Western mind addicted to the "go for it!" attitude.

In the same way, undertaking spiritual endeavors *for the purpose of physical enhancement* is likely to lead nowhere. For as long as one holds in the back of the mind that the cancer may be cured if only I can achieve enlightenment, a core of *desire* will remain—and the spiritual paths of all cultures would have us cast away all desire before the path can be traversed, even the desire to be healthy. Linking the desire for physical health to the task of spiritual enlightenment, therefore, is hopeless. We can begin to realize that only through a "noneffort" of "purposelessness," a doing by not doing, can we associate the goal of bodily healthiness to that of spiritual healthiness.

Physical health, if it cannot be *attained* by active effort, somehow must already *be*—and this is the vision that many mystics have given us. It is a vision that surprises us initially, for in it the meaning of health itself undergoes a transformation. It escapes a dualistic structuring, is seen to be tied hand-in-glove to illness, and cannot be separted from it.

Health and illness, when illuminated by spiritual light, are beheld for what they are: the moving principles of each other. No longer are they seen as eternal opposites engaged in titanic conflict. *This* is the sense in which spirit includes all below it in the hierarchical perspective we have been following. Spirit disallows nothing—including pain, suffering, infirmity— for on close scrutiny these hideous qualities of life are bound intrinsically to their opposites in a way in which opposition is transcended. When this is seen, spiritual health *does* include physical health—having, however, absolutely nothing to do with longevity, disease, and disability.

The mystical teacher and writer, Tarthang Tulku, once said, "Complete health and awakening are really the same." His words reflect, I feel, the conclusion we have come to above. At some fundamental level, health *is*. It is not a state to be attained through immunizations, exercise, blood pressure control, or diet. It has nothing whatsoever to do with the patency of one's coronary arteries. Health exists as a state which cannot be sundered by the appearance of cancer nor the eruption of a heart attack. It is a ground state, a state of wholeness which excludes nothing. It is lodged *in* spirit; it is subsumed *by* spirit. And the knowledge of health is made possible by spiritual awareness.

It may be objected that this view of health is so ethereal as to be useless, and that to suggest that health is some sort of ground state in which we all have our roots is rank mystical moonshine. It ignores the hunger, suffering, and death that are all around us. What is worse, it leads to self-deception and neglect of health and actually perpetuates disease. It is, thus, inhumane.

But there is nothing in this view that leads to a paralysis of our commonly accepted norms of health care. In my judgment, to the contrary, it may actually empower our efforts toward health. A comment by a modern mystic, Sri Aurobindo, may make this clear:

> It is necessary, therefore, that advancing knowledge should base herself on a clear, pure and disciplined intellect. It is necessary, too, that she should correct her errors, sometimes by a return to the restraint of sensible fact, the concrete realities of the physical world. The touch of Earth is always reinvigorating to the Sons of Earth. . . . It may even be said that the superphysical can only be mastered in its fullness . . . when we keep our feet firmly on the physical.[13]

Let us acknowledge that we *are* sons and daughters of the earth, and that we *do* have access to advancing knowledge of the earth we stand on. The scientific approach to understanding physical disease, based on the empirical-analytical dissections of the world, has yielded valuable insights. We *can* prevent polio, cure certain forms of cancer, and extend life. We *should* not, we *need* not, abandon the use of these tools and take refuge in the balmy, pop notion that "all is health" just because "all is one." Starving children and pain and suffering are facts of the material domain, and all the pious musing about oneness and unity will not make them any less real. As Sri Aurobindo said, we *do* touch the earth—an earth sometimes littered with thorns and barbs, and sometimes with disease.

The world of traditional medicine, thus, can continue to be used. Matter *can* act on matter, as the action of drugs and surgery on the body attest. But as we continue to use them, perhaps it can be from a less desperate posture than before. We do not need to continue to declare our interminable presidential wars on cancer and heart disease, as if we were facing some ultimate deadline. We need not be consumed by urgency and panic.

We can act on the material level much more sanely and wisely if our efforts are suffused with an understanding of the higher level of spirit, of the interpenetration of health and illness—if we know, to borrow Huston Smith's phrase, "the ways things are."

In matters of health, we become what we fear most. There is something pathetic about the person whose dread of aging or becoming ill leads him to consume dozens of vitamin pills a day, to drive his body to endless exercise, and to always look backward to make sure disease is not gaining. No matter that his physical examination is perfect, that his cholesterol level is admirable, and that his height and weight and body fat ratios are in balance. Living in the shadow of the fear of illness, he can never be his healthiest, for he is driven by something he does not control, his anxiety about his own mortality.

Such a person—and our society teems with such "health addicts"—is motivated as much by a fear of physical degeneration as by love of health. He structures his idea of health on the bottom rung of the ladder we have been using—on the hierarchical level of the material. Proper *physical* function—that's what health is all about.

But health in the hierarchical perspective of body-mind-spirit goes beyond the bottom rung. It includes, but transcends, blood pressure readings and cholesterol values. In the most radical sense, this view of health is *trans*physical.

It is not that our fictitious health addict, whose attention is focused solely on the physical, need abandon his discipline of self-care if he were to enlarge his perspective. It would demand, though, that he relinquish his grim imperative of health and his unconscious loathing of illness and aging and eventual death. His efforts in the larger view would become enriched with a deeper wisdom that health and illness, like inside and outside, are inseparable; and that the more actively one seeks to drive illness from one's sight the more acutely visible it becomes. He would understand that the acceptance of the ground that includes both health and illness enriches his experience of health and does not diminish it, as he feared. He would learn that to experience the quintessence of health he must paradoxically open himself to health's moving principles, disease and death.

There is the utmost squeamishness in holistic health care circles about doing this. Often the holistic philosophy seems just as tenaciously dedicated to emphasizing *only* health and exorcising illness as the orthodox methods of health care. What this leads to is mere trade-offs in techniques, with little advance in understanding and wisdom. "Natural" becomes preferable to "synthetic," "vitamins" are chosen over "drugs," and surgery and irradiation become abominations acceptable only as last resorts. Entirely new therapies emerge with little or no scientific base, whose legitimacy seems dependent primarily on the fact that they stand in sharp contrast to existing methodology. But this kind of "holistic" medicine is mainly a smokescreen, just another set of techniques as much a travesty of the deep meaning of the holistic hierarchical structure of reality as the existing methods. And at least orthodox methods make no pretense of their motives: they are admittedly based on the physical rung of the ladder; they strive to be empiric and analytic in their scientific base; and, in fact, owe their strength to this goal. And although holists can fret and grumble about the limitations of a vision that would focus mainly on the physical, nonetheless such an approach can point to spectacular achievements. Even those who object to its anemic definitions of man are themselves recipients of its benefits—usually well-immunized, well-nourished, and air-conditioned—evidence that modern medicine is not as hideous as it is sometimes portrayed.

The holistic health care movement has almost become a nonending cornucopia of new techniques whose conceptual basis leaves analytical critics baffled, with imprecise jargon such as "energy" and "vibrations." Yet the deepest power of holistic health care will never come from merely trading old methods for new, no matter if they are more "hands on" and compassionate and caring. At issue is not, even, whether such techniques work better than orthodox drugs or surgery, but that the essence of holism *does not come from technique*—and it is this fact which has yet to permeate the holistic health care movement.

It makes no ultimate difference from the perspective of the perennial philosophy whether we relieve pain by giving an injection of morphine or whether we massage our acupuncture points in an effort to release an endogenous burst of pain-killing endorphin chemicals in our brain. Both are examples of matter acting on matter—although one technique is called orthodox and the other is called holistic. It does not even matter from the perennial perspective whether we use meditation, biofeedback, autosuggestion, or hypnosis to eradicate pain—events which express the relationship between body and mind, the bottom *two* rungs of our hierarchical ladder. All these methodologies are still techniques, whether orthodox or holistic or "new age." The perennial philosophers would say ultimately that the pain we are experiencing may be dealt with in *any* way that works—but that, at the top rung of the ladder, the hierarchical level of spirit, a new level of understanding supervenes. "Pain" becomes something altogether different than the noxious sensation which we knew at the physical-sensory level and different from the way we perceived it at the mental level where we invested it with dark, symbolic meaning. At the level of spirit we transcend these material and mental investments, and pain loses its absoluteness as something sinister, as something other-than-pleasure. Pain "hurts" at the level of spirit, but it "not hurts" too—for it is at this level where, when opposites fuse and dualisms crumble, paradox reigns. Here the blind rush to escape pain and suffering abates—not that we cannot act to relieve pain, but that as we do so we see pain transformed into something other than the malevolent quality which threatened our psychological and material balance at the lower levels of being.

This perspective is, again, transphysical and transmental. It is holistic because it emphasizes all the levels of our being—the material, the mental, and the spiritual. By and large, this transphysical and transmental view has not been grasped by the holistic health care movement, and, although I do not doubt that there are wise adherents to the movement who understand these distinctions thoroughly, I fear that the movement is largely playing the game of orthodox medicine—the game of technique and method, albeit in a new guise. I realize, too, that any new movement in medicine never springs to life fully formed and in full philosophical flower. The holistic health care movement is no exception. It needs time and nurturing if it is to mature into the role it espouses for itself, that of a medicine which speaks to the whole person. These criticisms are offered, therefore, as an attempt to help in the maturational process.

My wish for the holistic health care movement is that it not reject the empirical-analytical methods of modern science, for bodies *can* be made healthier through applying the fruits of modern bioscience, as has been shown. I view it as alarming that some holists seem to reject anything that smacks too strongly of "left brain," a term frequently used to refer to the logical side of ourselves. I believe such an approach is naive and is itself a betrayal of the concept of the whole man. I urge the movement to use the scientific method unflinchingly in scrutinizing its own therapies and to cease hiding behind the recurring excuse that some holistic therapies, although they exert physical effects, may ultimately be too ethereal to nail down.

And, after all, it is empirical science that has yielded vast insights into the interconnectedness of mind and body, discoveries which serve as conceptual pillars of the holistic philosophy. Thus I am convinced that a rejection of science's methods will maim the holistic health care movement severely and retard the attainment of its goals.

CAN HOLISTIC HEALTH SUCCEED?

Why not continue to focus on a medicine for man's psyche and soma and leave the spiritual domain to the mystics? Why try to make it part of medicine?

First, for the reason that medicine should speak to all of man and not to some truncated version of him. And, most importantly, charts to the territory already exist. They exist in the rich legacy of the *philosophia perennis*, the records of the mystics of all the world's great spiritual traditions— that group of humans who, as Evelyn Underhill stated, "all come from the same country and speak the same language." It is the consistency and the depth of this knowledge that gives us reason to believe that it can become part of medicine.

Wilber has rightly described a community of experts that exists at both levels—the level of spirit and the level of matter. The spiritual scholars we call mystics, adepts, bodhisattvas, saints, etc., constitute this body of experts on the level of the spirit. And the scholars who know best how to scrutinize the material level we call scientists. In each case they form a body of critics who know the rules of the game in their respective domains. As evidence accumulates, whether of the material world or of the spiritual world, it is this community of scholars who pass judgment on it. At each level, if the data which is fed in is weak, the quality of evolving knowledge is weak: If the quality of the "referees" is poor, the quality of their judgments will similarly suffer. These problems exist in both the domains of science and spirituality. The point is that similar rules of scrutiny and discipline operate at both the levels of spirit and matter.

Thus a discipline *can* be maintained if a spiritual element is injected into medicine in an effort to devise something we do not now have, a truly holistic medicine. No matter that the rules of spirit are intuitive and transsensory; no matter that they are not the empirical-analytical methods which scientists would use to make sense of the material end of medicine's spectrum. There are many ways to gain knowledge of the world, as we have seen, just like there are different kinds of geometry, all of which operate according to repeatable, predictable, affirmable, and validatable principles.

HOLISM, YES; HEALTH, MAYBE

As physical health on the material level becomes equated with spiritual health ("take spirulina for health *and* enlightenment"), problems accumulate quickly. The most obvious one stems from the fact that the whole (spirit) contains all possible known parts, but the part (the material) does not contain the whole. Spirit *is*. The higher Self *is*. It cannot be developed or acquired, as can immunity to measles. As Sri Ramana Maharshi stated,

There is no reaching the Self. If Self were to be reached, it would mean that the Self is not here and now but that it has yet to be obtained. What is got afresh will also be lost. So it will be impermanent. What is not permanent is not worth striving for. So I say the Self is not reached. You *are* the Self; you are already That.[14]

On the contrary, most of us see health on the material level as something that has to be constantly coddled or it will fall apart. But Spirit cannot deteriorate like material health. It does not need booster shots or annual exams. It simply is. So we should be wary of equating spiritual health with bodily health for the reason that we are dealing with two distinct ontologic levels and two different levels of knowing.

On the other hand, there *is* a perfectly valid way of linking physical and spiritual health. It has to do with the concept of "no-health," described in Part I, Chapter 2. It is the recognition that longevity, absence of pain and suffering, and illness are inconsequential to health. It is not the collapse of one ontologic level onto another, nor the fusion of one mode of knowing into another, but the recognition that Spirit subsumes and includes all. Higher health, or no-health, is *trans*material (beyond the body) and *trans*mental (beyond the psyche). But this distinction is rarely made explicit by holistic health advocates who incessantly urge that one take this or that, or do this or that, to *achieve* a higher state of health. The highest stage of health cannot be *won*, or wrested from nature, nor kept from deteriorating into illness. Like Spirit, higher health or no-health *is*.

And like spirit, no-health or higher health is not in time or space. It is the all-at-once and the everywhere-at-once. As such, how can it be reached, achieved, or attained, since, being outside of time and space, it is already here at this very moment? And how can higher health be cared for, since, being beyond time, it can never fall apart? Falling apart implies process and thus linear time. But what is beyond linear time is not subject to process. Thus, for higher health, health *care* does not exist. It needs no health insurance, for it does not fail. It is perfection, for it is unmoved by the perturbations and vicissitudes that rock the world of material health. In the domain of higher health, Blue Cross has no subscribers.

The failure to distinguish between these two modes of health—pure bodily health and transmaterial and transpsychological health—has led to confusion in the holistic ranks. The point here is that the holistic health care movement cannot have it both ways. It cannot speak incessantly about "highest health and enlightenment" in the same breath and keep its feet planted solidly in the domain of the material body—with its endless array of prescriptions for diet, exercise, vitamins, relaxation, and God knows what. For these are accoutrements appropriate to enhancement of physical health; and as appropriate as they may be for that level, not even the greatest feat of the imagination will alchemically turn matter into spirit nor bodily health into spiritual health. Again spiritual health *is*; it is not something made from something else. Ken Wilber's words about the Absolute apply to perfect health:

> And so it is important to realize that since the Absolute is already one with everything everywhere, we can in no way manufacture or attain to our union with It. No matter what we do or don't do, try to do or try not to do, we can never attain It. In the words of Shankara:
> "As Brahman constitutes a person's Self, it is not something to be attained by that person. And even if Brahman were altogether different from a person's Self, still it would not be something to be attained; for as it is omnipresent it is part of its nature that it is everpresent to everyone." [15]

And still the temptation must be resisted over and over, that of turning "higher health" which exists at the spiritual level into "perfect health" at the material, bodily level—a trap into which many a holist has fallen. For we are wont to say that with spiritual perfection comes physical perfection—which again is the superposition of the highest level of being, the spiritual, onto the lowest level, the material. It cannot be stated too strongly nor too frequently that many a sickly mystic has existed, as has many a healthy, unenlightened spiritual profligate. Perfect bodily health is *not* given out with spiritual enlightenment like so many Green Stamps, a bonus for being good or for "making it." Higher health cares not a whit for (although it includes) numerical values of the cholesterol level, the amplitude and frequency of one's brainwaves, or the duration spent in twitchless relaxation. It is radically and fundamentally beyond all such measures of the flesh.

The temptation must be firmly resisted to equate the highest physical health with satori, enlightenment, or liberation. The same transformational rules *do not apply* to physical states and spiritual states. While it is true that *physical* conditioning can be achieved, that high blood pressure can be lowered, or that better cardiopulmonary performance can be developed, the same is *not* true for spirit. Spirit cannot be conditioned. It cannot be developed like one's aerobic capacity for exercise. If it were capable of improvement, Spirit would not be ultimate. It would not be the highest state—for there would be yet a higher level to which it would be inferior, to which it had yet to attain. But Spirit is all. There are no levels that lie beyond it. It is not "pre" anything. It is not "in training" for some higher state. As such, nothing lies outside it—including, let us always remind ourselves, poor physical health.

That is why the highest spiritual state is patently *not* the same as perfect physical health. The domains are different—because one is ultimate and excludes nothing, while one (the physical) does not. That is why we have seen and continue to see mystics die young, and why great spiritual masters contract tuberculosis, intestinal parasites, hemorrhoids, and athlete's foot like the rest of us—and why they also laugh about it. And that is why we should not be deceived into thinking that, just because a great leader *does* live to Methuselean old age, he did so *because* of his spiritual achievement. For he is beyond time, outside of it, where all considerations of longevity fall away to nothing.

This realization is frequently encountered by persons who confront death and dire physical illness. In extreme states of disease, or in actual physical danger when death seems imminent, a clarifying vision frequently unfolds so that one does feel, at least for the moment, outside of durational time. Longevity's concerns melt away, and the pervading sensation is an all-at-once, nonlinear temporal awareness. Even the disease itself is seen in a radically different way, as if it didn't matter—a nuisance and a bother, at most—something of utterly no moment. I do not believe these moments are products of deranged minds or of compromised mental faculties, for in some cases the faculties actually seem sharpened, as in the case of the person in grave physical peril. I think it more likely that the habitual, time-worn ways of thought fall away as so many constraining inhibitions so that the world, and one's place in it, can be sensed more clearly. Accounts in such cases reveal a sense of "is-ness," of timelessness, that is part of the domain of spirit we have been speaking about.

It is to this domain that higher health belongs. Because it is outside time, all elements of dread, suffering, pain, and fear take on different complexions. In the timeless domain of Spirit and higher health there is no place for the dark emotions we associate with physical ill health and disease—fear, depression, anxiety, and worry about what is to come—because there is, quite simply, *no* "to come."

Seen from this perspective, higher health is now. It is now because it is timeless. It is not something in the future, not something to be attained. And, also, it is every*where*. It is, thus, at all places at all times. As such, one cannot escape it. One cannot hide from it, since there is no place and no time it is not. It is here and now, and it belongs, like it or not, to everyone. It is in you, now.

This is the most shocking lesson of all, how we—with our bursitis, spastic colons, dandruff, heart disease, cancer—can possibly possess higher health. The acquisition of higher health is not an acquisition, we must continually remind ourselves. There is no effort to be expended. There is, even, nothing to achieve in terms of an increasing awareness—for this would simply be attainment in another form, that of attaining something through understanding. For events which lie beyond space and time, no attainment is possible.

Rest assured, therefore, that Perfect Health is your birthright, one which you cannot possibly renounce. Perfect Health is you, and it is now—just before it's time for your next pill . . .

"ARE YOU A HOLISTIC PHYSICIAN?"

One of the oddest questions I am ever asked as a physician is, "Are you a holistic doctor?" The question invariably comes from persons seeking more than the sterile, impersonal offerings of traditional medicine. They seek attention to their "whole," not just their parts. Although I realize this admirable goal underlies their question, I always wish it had been put differently.

The plain fact is that, if the underlying principles of the philosophy of holism are true, it is impossible to *not* be a holistic physician. Holism, as applied to the body, implies that one cannot understand the function of humans by attention solely to the operation of their basic parts, be they electrons, atoms, molecules, cells, or organs. Such an approach does not tell the entire tale. A vital extension of this notion is that consciousness or mind is inextricably part of body, so intimately connected with our own matter that the suggestion that they can be separated leads to errors in judgment. How could one treat *other than* the whole, if it is, in fact, indivisible? It is impossible to *not* treat the whole because of the unseverable connections between body parts, mind, and consciousness. To even suppose that there is such a thing as a nonholistic physician is to suggest that there are persons to whom the principles of holism do not apply—a possibility which, I believe, does not exist.

What is meant, I feel, when this question is asked, is not "Are you a holistic doctor?" but "How deeply do you sense the principles of holism, and to what extent do you attempt to implement them in your own practice of medicine?" For no doctor has ever "just" treated body parts, no matter how vigorously he may claim to have done so. It is even arrogant to suppose that as a physician, through the mere choice of my practice style, I could send the mighty principle of holism packing, banishing its applicability to *my* patients. Holism does not wait on me to call it into being, nor can I violate its existence through my own ignorance or stupidity. I can only cooperate with it, or fail to cooperate with it. In either case, holism *is*, and the most I can say as a physician is that I attempt to allow its ramifications to flower in my own practice of medicine, or I do not. But I do not have the choice of *being* a holistic physician or *not being* one; it is only my cooperation with this pervasive principle that is a matter of degree.

CONCLUSION

Consciousness progresses . . . from limited to wider, from lower to higher dimensions, and each higher dimension includes the qualities of the lower, i.e., it incorporates them into a higher system of relations. . . . Therefore the criterion of the consciousness or cognition of a higher dimension consists in the coordinated and simultaneous perception of several directions of movement within a wider unity, without destroying those individual features which had characterized the lower dimensions thus integrated.

It is important to stress this, for nothing would be more dangerous than a frivolous throwing over-board of the normal logical thinking appropriate to our world, in favor of seemingly profound paradoxes, as has become the fashion in some intellectual movements of our time. . . . Until we have achieved a clear dimensional world it is useless to be occupied with a higher dimension (whose substructure is represented by those laws). *We must first have reached the limits of our thinking before we are qualified to transcend them.* (italics added)[16]

Lama Govinda's words are worth emphasizing because of the tendency in some circles to suppose that "holistic" somehow means "nonlogical." This finds expression in the tendency to believe that unless a health care intervention is somewhat strange and ethereal, it isn't or could not possibly be holistic. "Logical" is a characteristic of orthodox, traditional medicine, not that of the holistic variety, and is thus the source of many of our troubles in medicine—increasing depersonalization, inhumane approaches to patients and persons, etc. We should abandon, or at least minimize, the strictly logical approaches to health care, therefore, if we want to re-humanize medicine. In a stronger version, "logical" is equated with "scientific," "scientific" is equated with the cold, the impersonal, the inhumane. Logical thinking, then, in holistic medicine is to be deemphasized in favor of paradox, intuitive modes of knowing, and nonlinear thought.

Lama Govinda's words (which are those of a mystic and a scholar of the first order) tell us that this attitude is shortsighted. For the higher, more holistic modes of thinking do not discard the logical and lower and more limited forms of knowing the world, they *include* them. There is no short-cut to the intuitive, the mystical. The knowledge of the heavenly must include the knowledge of the terrestrial. If this were *not* the case, then the realm of the mystical, the intuitive, would *not* be holistic—it would be a limited form of understanding, and would lose all claim to being called the whole.

I do not believe, then, that the path to more holistic forms of medicine can ride roughshod over the logical, calculated, linear and analytical-empirical ways of understanding health and illness that typify modern medicine. I have no sympathy with the urgings that we discard our rational faculties and "wing it" with intuition. There is no reason why we should ever substitute a "Trust me, this works" pitch to our patients for an approach which says, "Let me *show* you *why* you can trust this therapy." Intuition and higher forms of knowing, as Lama Govinda tells us, if uninformed by lower, "normal logical" means of perception, are not higher at all. They are a confusion, a lower state of knowing instead of a higher, and will never serve to advance the cause of a truly holistic medicine.

This means that we should neither totally substitute intellectual forms of knowing for spiritual forms, or subvert the intellectual mode of wisdom with an approach that is totally spiritual in quality. The correct approach is to know the applicability and the limitations of each. We must wisely choose *how* we know.

The proper balance of these two modes of knowing is stated by the physicist Ravi Ravindra:

Another extremely consequential aspect of the modern scientific procedures is that whatever is investigated is in principle capable of being subjected to control and manipulation by the scientists-technologists. The subject matter under investigation may be an elementary particle, or another culture, or human mind, or extra sensory perception; the general scientific attitude is of manipulation and control. What does this insistence on control and manipulation amount to in knowing something? Does it not guarantee that we cannot know, by these methods, anything subtler or more intelligent than we, anything that is higher than we are, if such a being, or force is not susceptible to our control? If scientists speak of lacking evidence of anything higher than man, that is to be expected, for their procedures specifically preclude the possibility of such evidence.[17]

Just so, the richness and diversity inherent in the concept of holistic health demand more than one mode of knowing. A *discipline* of knowing is called for, the implementation of which will hopefully lead to the full flowering of a medicine for the whole of man.

NOTES

1. Ken Wilber, *Eye to Eye* (New York: Doubleday, 1983), pp. 155–189.
2. *Ibid.*, p. 162.
3. *Ibid.*
4. For a thorough discussion of general systems theory, see James Grier Miller, *Living Systems* (New York: McGraw-Hill, 1978).
5. Arthur Koestler, *Janus: A Summing Up* (New York: Random House, 1978), pp. 27ff.
6. Fritjof Capra, *The Turning Point* (New York: Simon and Schuster, 1982).
7. Wilber, "Reflections on the New Age Paradigm—an Interview," in *Eye to Eye*, pp. 155ff.
8. E. R. Gonzalez, "Constricting Arteries Expand Views of Ischemic Heart Disease," *Journal of the American Medical Association*, 25 Jan. 1980: pp. 309–316.
9. S. J. Schleifer et al., "Suppression of Lymphocyte Stimulation Following Bereavement," *Journal of the American Medical Association* 250 (1983): p. 374.
10. Baruj Benacerraf, an interview, *OMNI*, July 1983: p. 107.
11. Naomi Remen, *The Human Patient* (Garden City, N.Y.: Anchor Press/Doubleday, 1980), p. 107.
12. Evelyn Underhill, *Mysticism* (New York: E. P. Dutton, 1961).
13. Lawrence LeShan, *The Medium, the Mystic, and the Physicist* (New York: Viking, 1966), p. 283.
14. A. Osborne, ed., *The Collected Works of Ramana Maharshi* (London: Rider, 1959).
15. Wilber, *Eye to Eye*, pp. 298–299.
16. Lama Govinda, "Logic and Symbol in the Multi-dimension Conception of the Universe," *The American Theosophist* 69 (November 1981): p. 288.
17. Ravi Ravindra, "Science and the Mystery of Silence," *The American Theosophist* 70 (November 1982): pp. 354–355.

XII

*The Wounded Healer**

Although life is an affair of light and shadows, we never accept it as such. We are always reaching towards the light and the high peaks. From childhood, . . . we are given values which correspond only to an ideal world. The shadowy side of real life is ignored. Thus [we] are unable to deal with the mixture of light and shadow of which life really consists; [we] have no way of linking the facts of existence to [our] preconceived notions of absolutes. The links connecting life with universal symbols are therefore broken, and disintegration sets in.

—Miguel Serrano
C. J. Jung and Herman Hesse: A Record of Two Friendships

In the treatment process, something happens to the clinician as well as to the patient (e.g., fear, distancing, anger, frustration, joy, satisfaction, etc.). Frequently, [there occur] defensive maneuvers on the part of the clinician to avoid confronting the emotions and memories which the patient evokes . . . in the clinician. In shutting out a part of the patient, we also close off access to an important part of ourselves. We can grow emotionally (if painfully) with our patients . . . if we can see beyond surgical "repair," patient "compliance," or drug "efficacy." Not that these latter are unimportant: but what whole are they a part of? What happens to us is as important as what happens to our patients. Indeed, what we allow ourselves to experience, both in ourselves and in our patients, decisively determines our diagnostic procedure, assessment of etiology, determination of prognosis, and formulation and implementation of a

*For Robert J. Sardello

treatment plan. The philosophical and psychological question is not whether we will use ourselves in the clinical encounter, but how. This is axiomatic in all medicine.

—Howard F. Stein

To say "Thou" to a patient, and mean it, one must be able to utter "I" to oneself. One can then stand *with* his patient, because he can stand alone with himself. This is the essence of medicine, of therapeutic communication, of life.

—Howard F. Stein

. . . Eliade says . . . "the myth reveals the *deepest aspects* of reality." . . . That is, the language and imagery of mythology might be much closer to the nature of reality than are linear logic and abstract thinking, for if the real world is indeed holographic, then only the multivalent nature of the mythic image would be capable of sustaining this vision and eliciting this understanding. The holographic-mythic image, wherein the whole is the part and the part is the whole, would be able to grasp [these] states of affairs. . . . Mythological awareness is holographic because it begins to transcend conventional boundaries—boundaries of space and time, and opposites and selves—and for that very reason alone, mythological awareness might be one step close to the real world, "the seamless coat of the universe," as Whitehead put it.

—Ken Wilber

One of the greatest obstacles in understanding how health and illness form a unitary fact of our existence, how illness is as necessary as health in our lives, is our tendency to ignore life's darker side. In matters of health we focus only on the light and the high peaks, cringing from pain, suffering, and illness. We ignore these ignoble aspects of existence until we confront them in stark and undeniable ways and can no longer run from them. They may surface as illness in our own particular life, or in the death of a friend. But following the anguish we continue to attempt the impossible: to banish them from existence, looking only to the light. Yet it is a futile task. Deep within us we know we have created a lie and that sooner or later the next confrontation with the shadowy side of life must inevitably occur.

I am not proposing that we renounce optimism about our own health and revert to a morbid disposition wherein we continually dwell on our inevitable decline and demise, for this extreme is as one-sided as its opposite. I am not suggesting that physicians cease to hold out hope to those who are ill, assuring them instead that they must inevitably die—if not this time, then perhaps the next. I am proposing instead that we simply cannot have it the way we want it, for the simple and plain fact that light is not to be found without shadows, nor health without illness. To suppose otherwise is to live a fantasy, a make-believe world of presumed uninterrupted healthiness which has no basis in the real world. And to fail to acknowledge the dark side of health actually diminishes the healthiness we do feel—for it takes energy to live out falsity; it is draining to attempt to always keep the lid on the pot of grimness. We pay a penalty for supposing that there is only the light, and the penalty is that the intensity of the light, our healthiness, is diminished.

THE MYTH OF THE ALL-POWERFUL PHYSICIAN

One of the most curious traditions that has persisted in modern medicine is the tradition of the all-powerful physician. This belief is pathological because it is a distortion to the grossest degree. It is a belief that endures because it fills a need—the need of the patient to deify his healer and to imbue him with superhuman abilities, and the need of certain physicians whose egos need the fantasy to continue. As long as the patient has a godlike figure looking after his welfare, things are safe. Any self-responsibility he might need to invoke in his own behalf to be healthy is minimized, for with an all-powerful physician at hand he is secure. After all, gods can "fix" anything. No matter the degree to which my health might fail, my physician-as-god can set it straight. And it is not surprising that many physicians do little to disavow this saintly mantle with which they are invested, allowing the show to go on rather than acknowledge their own limitations and ignorance.

This mutual participation by both doctors and patients in the myth of the all-powerful physician is one way in which we hide from the shadows. We need not acknowledge the dark side of illness and suffering as long as we have a god-healer at our disposal. True, illness will one day occur; but the mythological, godlike healers will summarily sweep it aside when it does supervene as if it were little more than a nuisance and a bother. With gods as our healers there is nothing but the light. The valleys and the shadows can be ignored.

The greatest healers, however, do not participate in this myth. They sense their own limitations as surely as they know their strengths. They know, too, the necessity of illness in human life and its dynamic interrelatedness with health. For them the light and shadows are both essential ingredients of healthiness, and they do not attempt to ignore one in favor of the other.

THE MYTH OF CHIRON

Nowhere is the intrinsic fusion of health and illness more vividly illustrated than in the Greek mythological figure Chiron, whom the brilliant contemporary mythologist Carl Kerényi calls the wounded healer. Chiron was a centaur, half man and half horse. According to myth, the hero Heracles was received by the centaur Pholos at his cave. He was presented with a jar of rich wine as intended by Dionysus, the scent of which attracted the other centaurs. Unaccustomed to the wine, the centaurs began to fight; and in the battle which followed, one of the arrows shot by Heracles wounded Chiron in the knee. Following the instructions of Chiron, Heracles tended to the wound, but because the arrow's tip bore the poison of the hydra the wound was incurable. Chiron thus could not be cured nor could he die, since he was immortal. He is an enigmatic figure: immortal but wounded, carrying within himself the godlike and the mortal at the same time.

From Mount Pelion, the site of his cave, he received and taught heroes their craft. Among them was Asclepius, who learned from Chiron the knowledge of herbs and the power of the snake. Yet Chiron, the greatest teacher of medicine, ironically, could not heal himself. This was part of the wisdom which Chiron passed to Asclepius, the wisdom embodied in the wounding of the great healer.

PHYSICIAN AND TEACHER:
AN INTIMATE RELATIONSHIP

The etymological meaning of the word "physician" is "teacher," an association symbolized powerfully in the relationship between Chiron and Asclepius. Robert J. Sardello, the psychologist and writer, has drawn attention to the similar role of the teacher and healer. In his penetrating treatise, "Teaching as Myth," his observations about teaching have the strongest relevance to the role of the physician:

> Our teaching often does not resemble that of this greatest of mythical teachers, Chiron. As long as a teacher stands totally in the light, stands as one who knows, facing those who do not know, the teacher remains unaware of his own woundedness and does not participate in the learning enterprise. An original and originating image of teaching is split

radically into two parts as long as the teacher imagines himself as one who knows and the student as one in need of instruction. The student must stand in total darkness if the teacher stands totally in the light. Such a split image identifying teaching with knowledge and learning with ignorance can be maintained only through power. This attitude is like that of the physician who believes that he does the curing rather than being the occasion through which a curing comes as a gift. And like such a physician, such power is maintained by authority, by speaking in jargon, presenting oneself as a specialist, and seeking professional status.[1]

This is a grotesque view of teaching, a dehumanizing, inhumane scenario which places one human in domination over another who becomes the inferior supplicant. It is the role all too often enacted in the doctor-patient relationship. The physician forgets his own woundedness, his own imminent or potential sickness, his own inexorable death. He is willing to be elevated by the patient to the role of the godlike. The error occurs on both the parts of the physician *and* the patient—the physician, renouncing his own fallibility and woundedness in favor of deification, and the patient, who creates a god and claims him for his own private healer.

It is frequently supposed that this type of relationship is actually desirable, for from his position of ultimate respect and admiration the physician can motivate the patient to make certain changes, to follow advice, to have surgery, to take medications, etc. Nothing is lost if the all-powerful, glorified, and deified physician uses his power benevolently. If the patient's best interests are kept in the foreground, this type of relationship can be tremendously therapeutic, it is alleged. It does no good in this scenario to remind the physician of his own woundedness, for it is power that counts in this relationship, not weakness. Why, if the patient actually felt his physician to be "wounded" he would lose respect. After all, who wants his physician to be compromised in some way? It is best to let the concept of the wounded healer remain in mythical lore.

I believe that this kind of relationship, in spite of the fact that it is frequently preferred by *both* doctors and patients, is sadly off base. It perpetuates the idea that woundedness is abhorrent; we especially must not speak of it in healers; it is only power and health that count. The interconnectedness of health and illness in human lives goes unnoticed. It might be argued that we should not object to this sort of doctor-patient relationship if it were highly effective. But here is the point on which it most miserably fails: it simply does not work therapeutically as it ought. We must now see why.

THE DOCTOR-PATIENT RELATIONSHIP:
A LIVING ARCHETYPE

The Jungian psychiatrist Adolf Guggenbühl-Craig has described the doctor-patient relationship in a provocative way. In his book, *Power in the Helping Professions*, he states:

> The "healer-patient" relationship is as fundamental as is that of man-woman, father-son, mother-child. It is archetypal, in the sense expounded by C. G. Jung; i.e., it is an inherent, potential form of human behavior. In archetypal situations the individual perceives and acts in accordance with a basic schema inherent in himself, but which in principle is the same for all men.[2]

The doctor-patient relationship, then, is contained within nature. It is primordial, something inborn, an innate behavior seeking expression in the appropriate circumstance. It is called forth when we are sick, injured, or about to die. At those times we look to healers as naturally as a mother looks to her child. At such times we are duplicating behavior of countless members of our species who have looked to their own healers, persons who have had names other than "doctor": shaman, curandero, witch doctor. To look to the healer during times of affliction is as natural as seeking food or water.

On the surface, archetypal behavior seems simpler than it is. It seems as if, for example, the mother is simply reacting to her child, an object "out there." A woman responds to a man, who is himself an object apart from her. Patients respond to healers who, too, are objects possessing some fundamental status of their own distinct from that of the patient. But the basic situation is more complex. Every archetypal situation contains a polarity—that is, both poles are contained within the same individual. To reiterate, as Guggenbühl-Craig says, "Each of us is born with both poles of the archetype within us." And, ". . . in human psychology as we know it, both poles are contained within the same individual."[3]

This is a crucial point because it flies in the face of our ordinary concept of the doctor-patient relationship. We suppose that on the one hand there is the healer, and that on the other stands the patient, who is little more than a passive object to whom and for whom certain things are done. But the concept of archetype tells us that this way of thinking is misconstrued. It suggests that a polarity exists within both individuals that constitute the archetype, the healer and the patient. It suggests in no uncertain terms that the patient contains something of the healer within his being, and that the healer is simultaneously the patient as well—containing, as it were, his own woundedness.

Guggenbühl-Craig clarifies how the polarity of the archetype operates:

A child awakens maternal behavior in its mother. In the psyche of every woman there is the inborn potentiality of motherly behavior within the mother-child situation, which in some mysterious way must mean that the child is already contained within the mother, somewhat in Goethe's sense when he wrote: "Did our eye not contain sun's power, how could it perceive the sun at all?" Perhaps we should not speak of a mother archetype, a child archetype or a father archetype. It might be better to talk of a mother-child or a father-child archetype.[4]

Extending these analogies to the doctor-patient relationship, there is, then, something of each in both: the polarity of the healer and the one-to-be-healed are contained within the healer and the patient, and there is, in fact, only a single archetype which embraces both doctor and patient, not a different archetype for each.

Why bother to struggle with formulations such as these? What difference does it make what ancient mythology has contended about "wounded healers," or what Jungian psychological theory asserts about arcane constructions such as archetypes and polarities? It is my belief that there are few things more important in modern medicine than that we get these issues straight—far more important than, for example, setting up a Manhattan-type Project to search for "the cure" for cancer, heart disease, or any malady whatever. Unless we understand such basic notions as how we ourselves, patients and physicians, are constituted at heart, all subsequent attempts at healing will, in some sense, fall short, and all apparent cures will be nothing more than counterfeit. We will continue to flail about in medical research and in clinical medicine in our endless attempts to banish the shadows and retain only the light, or attempt to fill in all the valleys in our lives while retaining the peaks. It will not matter greatly whether we actually do find "the cure" for whatever affliction, for, without a sure knowledge of how we are constellated, we will never know, even who it is that has been cured, nor who it was that did the curing.

Yet what does it mean to say that both poles of the archetype exist within the physician and the patient? The statement need not be defended simply through metaphor or psychological theory. It can be taken literally, and it can be described in strictly scientific terms. Let us consider that the sick person contains his own healer. What is the proof?

THE INNER HEALER: MORE THAN MYTH

Examples could be endlessly produced, one of which is the careful study of Jerome Frank, at Johns Hopkins Medical School.[5] Frank studied the speed of healing of surgical wounds in the immediate post-operative period. He found that those patients healed fastest who had faith, trust, and confidence in the surgeon and the nursing staff. On the other hand, slower wound healing occurred in those patients who did not trust their physicians, and who were reluctant and afraid. This type of study goes beyond the *metaphorical* use of the term inner healer, and relates the concept to something as concrete as the healing of actual surgical wounds. The end point is measurable: The inner healer is something inward, whose effects are quantifiable. As such, it is not just a topic that must be dealt with by mystics and philosophers, but it is a fit concern for bioscientists as well. It is important to point this out, for we must constantly remind ourselves that we are not just speaking psychologically or poetically, but physiologically as well.

The polar expression, then, of the wounded healer who is mythically represented by Chiron, the centaur-teacher of Asclepius, is that of "the healthy wounded." The healthy wounded are all of us, for we all have within us the inner healing potential demonstrated in Frank's study. It is not for us to create, for it is there, existing inwardly as a force for healing as surely as there exists within us the capacity to fall ill. This is the polarity of the archetype which all men contain.

It is becoming recognized, through the best of medical research, that patients do have self-corrective, innate, inward, self-healing capacities. In a variety of disease states these so-called "factors of consciousness"—emotions, attitudes, feeling states of various sorts—have emerged as potent factors in healing.[6]

THE INNER PATIENT

But the sword of the archetypal polarity cuts both ways:

> It is not very difficult to imagine the healing factor in the patient. But what about the physician? Here we encounter the archetype of the "wounded healer." Chiron, the Centaur who taught Aesculapius the healing arts, himself suffered from incurable wounds. In Babylon there was a dog-goddess with two names: as Gula she was death and as Labartu, healing. In India Kali is the goddess of the pox and at the same time its curer. The mythological image of the wounded healer is very

widespread. Psychologically this means not only that the patient has a physician within himself but also that there is a patient in the doctor.[7]

It is this concept that is much harder for healers to swallow, for it is an admission of an integral, inescapable weakness. The recognition of fallibility comes hard for many modern healers. And, not surprisingly, we physicians expend ingenious efforts to conceal this eternal fact. This dilemma, however, has been faced by healers of all times, not just our own, and is expressed by Guggenbühl-Craig:

> It is not easy for the human psyche to bear the tension of polarities. The ego loves clarity and tries to eradicate inner ambivalence. This need for the unequivocal can bring about a certain splitting of polar archetypes. One pole may be repressed and continue operating in the unconscious, possibly causing psychic disturbances. *The repressed part of the archetype can be projected onto the outer world.* (italics added)[8]

One of the most difficult admissions for many modern physicians, who have been schooled in an era when the medical credo is to do, to act, and to cure, is that of woundedness. It becomes more expedient to do something, sometimes anything, for which the doctor is frequently praised ("He was willing to take her case when no other doctor would; he was willing to operate in spite of overwhelming odds; no matter that Mother died, the doctor tried!"). It has become extraordinarily difficult in modern clinical medicine to do nothing. Doing nothing is taken too frequently as an expression of impotence, of fallibility. It is a reminder to the physician of something he'd rather forget: the fact of his own woundedness.

There are many physicians to whom the fact of their own woundedness is apparent, and they handle this knowledge with a grace that *empowers* them as healers. Yet others do not. And the unfortunate way that the inner fact of woundedness is too often dealt with is through projecting it onto the external world in an attempt to rid oneself of something painful. Far better that someone else should be wounded, weak, or fallible than I, so the rationalization goes. And the object of the physician's projected weakness is all too often the patient, as the following incident illustrates.

THE STORY OF TOM B.

Tom B. was taken to the coronary care unit of a major hospital after collapsing with chest pain and shortness of breath at home. He was seventy-eight years old, had already sustained two heart attacks, and suffered from high blood pressure. Although he took his prescription medications religiously, he had been unable to stop smoking and lose weight, a fact which always irritated his doctor who never failed to remind Tom about it.

Tom's wife had called an ambulance immediately and then called Dr. Ponder, who said he would meet his patient in the emergency room. Upon arrival of both patient and physician at the hospital's emergency room, resuscitation efforts were continued, having been initiated by the paramedics who found Tom without any detectable blood pressure and with an erratic, ineffective heart rhythm. Finally, with intravenous tubing streaming from both arms, Tom was moved to the coronary care unit of the hospital with the diagnosis of acute myocardial infarction and congestive heart failure.

Tom's elderly wife remained in the background all the while; she didn't want to interfere. After all, Dr. Ponder had rescued Tom on two previous occasions following heart attacks, and she had to believe he would do so again. Even though she was burning with a desire to hear from the doctor about how her husband was doing, she remained unobtrusive, getting secondhand bits of information from the nurses who were scurrying in and out of the room. She thought it odd, though, that Dr. Ponder had no time for her. After all, he had to know she was there, for it was she who had placed the call, telling him she was en route to the hospital with her husband.

An hour later, following her husband's transfer to the coronary care unit, she stood weeping outside the swinging doors that guarded its entry. Still no word. Then without warning both doors burst open and Dr. Ponder emerged, obviously very angry. My God, she thought, why is he angry? Any emotion, she allowed herself to think, would be more appropriate than anger.

Fuming, Dr. Ponder exploded, "Your husband is making this very difficult! He refuses to cooperate with anything I do!"

Dr. Ponder stood there, glowering at her, his face flushed and diaphoretic, gripping a stethoscope in one hand. Mrs. B. sensed he was waiting for some response from her. She knew she had to say something, anything, and through her tears she stammered, "Oh Dr. Ponder, please forgive Tom, I know he doesn't mean it!"

Dr. Ponder did not acknowledge the apology, but wheeled abruptly, disappearing through the double doors, still streaming anger behind him. Mrs. B. never saw her husband alive again. Within an hour he was dead.

I fortunately do not believe most physicians behave in crucial situations like Dr. Ponder; this incident is related only as a classic example of how healers repress part of their own archetype (their woundedness, their weakness, their fallibility, their helplessness) and project it onto the external world where it frequently becomes the patient's weakness, not the doctor's ("He refuses to cooperate with anything I do!"). But the healer may project his own wounds in a more subtle way than did Dr. Ponder. For instance, it may not be the poor patient himself onto whom the physician projects his weakness, but the disease itself ("This is the worst case of high blood pressure I have ever seen in my career as a physician!"). In this case, the patient does not answer for the doctor's weaknesses, but some impersonal entity called disease. This disease-as-enemy approach is very common. The doctor-patient relationship can constellate strongly around this common foe without either having to admit to the shadows within themselves.

Another variation on the theme of how the healer avoids the recognition and admission of his own woundedness is by projecting the failure onto "the system"—"We just don't have a cure for this problem yet." Here the scapegoat becomes the entire medical edifice itself, which has so far failed to produce a suitable remedy. It is not the physician who is weak. He is simply making-do the best he can, working with the tools at hand.

THE HARM IN DENYING THE INNER POLARITY

I am not suggesting that there is not some justification to the occasional use of statements such as these. It is when patient and doctor actually begin to believe that these postures represent reality that great harm occurs. For when each denies the inner polarity of his own archetype, certain events predictably follow: for the physician, his own inner psychic processes are blocked; he sees a distorted view of himself and may begin to live a lie to his patients. As long as he persists in denying his own woundedness *he cuts off from himself an essential part of his healing power*, preferring to assuage his own ego rather than confront the shadowy elements that are a part of himself. He glues together this distorted view of himself with the element of power—personal power, his imagined notion of what healers should be like. He becomes a doer, for it is only through doing that he believes power can be wielded. This strategy transforms his patients into the recipients of his doing; and it is on "the doing of the doctor" that cure and healing must hinge. He becomes a peddler of techniques; no matter that they are sophisticated expressions of biotechnology, they are techniques nonetheless. And no matter that they occasionally seem to work, as they indeed do. What has occurred is that a deeper, more profound potential for healing and wholeness has been sacrificed.

How? *The patient becomes the sacrifice*—for in projecting his own wounds onto the patient, the patient is further crippled. It is only the healer now who can save him through the incessant round of doing, of the endless wielding of technique. The stage is set for the "fix it" mode of medicine that has become the hallmark of our day.

The physician is an easy target in our time, but we should not forget that this scenario could not go on *but for the complicity of the patient*. It is the patient who allows the doctor's strategy to be enacted. After all, it fulfills a need for himself, too—for by repressing his own power, his own "inner healer," the polarity of his own archetype, he escapes having to acknowledge that he is "the healthy wounded." He can project his own inner healing power onto the physician, whose job it becomes to then do all the work. It is an escape of responsibility that the patient has engineered. He has become the genuine article: the helpless, woeful, innocent person who is stricken down by illness which he cannot possibly control, and who must, therefore, look to the source of power, the physician, for cure.

Most doctor-patient relationships are constituted along these lines. When a physician and a patient come together who have repressed, respectively, their woundedness and healthiness, a silent bargain is struck. The physician unconsciously agrees to de-emphasize the inner power of the patient in bringing about his own healing (he must reserve the power for himself, for it is only through this mechanism that he can disguise the fact of his own woundedness); and the patient silently agrees to not acknowledge his own power (to do so would create a responsibility for himself in getting well), not to point out the wounds of his healer (this would constitute such a threat that the entire relationship might crumble). In the context of such an agreement the average doctor-patient relationship limps along—sometimes working, sometimes not.

AN ALTERNATIVE APPROACH TO TRANSFORM
THE DOCTOR-PATIENT RELATIONSHIP

What is the way out? The admission by the physician and the patient of the murky shadows within each—the woundedness of the healer and the latent healthiness of the patient. Such a recognition would create the atmosphere wherein a new kind of healing could flower. It would entail no less than a radical transformation of the doctor-patient relationship.

The image of the wounded healer symbolizes an acute and painful awareness of sickness as the counterpole to the physician's health, a lasting and hurtful certainty of the degeneration of his own body and mind. This sort of experience makes the doctor the patient's brother rather than his master. . . .

In the final analysis [the physician] must always strive to constellate the healing factor in the patient. Without this he can accomplish nothing. And he can only truly activate this healing factor if he bears sickness as an existential possibility within himself. He is less effective when he tries to unite the two poles of the archetype through petty power.[9]

Thus a new vision of the doctor-patient relationship begins to take shape as both doctor and patient become attuned to the two poles of their archetype. The traditional hierarchical stratification wherein the physician is seen as a powerful master directing the inner workings of the body of the subservient patient is transcended. This *does not mean* that in admitting his own woundedness the physician must actually take on the illness, for this would be a sentimental perversion of the recognition of weakness. And it *does not mean* that the patient, secure with the awareness of his own inner potential for healthiness, must never seek out a healer. For this, too, is an improper and shallow conclusion. The healing relationship goes beyond hierarchy, wherein neither healer nor the one to be healed stands above the other.

In the new context a basic humanism emerges, a quality that in the ordinary doctor-patient relationship is decidedly suppressed. Robert J. Sardello has described the flowering of this humanistic quality in speaking of the proper relationship between teacher and student. Bearing in mind that the root meaning of the words "physician" and "teacher" is the same, Sardello's observations are keenly applicable to the doctor-patient relationship:

When teaching and learning are imagined as a single action occurring for both teacher and student, a model of teaching more closely corresponding to the perennial pattern of the teacher is enacted. The teacher admits to being a student and students experience the desire to know awakened in their relationship with teachers. The teacher is touched by a certain vulnerability, is reminded over and over again that there is much that he does not know. He is deeply touched by students, excited, frightened, shaken by them. Only when the teacher is a perpetual learner does a learner desire knowledge. Like Chiron, whose very name refers to the hand and has connotations of touching with the hand, working by hand, practicing a handcraft or art, the teacher who allows himself to be touched, touches in turn.[10]

As Sardello has described the teaching-learning experience, the new vision of healing is that it is "a single action." Hierarchical differences, contingent on the wielding of power by one person over another, take a backseat. Power can be brought into play, *but it does not flow only from the doctor to the patient*. In full knowledge of the polarities within himself, the patient also uses power—this time in his own behalf, not content to let the doctor do it all. The appeal of the patient to the physician of "Fix it!" dissolves in the "single action" of mutual effort.

This mode of interaction will suggest to some the impossible. How can healing possibly occur as a "single action" unless a single person is involved? This sounds suspiciously like the mushy appeal to "oneness" and "sharing" and "uniting" of the transpersonalists, who would have us, in effect, forget who we are, dissolving into some featureless relationship wherein one cannot tell doctor from patient or patient from doctor. We can't forget who we are and what we are, and this "single action" mode of healing is nothing but words.

Yet the "singleness" that we are speaking of is not a featureless blending of identities, a fusion of disparate qualities into some unrecognizable blur, but exactly the opposite. It is a mode of bringing about healing not through *forgetting* all the various qualities that make us who we are, *but in acknowledging them*. It is a new way of doing and being that becomes possible because we know *all* that we are. Because we now sense within us the shadows as well as the light, we are empowered into a new existential set of premises which say something entirely different about how healers and patients can interact and about how healing can come about.

Lewis Thomas once observed that, instead of always emphasizing what we actually know in science, it would be enormously fruitful to focus alternatively on what we do *not* know. For it is here that the wonders lie. The known is the domain that is safe, where risk taking is no longer necessary. To dwell in it forever is not only to never advance, it is to promote a deceptive and false view of ourselves as knowing more than we do, of being more powerful than we really are.

I can conceive, too, that one day medical schools will emphasize not entirely the known, but a healthy dose of the unknown as well. It might give us not only a true picture of medical science, but a truer vision of ourselves as well. It might remind us of something we have almost forgotten as modern physicians, and which we desperately need to remember: that first, and finally, and without exception, we are wounded healers.

NOTES

1. Robert J. Sardello, "Teaching as Myth," in *The Soul of Learning* (Dallas: Pegasus Foundation Press, forthcoming).
2. Adolf Guggenbühl-Craig, *Power in the Helping Professions* (Dallas: Spring Publications, Inc., 1982), p. 85.
3. *Ibid.*, p. 89.
4. *Ibid.*, p. 90.
5. Jerome Frank, "Mind-Body Relationships in Illness and Healing," *Journal of the International Academy of Preventive Medicine*, 2:3 (1975): pp. 46–59.
6. Larry Dossey, *Space, Time and Medicine* (Boulder, Colo.: Shambhala Publications, 1982); and Kenneth Pelletier, *Mind as Healer, Mind as Slayer* (New York: Delta, 1977).
7. Guggenbühl-Craig, *Power*, p. 91.
8. *Ibid.*
9. Guggenbühl-Craig, pp. 97, 100–101.
10. Sardello, "Teaching as Myth."

Also in New Science Library

Awakening the Heart: East/West Approaches to Psychotherapy and the Healing Relationship, by John Welwood.

The Holographic Paradigm and Other Paradoxes, edited by Ken Wilber.

Jungian Analysis, edited by Murray Stein. Introduction by June Singer.

No Boundary: Eastern and Western Approaches to Personal Growth, by Ken Wilber.

Order Out of Chaos: Man's New Dialogue with Nature, by Ilya Prigogine and Isabelle Stengers. Foreword by Alvin Toffler.

Perceiving Ordinary Magic: Science and Intuitive Wisdom, by Jeremy W. Hayward.

Quantum Questions: Mystical Writings of the World's Great Physicists, edited by Ken Wilber.

A Sociable God: Toward a New Understanding of Religion, by Ken Wilber.

Space, Time and Medicine, by Larry Dossey, M.D.

The Sphinx and the Rainbow: Brain, Mind and Future Vision, by David Loye.

Staying Alive: The Psychology of Human Survival, by Roger Walsh, M.D.

The Tao of Physics: An Exploration of the Parallels between Modern Physics and Eastern Mysticism, second edition, revised and updated, by Fritjof Capra.

Up from Eden: A Transpersonal View of Human Evolution, by Ken Wilber.